**St. Louis Community
College**

Forest Park
Florissant Valley
Meramec

Instructional Resources
St. Louis, Missouri

GAYLORD

Teotihuacan

Teotihuacan
An Experiment in Living

By
Esther Pasztory

Foreword by
Enrique Florescano

UNIVERSITY OF OKLAHOMA PRESS : NORMAN AND LONDON

Library of Congress Cataloging-in-Publication Data

Pasztory, Esther.
    Teotihuacan : an experiment in living / by Esther Pasztory ; foreword
by Enrique Florescano.
       p.   cm.
    Includes bibliographical references and index.
    ISBN 0–8061–2847–X (alk. paper)
    1. Teotihuacán Site (San Juan Teotihuacán, Mexico) 2. Indian art—
Mexico—Teotihuacán Site (San Juan Teotihuacán, Mexico) I. Title.
F1219.1.T27P37   1997
972′.52—dc20   96–32775
                                                  CIP

The paper in this book meets the guidelines for permanence and durabil-
ity of the Committee on Production Guidelines for Book Longevity of the
Council on Library Resourses, Inc. ⊗

1 2 3 4 5 6 7 8 9 10

For Adam

Contents

Illustrations

COLOR PLATES

Foreword

By Enrique Florescano

WE ARE DRAWN TO ANCIENT CITIES IN PART BY THEIR EXOTIC architecture, followed by the mystery shrouding their inhabitants and creators. When we visit these cities, we are captivated by their scale, the symbolism of their monuments, and the impact of seeing them vibrantly set in the midst of magnificent scenery, yet deserted. What strikes us is their will to seem both splendid and strange at the same time. After this initial seduction comes the perplexity of not knowing their origins, and the shock of not knowing who built them.

Teotihuacan embodies these charms and mysteries. It is the largest, most ordered American city built in antiquity. From its inception, it was planned to adhere to an astronomical orientation different from that of other cities, and it was conceptually situated at the center of the cosmos. The great avenue, called the "Street of the Dead," traversing it from north to south, was converted into its central axis, and each one of its barrios and monuments adopted a stylistic order that imparted to the entirety the aura of a sacred city.

The site's life-span covered almost eight centuries, but there is not a single written account describing it. Based on archaeological inquiries, we know Teotihuacan was built at the beginning of the Christian era, and its splendid original design was respected until the time of its abandonment, around the mid-eighth century. Based on diverse evidence, archaeologists conjecture it was a political, religious, commercial, and cultural center whose influence extended throughout all of Mesoamerica. Nevertheless, in contrast to what is known of contemporary Maya and Zapotec cities, the ethnic identity of its inhabitants, what language they spoke, the names of their rulers, and the original name of the metropolis continue to be a mystery.

The Teotihuacanos themselves added to the enigmas created by the passage of time. They constructed the center of greatest political power and cultural influence of the Classic period, but its rulers voluntarily omitted their presence in the city's monuments; contrary to the leaders of other states, they decided not to record the city's public history in artworks. Evidence indicates that, like the Mayas and Zapotecs, the Teotihuacanos relied on refined calendars and sophisticated astronomical computations as well as a system of writing to record supernatural and earthly events affecting the lives of the site's inhabitants. Nevertheless, Teotihuacan monuments lack glyphs or pictographic texts listing the names of their rulers and commemorating their deeds. Not a single record has been found alluding to a historical event and providing the date on which it occurred. The city built to last for eternity chose not to record passages from its earthly life.

Unlike the ruler effigies and monuments commemorating events shaping the history of Maya and Zapotec kingdoms, temples, gigantic pyramids, and impressive apartment compounds decorated with paintings alluding to religious scenes and acts propitiating fertility fill Teotihuacan. Only a few sculptures represent the main gods of the city, while tons of sherds, rubble, and different types of utensils constitute the puzzle behind which are hidden the activities of the site's inhabitants.

In the 1960s, William T. Sandes and René Millon directed two ambitious archaeological projects, one dedicated to understanding human settlement patterns and ecological evolution in the basin of Mexico, and the other focusing on the process of urbanization in the Teotihuacan area. Both produced fundamental information on the development of this great center and raised new, provocative questions. What kind of government forged the power of this city? Why are there no representations of rulers, nor a cult of dynastic power? How can we explain that the majority of the population lived concentrated within the limits of the great city, divided into barrios and apartment compounds? Instead of revering a supreme ruler, why did this large, diversified population honor collective values and deities propitiating fertility and agricultural abundance?

Intrigued by the mysteries of this great city, Esther Pasztory decided to write this book to address some of its enigmas. Her study is highly original. Based on an approach that she calls structural and semiotic, she analyzes the symbols expressed by the pyramid, the gods, the precinct of power, the apartment compound, painting, ceramics, and the representation of the human body. Immersed in the study of symbols, this book adopts the perspective that art is a reflection of the society that creates it. Art is a mirror in which ideals can be perceived that do not always coincide with the reality producing them. Nevertheless, these manifestations give us a notion of the depth of the problems that had to be resolved through the formation of collective values and images.

The chapters dealing with the significance of the so-called Pyramids of the Sun and Moon exemplify the advances achieved in recent years through symbolic analysis. Pasztory believes that the Pyramid of the Sun is a monument dedicated to the Goddess, the most prominent deity at Teotihuacan. Evidence includes studies revealing that this pyramid was constructed over a cave running deep through its interior. This fact is tied to the deeply rooted Mesoamerican cosmogonic tradition of the first mountain, which arose from the primordial waters of a cosmic ocean and which contained in its interior the fertile waters and nourishing seeds providing basic sustenance for the first human beings. Representations of the Goddess allude to the germinating powers of the earth's interior, to the generative womb of plant renewal, and to the cycle of death and the resurrection of life. The Pyramid of the Sun, as the original mountain of creation myths, would then be the sacred place of origins, the place where the first human beings and foodstuffs emerged.

In Pasztory's stimulating interpretation, the so-called Pyramid of the Moon is a monument dedicated to the god Tlaloc, the deity next in importance to the Goddess. In contrast to this telluric deity, Tlaloc is a celestial being, the manipulator of thunder and lightning provoking rainfall. He is a masculine deity linked at Teotihuacan with water, the calendar, warfare, and foreign affairs.

Esther Pasztory emphasizes one of the most surprising characteristics of Teotihuacan: its image as a planned city. Carefully organized into barrios and large apartment compounds each with its own temples, the entire city depended on a central order to oversee its construction, permanent maintenance, and decoration. This powerful organization would seem to indicate the presence of a strong central authority, which is paradoxically hidden in the public art of Teotihuacan. Instead of a personified central power, paintings display groups of figures, dressed in rich priestly or military garb, who are not shown as individuals, but rather as anonymous, collective groups. In the final stages of Teotihuacan some of these figures display headdresses that seem to indicate political or military rank or title, and isolated glyphs positioned next to some of them seem to refer to their names. However, never do we find the exaltation of an individual who may have occupied a supreme position of power, nor is there any evidence of a dynastic cult.

Pasztory's fine analysis of objects of daily use and of other collective manifestations of social life reveals these are characterized by uniformity, simplicity, and mass production. Most objects of everyday use, such as incense burners, the heads and bodies of abundant human figurines, architectural styles, and the very murals decorating temple and apartment compound walls are reproductions of a previously established model, repeated without great variations in different barrios of the city and through the centuries. In this way, the leaders of Teotihuacan, by subjecting both ordinary objects and public art to a uniform stylistic and symbolic canon, gave the population a shared identity. At the same time, they singled out their city in relation to other contemporary or rival cities and cultures.

In Teotihuacan artistic and symbolic representations, human beings appear in the guise of diminutive, inconsequential figures, secondary to the acts or ceremonies carried out by priests, figures in military attire, and gods. The most frequently represented human figures are those of functionaries responsible for public rituals, dressed in rich clothing and ornaments, performing ceremonies to propitiate fertility and human sacrifice by heart extraction. Deep down, as Pasztory indicates, human beings, priests, religious ceremonies, architecture, and all symbolic expressions of the city seem to celebrate the natural and cosmic order established in primordial creation myths. "Teotihuacan presented itself as a cosmic place, without history." What distinguishes Teotihuacan from other Mesoamerican cities, underscores Pasztory, is its insistence on "the appearance of impersonal order and organization. The mechanics of order and organization are so clear in the city plan, in the murals, in the censers and host figures as to suggest an obsession." Another obsessive focus "is on nature and the divine, which are conflated as one. Insistent images of a paradisiacal, verdant nature, flora and fauna, deities and elite in the act of giving, create a benevolent semblance of flourishing life."

The presence of these collective values, the will to create a language of signs and symbols capable of being understood by different ethnic groups and wide sectors of the population, plus the absence of the centralized authority of a supreme ruler, are what leads Pasztory to say that Teotihuacan "seems to have emerged in contrast to dynastic and aristocratic cultures, such as the Olmec and Mayan, and to have created and idealized more participatory institutions than were common at the time. Teotihuacan was, therefore, not just one of the many Mesoamerican cultures, but a remarkable, unique one." This "portrait of a civilization through its art" is the new image of Teotihuacan that Esther Pasztory offers to the readers of this fascinating book.

Preface

IT SEEMS PARADOXICAL TO ENTITLE THIS BOOK AN "EXPERIMENT IN LIVING" when the book is more properly the portrait of a civilization through its art. However, what the portrait shows is that Teotihuacan was no ordinary ancient civilization, but one that developed such different ways of governing itself that it can be described as an experiment. The idea of a "portrait" is also paradoxical, since portraits were precisely the sort of representations not made at Teotihuacan. Teotihuacan has remained little known because its images consist so often of masks, and what is a mask if not a hider of the real self and the pretender of an artificial persona? This theme is the outline of my portrait: Teotihaucan in this view is all opposites and contradictions. As with Alice's Wonderland, one cannot assume that anything is what it appears to be.

What measure can be applied to test whether my "portrait" is appropriate? Of course, no portrait can really be accurate—even a photograph often shows us to be "unlike" ourselves to us and to others. Nevertheless, four aspects of Teotihaucan studies allow a sketch of this civilization. First, traditional "truths" about Teotihuacan are considered true because they are traditional. Second, probabilities about Teotihuacan in comparison to other ancient cultures provide a particular set of parameters. Third, certain features of Mesoamerican civilization provide another set of parameters. Fourth, a vast number of "facts," from the sizes of pyramids to the types of figurines, are more or less scientifically accurate and provide data. Within these four poles—traditional truths, ancient cultures, Mesoamerican features, and scientific facts—is an enormous latitude for interpretation.

What do you know about me if you know that I am five feet nine inches tall, a professor of Pre-Columbian art, a woman, and a United States citizen of Hungarian origin? Those facts provide little information from which to create my portrait without considerable recourse to the imagination.

One need not deconstruct the entire scientific enterprise to know that the reconstruction of all archaeological societies is, at least in part, fiction. Neither irrefutable logic, nor facts, nor inner coherence, nor parsimony of explanation can truly uphold the rightness of any interpretation. I used to believe that if new finds, not known at the time of writing, "supported" a theory, then the validity of the theory was proved. Now I believe that new finds are at best part of the same network of facts being analyzed and do not really support theories of any kind. Interpretation is an aesthetic activity whether it is done by humanists or scientists.

Moreover, anecdotes on portraiture are redolent of paradoxes. The seventeenth-century Italian sculptor Giovanni Lorenzo Bernini said that he put indentations and projections on the faces of his sculptures where none were in the original person's face because he could thus better capture the person's appearance than in an exact likeness. Similarly, when Michelangelo's sculptures of Lorenzo and Giuliano de Medici were criticized for not looking like the recently departed dukes, Michelangelo retorted that in two hundred years no one would know what the dukes looked like. I do not claim that my portrait of Teotihuacan is *the* true one. I merely claim that I have given the city a certain personality and character it lacked and that thus I am giving it the visibility it has not had. In the end the portrait is just another kind of mask, in an endless sequence of masks.

This book is written as a story, full of imagined human thought and action. Narratives, like portraits, were also not a Teotihuacan form. In the words of Hayden White, "Every historical narrative has as its latent or manifest purpose the desire to moralize the events of which it treats."[1] I accept that premise as both a limitation and an opportunity. And in so doing, I give my version of an encounter with Teotihuacan, knowing full well that it will not accord with the accounts of others.

Although most of my methods are alien to Teotihuacan thought, I learned from Teotihuacan something very important: the beauty of an open structure. I hope that the construction and artificiality of my portrait and narrative are always fully visible.

ESTHER PASZTORY

New York, New York

Acknowledgments

IT IS DIFFICULT TO KNOW WHERE TO BEGIN ACKNOWLEDGING THE HELP AND contribution of everyone to a book that has been in the making for more than twenty-five years. This list can be only a partial one of those who have been the most significant.

First and foremost I would like to express my appreciation to those Mexican scholars and friends who have been generous with material and information over many years: Jorge Angulo Villaseñor, Rubén Cabrera Castro, Clara Luz Díaz Oyarzabal, Enrique Florescano, Beatriz de la Fuente, Leonardo Lopez Luján, Linda Manzanilla, Eduardo Matos Moctezuma, Felipe Solís Olguin, and Mari Carmen Serra Puche. I would like also to note in retrospect my long interviews with Pedro Armillas, Laurette Séjourné, and Agustín Villagra.

My most sincere thanks are to archaeologists working on Teotihuacan material, without whose research, information, ideas, and help this book could not have been written: Warren T. D. Barbour, George L. Cowgill, Clara Millon, René Millon, Evelyn Childs Rattray, Sue Scott, Michael W. Spence, and Saburo Sugiyama. I am especially indebted to William T. Sanders, whose long critique of the first draft greatly strengthened the final version of the book. Gordon F. Ekholm is remembered for his initially introducing me to the field and his unstinting criticism of my beginning work.

In the field of art I would like to express my intellectual debt to George Kubler and his pioneering work on Pre-Columbian art. Scholars who have provided the most relevant material and ideas for which I am grateful (whether I agreed with them or not) include Janet C. Berlo, Clemency Chase Coggins, Cecelia F. Klein, James C. Langley, Arthur G. Miller, Robert Sonin, Karl A. Taube, Stephen Tobriner, Richard F. Townsend, and Hasso von Winning. Christopher Couch and Marvin Cohodas read earlier versions of the manuscript and gave valuable advice.

It has been my special privilege to be involved with Teotihuacan through the San Francisco De Young Museum since the 1976 bequest of the Wagner murals, and I would like to express my thanks for years of cooperative effort. It is not possible to thank everyone here in connection with the exhibition *Teotihuacan: City of the Gods* in 1993. I would just like to single out Harry S. Parker III, director of the museum, whose vision made it a reality; Thomas K. Seligman, who initiated the project and got me involved; and especially Kathleen Berrin, who was my co-curator. Although putting that exhibition together seemed at times as labor-intensive as building a pyramid, seeing the objects together was an invaluable experience.

I would like to thank all the students who have worked on Teotihuacan topics in seminars over the years both at Columbia University and for one quarter at the University of California, Los Angeles. Their questions and projects have been the testing ground for many of my ideas. Special thanks are due to those who were my assistants in various phases of the project: Ann Walke Cassidy, Cynthia Conides, Kate Morris, Patricia Sarro, and Sarah Travis. I would also like to thank Janice Robertson for a number of drawings. I owe a special debt to Debra Nagao, who has helped with everything from research and translation to the acquisition of illustrations in Mexico.

My oldest friend in Mexico is Doris Heyden, whom I first met as the curator of the Teotihuacan hall in the National Museum of Anthropology. She has been a friend, a host, an intellectual, and a practical resource for everything imaginable over the years, and I cannot thank her enough.

Teotihuacan

I

Personal Discovery

BORN DURING THE SECOND WORLD WAR IN A LITTLE COUNTRY CONQUERED
by foreign armies, growing up under communism, experiencing an un-
successful revolution in my teens in which some of my age-mates died,
I was probably ready to identify with a people who were similarly ruth-
lessly conquered by great outside powers. My arrival in America in 1956
from Hungary seemed a strange accident of fate, and of course back then I
knew nothing much about "Indians." The urgent subject I needed to understand was the United States. Like so many Europeans, I could have
become fascinated by the world of modernity—fast food, superhighways,
and skyscrapers. But the real surprise was that America had a great "antiquity" of its own, one that I did not "discover" until graduate school. In
trying to understand the United States, it seemed best to start at the beginning, with this glorious Native American heritage. It was a way both
of assimilating and of retaining symbolic links to my past. Moreover, the
way back to Hungary seemed until the 1970s permanently forbidden, and
once permitted, a nostalgic but difficult experience. But the ruins and cultures of the ancient Americas were available to anyone with the ability
to read, the small sum then of a ticket to Mexico, and the desire to imagine past ways of living. Mexico—with its colorful costumes, chili peppers
drying in the yards, peasants living in thatched huts, lively folk music,
and general appreciation of the joys of living—was similar in some ways
to the Hungary of my childhood, from paprika to folk art and even the
snappy csárdás. The old-fashioned way of life in general and the clear class
structure were also familiar territory. Mexico became an adopted "home"

I could visit without political and emotional complications.

Hungary, of course, did not have Indians; the major ruins in the domain are of provincial Roman settlements. But the Hungarians are "Indians" in that they see themselves as the descendants of "noble savages"—horse-riding nomads speaking a non-Indo-European (Ural-Altaic) language, who followed a magic "elk" that led them to their homeland in the ninth century A.D. They were brutal warriors raiding far into western Europe until, led by their first king, St. Stephen, they finally became Christianized and settled down. The story is not unlike the migration myth of the Aztecs, who were nomadic barbarians equally impressive in war, led by their god Huitzilopochtli, who promised to settle them in a land where they would see an eagle perched on a cactus. Both the Hungarians and the Aztecs adopted the religion and customs of the settled civilizations into whose midst they managed to enter.

Hungarians see themselves as both "Western" and "Other." They pride themselves that Budapest is the "Paris" of the East; that they had been the eastern bulwark against the Turks for centuries, thus providing the West with security to develop its unique "Westernness"; that their fifteenth-century king Matthias was a Renaissance ruler with a court that was run in the best Italian style. At the same time, Hungarians are forever searching for their roots in their customs and language among contemporary and ancient non-Western peoples. Ida Bobula, for example, had been trying to prove on the basis of linguistic similarities that the Sumerians were the ancient Hungarians, who would thus have been the originators of Western civilization.[1] She was laughed at, but indulgently. In my research in the library I kept coming across strange books by obsessed amateurs searching for Magyar origins. My favorite was *Munda, Magyar, Maori*,[2] in which the author saw a kinship with both the Munda of India and the Maori of New Zealand. We must have really gotten around! Generally, it seemed that in searching for forebears, Hungarian scholars considered only noteworthy cultures. A strongly nationalistic strain was evident even in the work of anthropologists. In the 1970s in a seminar on shamanism, I discovered the work of Vilmos Dioszegi, who at the height of communism (which discouraged the study of ethnic roots) managed to find and document Siberian shamans in Russia believed to be related to Hungarian ones.[3] He died as a result of the difficulties and privations of his trip and became something of a national hero. Otto von Sadovszky recently proposed that the language of the California Indians and hence of the original migrants from Asia was related to Ural-Altaic. In other words, Hungarians and Native Americans are related.[4]

Not as literal as Ida Bobula, but perhaps infected with the same national fascination with ethnic origins, in 1967 I found myself in Mexico, on a three-week tourist trip, looking for a dissertation topic. I had an idea of studying Aztec sculpture, and since that was a large subject, perhaps concentrating on the female deities. I had written my master's essay on African art but became fascinated by the mysteries and complexities of Pre-Columbian art, with its stone cities, stone sculptures, murals, and books. The only course I had had on the subject was given by the Africanist Paul Wingert, whose knowledge was sketchy and whose enthusiasm was much less than what he accorded the art of Africa and Oceania. The complexities of Pre-Columbian art he saw as unnecessary fussiness. However, dutifully he covered all the Pre-Columbian Mesoamerican civilizations: the Maya, the Olmec, the Zapotec, the Mixtec, and Teotihuacan.

So when I stepped out of the Teotihuacan site museum onto the Avenue, I pretty much knew what to expect—two of the greatest pyramids of Mesoamerica and the remains of a metropolis once inhabited by 100,000 to 200,000 people. I knew that Teotihuacan had flourished between 100 B.C. and A.D. 750, six hundred years prior to the Aztecs, and that the ethnic group and language of its people were unknown. I knew that it was big and awesome and that Wingert thought it was too rigid and inhuman in scale and form. I do not know if he had ever actually seen it. However, we had all seen slides of it: maps, plans, detailed visual documentation. Sometimes after such preparation, seeing the ruins themselves can be an anticlimax.

But that was not the case with Teotihuacan. Teotihuacan was an overwhelming experience for me that first time and has remained so no matter how many times I have returned. It is hard to grasp that a people without wheeled vehicles built an avenue more than three kilometers long, often fifty meters wide. It does not just look long, it feels long: walking from one end of it to the other is utterly exhausting. The Pyramid of the Sun is as great in mass as the largest pyramid at Giza in Egypt, although it is not as tall. It and the Pyramid of the Moon at the end of the Avenue rival in size and majesty the mountains that ring the Valley of Teotihuacan. Because the terrain slopes upward toward the Pyramid of the Moon, the perspective in which we experience the Avenue is tilted up, rising toward Cerro Gordo ("Fat Mountain") and the sky. Add a dramatic thunderstorm or a rainbow, and the whole is stupendous.

Figure 1.1. Aerial view of the Avenue of the Dead with the Pyramids of the Sun and the Moon, Teotihuacan. Copyright © 1973, by René Millon.

By the time the Aztecs saw Teotihuacan, it had been abandoned and in ruins for centuries. They named it Teotihuacan, usually translated as "The Place of the Gods," because they imagined that at the last creation of the world the gods gathered together there. The name may mean more precisely "Where the Gods Are Made." They also thought of the ruins as the tombs of ancient rulers. In both cases, the Aztecs saw Teotihuacan as more awesome and impressive than anything they had seen or anything they eventually built. Most of the Aztec Temple Precinct can fit into the Ciudadela at Teotihuacan, which is less than one-sixth of the ceremonial complex.

As modern Americans, we tend to mistrust monumental building on such an awesome scale. Although we take pride in our own giant skyscrapers, we have an ambivalent attitude toward them: on the one hand, they are good, the result of technology and American know-how, but on the other hand they are potentially bad, in that they may be owned by corporations not interested in public welfare. As an example of this ambivalence, until recently people assumed that the Egyptian pyramids had been built by slaves whipped on by their merciless masters. Views of most ancient monumental architecture are tainted by the notion that only some totalitarian form of government could have forced people to make such huge piles of stone. Add to that the general supposition that the pyramids were probably used for human sacrifices in Mesoamerica, and visitors can add a pleasantly perverse shudder to their contemplation.

The awe I experienced at Teotihuacan that first time and on every subsequent visit had two curious aspects. On the one hand I felt dwarfed and overwhelmed by the colossal size of the city and the power that built it. It made me feel small, insignificant. That impression is what people often refer to as the "inhuman" scale of Teotihuacan. Many Maya sites, such as Palenque, are small, charming, exquisitely decorated, and fit our current notion of "human" scale. Teotihuacan by contrast seems to be built on the scale of nature, like Mount Everest and the Grand Canyon. On the other hand, facing such awesomeness I felt a sense of belonging, even of being *privileged* to be part of something grand and inspiring. I felt as if the stones of Teotihuacan were saying, "This is a city built on a universal scale, and you are lucky to be here rather than elsewhere." Perhaps the fact that I am a New Yorker, used to sky-high monuments, has predisposed me to awesome places. But the skyline of Manhattan in no way overshadowed my experience of Teotihuacan—even in that comparison the ancient city remained colossal. But living in New York may have made such structures familiar and a part of "home," so that the awesomeness I experienced at Teotihuacan was not unpleasant (as it is for others), and I could easily make for myself an intellectual abode of the site. All this is a way of saying that I fell in love with Teotihuacan at first sight.

The "home" I found at Teotihuacan was literally that—a dwelling complex covered with murals, which was eventually the subject of my dissertation. Everywhere I went on that first visit, I saw the remains of painted walls (never discussed by Wingert in his course) consisting of enigmatic faces, hands scattering jade ornaments, animals such as birds and turtles, flowers, plants, drops of water, and mysterious signs. The colors were a resonant combination of reds, greens, blues, and yellows. The surfaces were hard like a glaze, due perhaps to polishing, and shimmered with tiny mica pieces embedded in paint—red specular hematite. As far as I could tell, no one knew anything much about them.

Scouting the bookstores along the Reforma Avenue brought to light three books on Teotihuacan written by Laurette Séjourné in 1966.[5] There in drawings, photographs, and color reconstruction were the curious faces and beings that I had seen. However, the text of the books was quite vague and disappointing. On returning to New York, I found that as early as 1956, Vanguard Press, one of the experimental publishers of the cultural works of the 1960s, had published Séjourné's *Burning Water: Thought and Religion in Ancient Mexico*, in which she first developed her interpretation of ancient Teotihuacan.[6] In her 1956 foreword she wrote that as a result of her work at Teotihuacan she hoped that "Pre-Columbian religion will be acknowledged to rank among the highest manifestations of the human spirit."

Because the Aztecs had come to power in the same central Basin of Mexico six hundred years after the fall of Teotihuacan, Mesoamericanists viewed the great ruined city as a forerunner of Aztec culture, a view that in many ways still predominates. Séjourné was the first to argue in forceful terms that Teotihuacan was different from the Aztecs. She described the Aztec sacrifices and showed the bodiless hearts, heads, and hands represented in Aztec sculpture. She was the first to identify various designs as "hearts" in Teotihuacan art (impaled on sacrificial knives, in front of the mouths of felines and coyotes, as well as in the headdresses of deities). But evidently she had fallen under the spell of Teotihuacan, because she argued that in that ancient city the heart was not the literal symbol of sacrifice but a metaphorical symbol of the *soul* in search of perfection and self-realization. She insisted that because of Teotihuacan's greater wisdom and spirituality, all the symbols referred to immaterial and mystic concepts. The conquering Aztec barbarians were the ones who misunderstood this religion and turned its transcendent concepts into a literal bloodbath.

I had tea with the elderly Laurette Séjourné in the garden of her house in Mexico City a year or two after my first visit to Teotihuacan. She was then in something of an academic decline. The garden of her Mexico City home—she was married to the publisher who had published her three books—seemed pleasantly but also restrictively isolated from the rest of the world. She was small and plump, dressed simply in black. It was unclear why, with her lack of qualifications, she had been given the opportunity to excavate at least two apartment compounds at Teotihuacan (Zacuala and Tetitla) and a part of one she called Zacuala Patios because she did not recognize the fact that it was yet a third. She thought that these were palaces. Her ideas were an embarrassment to archaeologists in Mexico, and as far as I could tell she never appeared at conferences and meetings. In fact, I do not quite know why I looked her up. I did not expect to find out any new information from her, did not bother to ask her too many questions because I knew that our ideas were a world apart. But still, I was evidently curious enough to see the person behind the books to go to the trouble of finding her. She was then excavating at the Aztec site of Culhuacan, but her finds were limited to potsherds and figurines.

She was delighted that someone had sought her out. She complained that, with all their scientific apparatus and high academic qualifications, the modern university-trained anthropologists and archaeologists were missing out in reconstructing the heart and soul of an ancient civilization. She admired most the nonprofessional scholars and thinkers of an earlier generation, such as Paul Westheim and Miguel Covarrubias. She believed, following Carl Jung, that intuition could explain art, because all art ultimately derives from a collective unconscious. Her books are a treasure trove of illustrations of Teotihuacan objects and images, floating as free of reality as the photographs in a fashion magazine. They evoke, they suggest, but they never explain. Though her ideas remain near the fringe, her illustrations are found in all studies of Teotihuacan art and culture. She made it come to life visually.

Séjourné was where I began; evidently there was room here for an art historian, since hers was clearly not a definitive study of Teotihuacan art. The first paper I wrote on a Teotihuacan subject back at Columbia University was to prove her wrong. As far as I could see, the hearts were hearts and indicated that Teotihuacan had a cult of war and warriors not unlike that of the Aztecs.[7] Nevertheless, Séjourné had a legacy for which I had not given her credit. She had begun the process of severing Teotihuacan from Aztec culture, a subject to which I turned in the 1980s. The people of Teotihuacan may not have been more "spiritual" in the Jungian sense, but they were certainly different from the Aztecs.

I can remember, as if it were yesterday, the first time in the town of San Juan Teotihuacan when I plucked up the courage to talk to the archaeologists René and Clara Millon. I was in Mexico City doing preliminary research for my dissertation, staying in a fine hotel for four dollars a night, going out to the site every day. No sign indicated the location of the Teotihuacan Mapping Project, so I had to find out, from the severe-looking men who populate the central squares of Mexican villages, which door to knock on. I was fearful, since I had discovered at Columbia University that archaeologists found art historians silly and irrelevant. (This was in the beginning years of the "New Archaeology," designed along scientific lines.)

The Teotihuacan Mapping Project was the first major archaeological project for which a computer program, run by George Cowgill, recorded its vast quantity of data. The aim of the project was to map the entire city, to create a better history and chronology, and to try to understand how it functioned economically and politically. The area had been divided into a grid; teams of workers analyzed every area for architectural, ceramic, lithic, and other remains.[8] The samples were stored in shoe boxes that occupied the many rooms of "the Lab" on shelves that covered the walls from floor to ceiling, while the information was entered into the computer program. This study demonstrated an idea first proposed by the Mexican archaeologist Pedro Armillas that Teotihuacan had been a huge city, not just a temple complex. René Millon was the director of the project, and Clara Millon had written the first scholarly dissertation on the murals in 1962, in which she put them in chronological order.[9] She was the recognized expert on Teotihuacan art and seemed to have a slide of every work of Teotihuacan art ever found.

Together the Millons were formidable. I explained that I had conceived the notion of writing a dissertation on Teotihuacan mural painting and that for the sake of coherence and simplicity I wanted to focus on Tepantitla. The paintings of this dwelling were accidentally revealed by a farmer digging in a field in 1942. The murals were well preserved and had already been studied by the Mexican archaeologists Alfonso Caso[10] and Pedro Armillas.[11] The fact that I was an art historian displeased the Millons. They cross-examined me for nearly an hour. When they asked with whom I was studying, I explained that Columbia University had no Pre-Columbianists and that my sponsor was the primitivist Douglas Fraser. This detail displeased them even more, since Douglas Fraser had just written a book, *Primitive Art*, in which he argued that art all over the world derived from a few centers of power, such as the ancient Near East or ancient China.[12] Such theories were called diffusionist, and though popular in the 1950s, they had become unpopular by the late 1960s. So the Millons asked whether in my work I would find "Chinese influences" in the art of Teotihuacan. I assured them that my dissertation would contain nothing "diffusionist," and eventually we settled on amicable terms.

The Millons' front room in the town of San Juan Teotihuacan became a place to discuss questions about Teotihuacan and the projects of the day and provided a chance to meet other project members such as Warren Barbour, who was assembling all the data on figurines, and Evelyn Rattray, who was in charge of ceramic studies. Mexican archaeologists such as Jorge Angulo stopped there during their visits to the site. Although "the Lab" (which includes living quarters) was moved to another, larger location in the village a few years ago, it has been a fixture in the life (and I imagine some of the legend) of San Juan Teotihuacan for nearly thirty years. Generations of graduate students and visitors have left piles of mysteries and other decaying light reading for the newcomers in various corners. A number of couples have argued themselves into divorces, or romanced one another into marriages, while René Millon and George Cowgill kept up intense work schedules. I once asked René if his team would stop excavating as we stood in the middle of a tropical downpour. He looked up at the sky and said, "Rain? What rain?" The digging continued, under plastic tarps, as if nothing had happened.

Back in the United States, I later saw an article in the *National Enquirer* entitled "Your Tax Dollars Wasted," on the study of irrigation agriculture at Teotihuacan. René Millon was reported to have received millions of dollars(!) from the National Science Foundation to study an ancient pile of rocks—as if studying Teotihuacan reached the greatest heights of absurdity. Was it indeed a useless luxury?

Most people, like the Hungarians, study the past to find themselves and their ancestors. Teotihuacan has no direct descendants. Its population became part of the Toltec and Aztec worlds and is now a mixture of Indian and Spanish. The population of the area spoke the Aztec language, Nahuatl, at the time of the Spanish conquest, and Nahuatl names are still given to Teotihuacan and its compounds by the people living there today.

Like modern Italians who have little firsthand information about ancient Rome, the modern people living at Teotihuacan have no memory of ancient Teotihuacan. Their emotional identification is with the culture of the Aztecs. Teotihuacan is, therefore, like some other great early cultures such as the Olmec or the Moche, without direct descendants who can speak about its traditions. This discontinuity leaves modern observers bereft of information but also free to tell our stories.

Whether our approach is scientific, like that of the Millons, or romantic, like that of Séjourné, we use ancient cultures to project aspects of our own lives and civilizations. We *say* that we are trying to find out what earlier cultures were *really* like, but that reality seems to escape with time—why else would so many early interpretations be so inadequate? These sites are laboratories for testing how we think, at this moment, human groups might have lived back then. Sometimes we consider previous cultures as ideals to follow; sometimes as hells to avoid. I have changed my own concepts radically since the 1970s. I will even argue that though many of our ideas may prove to be ephemeral, something is carried along from every time and every one of us, as a kind of sediment in which some of the unique reality of Teotihuacan is condensed. Every time we state a view of the culture, we get a little something right. But only history will tell what that is. In the meantime, we write for our *own* time, telling morality tales of the past, so that we can understand and recast our present in better ways.

During most of the twentieth century, Western observers have extolled the ways of life of "primitive" or "tribal" cultures, such as those of the Native Americans of North America, Polynesians, or Africans. These relatively small societies impress us because they appear to place greater emphasis on community life and on family relationships than on work, the accumulation of goods, or the building of superhuman monuments. We imagine that the people of these societies live closer to the land, that they are ecologically less ruinous, and that they are emotionally more fulfilled. We are looking for what we lack in our decaying cities and polluted world. Other eras have seen such societies in a less romantic light. The philosopher Thomas Hobbes summed up the view of many in the seventeenth and eighteenth centuries that in the state of nature human life was "solitary, poor, nasty, brutish, and short."[13]

In contrast to the romanticized small societies, the ancient civilizations built around cities by politically more complex states make great ruins for tourist pilgrimages but do not inspire anyone with ways of living. For example, Egyptian culture, with its morbid mummies and apparent artistic monotony, is a staple in cartoons about cultures that are unwilling to innovate. The notion of slaves dying in the task of building monuments is still the popular idea of ancient Egypt, even though recent research has shown that the laborers came from the agricultural peasantry, that they worked during the slack, nonagricultural season, that they were paid, and that (according to the graffiti on the barracks that housed them) the work groups competed for achievement.[14]

Try as we might, our twentieth-century idea of paradise on earth is not Giza or Thebes, but more likely ancient Tahiti or the homeland of the Iroquois or the Hopi—rural rather than urban. Yet at the time of the building of these ancient cities, they must have been presented to their inhabitants as something far more splendid than the "mere nature" we pine after. Can we discover from the ruins and the images what these ideals might have been? Our fantasy has concentrated on the "sticks"—what could have been the "carrots" in each case?

Ancient Teotihuacan has to have been a success, judging by the fact that it lasted over seven hundred years. (The United States recently celebrated only its two-hundredth anniversary, and there is much talk of its decline already.) Teotihuacan is unique in Mesoamerica for several reasons: almost all the population of the valley resided in one large town; the town was highly organized on a grid plan; and the general population was housed in apartment compounds made well enough to qualify as "palaces" elsewhere. No evidence indicates that residents of Teotihuacan glorified their rulers in art as did the Maya or the Egyptians. Instead, the emphasis of the art is on the gods, especially a Goddess. What then were the ideas and forces that brought this city into being and allowed for its long period of power and influence in Mesoamerica?

I am going to suggest that Teotihuacan was a Pre-Columbian experiment in living. Like the United States, which defined itself against the monarchic governments of Europe, Teotihuacan seems to have emerged in contrast to dynastic and aristocratic cultures, such as the Olmec and the Maya, and to have created and idealized more participatory institutions than were common at the time. The cultural identity of Teotihuacan has been hard to define, because it has long been assumed to be merely an earlier version of Aztec culture and because no written texts are associated with it. Who the people of Teotihuacan were and what they thought they were doing can be interpreted only from the nature of the things they made—the city with its temples and habitations, the sculptures and mural paintings, the objects buried with the dead or placed in offerings, the trade wares they valued, the everyday things they threw out, the rituals they celebrated, and the perfection they seem to have sought. To that list we can add the speculations of earlier generations of scholars, which are full of bright ideas despite an obsession with certain interpretations that hindsight finds inadequate.

This analysis falls between disciplines. It is too heavily anthropological to be art history and too obsessed with artistic readings to be anthropology. It ranges from "scientific" proofs to "humanistic" interpretation but also includes suppositions that are frankly fantasy and perhaps outside of what can be called disciplines altogether. I hope that the reader will engage with each type of "truth" in its own spirit.

After many years of planning and many trips to museums in Mexico, the United States, and Europe, Kathleen Berrin and I organized the first exhibition of Teotihuacan art in San Francisco in 1993. Few people shared our enthusiasm that such an exhibition would be interesting for the public, a significant cultural and aesthetic experience, and a major step in the emergence of Teotihuacan from obscurity. However, nearly 250,000 people saw the show, more than the population of Teotihuacan at its height. The exhibition affected its curators as well. All the objects of Teotihuacan art looked more impressive than we had hoped: we had been working with bad photographs taken in dim conditions and were awed by the actual objects all together in the halls. The museum chose to treat the objects as the treasures of a mysterious ancient civilization and all attempts were made to provide adequate archaeological context. By contrast, the public seemed to see the exhibition as "spiritual." Despite both the conventions of museum exhibition practice and popular sentimentality, Teotihuacan came to life through its objects. Seemingly familiar after years of research, the objects nevertheless took on unexpected dimensions when treated like the treasures of a mysterious ancient civilization. The exhibition emphasized the impressive aspect of the objects, which was indeed considerable. The impersonality, intricacy, and fragility of the objects were also dramatic. Missing, though, was a sense of casualness, playfulness, unpretentiousness, and intimacy. It is not in the nature of a modern art exhibition to encourage such values. What was impressive was that although Teotihuacan lacked a cult of the aesthetic such as that of the Classic period Maya, its objects, once turned into aesthetic objects by the museum display, could rise to the competition.

II

The Paradise of Tlaloc

The Aztec Hypothesis

ALTHOUGH THE CULTURAL IDENTITY OF TEOTIHUACAN HAS BEEN ELUSIVE, the ruins have never been "lost" for any period of time. According to one source, Motecuhzoma Xocoyotzin (the last Aztec ruler) went to perform rites at Teotihuacan every twenty days, and Aztec-style sculptures have been found near the Pyramid of the Sun, supporting the idea that it was a shrine for the Aztecs.[1] Moreover, the ruins were correctly placed on sixteenth-century colonial maps such as the Mapa Tlotzin, which were probably copied from Aztec originals.

The Aztec accounts began much of the confusion surrounding Teotihuacan. Many of the Spanish chroniclers recording Aztec history refer to a golden age prior to the time of the Aztecs, when the greatest city was "Tollan." Before archaeological excavations provided a history, these texts were the authoritative sources. It did not require much imagination to cast Teotihuacan as the ancient "Tollan." The trouble is that other cities, such as Cholula, were also sometimes called "Tollan;" the Aztecs might have called all great ancient cities "Tollan." Some accounts describe the architectural features of "Tollan," which include serpent columns, "with their heads resting on the ground and their tails and rattles in the air."[2] Such columns had not been found at Teotihuacan but were located at Tula, the capital city of the Toltecs, who ruled before the Aztecs. Evidently, to the Aztecs "Tollan" and "the Toltecs" referred in general to the people of antiquity, and more specifically to Tula and Teotihuacan. The Aztecs were apparently not aware of the chronological differences between the two, since they treated both in the same way and imitated the sculptures and architecture of both.[3]

Until 1940, modern scholars accepted the Aztec concept of their past, considering Tula and Teotihuacan the Toltec predecessors of the Aztecs. In 1940, at a roundtable conference of the Mexican Society for Anthropology, the ethnohistorian Wigberto Jiménez Moreno demonstrated conclusively that the "Tollan" of the Aztec texts referred primarily to Tula, in the state of Hidalgo, whose builders were the Toltecs.[4] A growing body of archaeological excavation between 1900 and 1940 had shown that Toltec Mazapan pottery was generally found above Teotihuacan types of pottery, and that therefore Teotihuacan had to have preceded the Toltecs, that is, before A.D. 900. Teotihuacan was thus extricated from its "Toltec" identity but had not yet acquired very much of its own.

Not only the Aztecs have caused confusion about Teotihuacan; modern popularizers do the same. Whenever there is a television special on Mesoamerican cultures and the Aztecs are being described, the camera pans up the majestic Avenue and pyramids of Teotihuacan! Partly filmmakers use this scene because Teotihuacan is more impressive than what remains of Aztec architecture, most of which was consumed to build the cities of colonial Mexico. But can one imagine a special on the Romans in which the Athenian Acropolis stands for Rome? One cannot blame the popularizers for this confusion—we scholars have not provided adequate alternatives for the "Aztec" interpretation.

As early as the sixteenth century the Indians of Mexico and their monuments were identified with other peoples (the lost tribes of Israel were a popular early choice). Likewise, many of the nineteenth-century interpretations of the ruins of Mesoamerica by European travelers and theorizers were so wild and fanciful that seeing Teotihuacan as Aztec appeared to be the height of sober reason. In 1803, for example, the famous visitor Baron Alexander von Humboldt, whose travel account was published in several languages, compared the ruins of Teotihuacan to the pyramids of Egypt, a comment that became a commonplace of nineteenth-century authors.[5] In 1882, as another example, Hubert Howe Bancroft quoted Antonio García y Cubas's study, *Ensayo de un estudio comparativo entre las pirámides egipciles y mexicanas* (1871), and concluded that the layout, orientation, and nature of the pyramids of Teotihuacan were *identical* to those of Egypt![6] Similarly, Désiré Charnay picked up figurine heads in the ground while walking toward the Pyramid of the Sun, and he saw Negro, Caucasian, Mayan, Japanese, and Greek physical types in them.[7] Since authors routinely invoked all other known cultures for comparison with Pre-Columbian ones, the insistence that they were local and related to the ones known was the most scholarly position of the time.

Charnay's excavations resulted in the finding of an enigmatic sculpture that became identified as the first Tlaloc, or Aztec rain god, at Teotihuacan. This 1880 excavation was near the Avenue of the Dead, which Charnay called a "Toltec Palace," now known as a part of the Street of the Dead Complex. After Charnay took the sculpture back to France, E. T. Hamy, at the Paris Trocadero Museum, identified the stylized forms as the upper lip, fangs, and bifurcated tongue of the rain god.[8] Hamy had seen the illustration of such images made in clay on Aztec period Tlaloc shrines and in Aztec pictorial manuscripts. Tlaloc creates thunder and lightning by striking a vessel with an axe. Among the Aztecs, he was one of the two major deities—the other was a patron war deity. The recent excavations of the Aztec Templo Mayor unearthed many Tlaloc images in stone and clay vessels.

This identification by Hamy was rather clever, since instead of a whole face only a few isolated aspects are shown on the sculpture. It is still the best iconographic definition we have for this image, which has come to be called the "cross of Tlaloc." Moreover, in a mural found at Tetitla in the 1960s, a goggled and fanged Tlaloc holds a weapon and pours water from a vessel as in the Aztec codices, thus proving the existence of such a rain god at Teotihuacan and a certain continuity with the Aztecs.[9]

However, between 1900 and the 1970s, nearly every figure found in Teotihuacan art was called Tlaloc—perhaps because of the goggles, which at Teotihuacan turn up in imagery in a bewildering variety of ways. Between 1917 and 1922, the so-called Ciudadela was excavated. Excavators found that the largest structure of the precinct had been built over an earlier pyramid that was faced with a sculptured stone facade featuring two major figures: a fanged serpent and a composite creature with a big upper jaw, fangs, scales, and goggles on its forehead. This creature, still unknown and unidentified, was also dubbed "Tlaloc," though it looked not at all like the "cross of Tlaloc" (page 123).

By the 1940s, enough murals and frescoed vessels were found to indicate that a major theme in Teotihuacan art was water, water creatures, blooming plants, and other symbols of a fertile and verdant world. It was

Figure 2.1. Storm God mural. Copy of a mural painting at Tetitla, Teotihuacan. Metepec phase, A.D. 650–750. From Séjourné 1966b, fig. 160.

perfectly reasonable that the rain god Tlaloc should have been master of this domain. Then, in 1942, excavators discovered the murals of Tepantitla in a remarkable state of preservation. Alfonso Caso wrote the most widely quoted essay on one of these murals, entitled "The Earthly Paradise of Teotihuacan."[10]

The central figure of the Tepantitla mural stands frontally with arms outstretched holding giant drops of water. It is the center of an elaborate image of nature, emerging from the waves of a "sea" and standing beneath a flowering tree. Although its eyes are rhomboid and not goggled, Caso dubbed it (and every other figure in a context of wetness) "Tlaloc."

The mysterious scene of the little human figures beneath the "Tlaloc" Caso identified as the "paradise of Tlaloc," or "the Tlalocan," on the basis of Aztec information. According to the Aztecs, the disposition of the dead in the afterworld did not depend on how virtuously or how sinfully they had lived but largely on the manner in which they died. If they died a natural death, they went to a colorless but not pleasant underworld like the Greek Hades. If they died on the sacrificial stone, they rose into the sky to accompany the sun on its daily path. They could also return to earth in the form of hummingbirds or butterflies and suck the nectar of flowers. Since that activity was a metaphor for sexuality and the joy of living, this was the most splendid fate an Aztec could expect after death. Tlalocan was in an intermediate place, on mountain peaks where the clouds gather. Those who died by the agency of Tlaloc—being struck by lightning, drowning, or succumbing to certain diseases under his aegis—went to the verdant place. Caso therefore saw this mural as the realm of Tlaloc. The many big and prominent butterflies he saw as the souls of sacrificed warriors "visiting" the earth.

As a result of Caso's interpretation, the first identity Teotihuacan acquired was that of a culture preoccupied by water and agricultural fertility. Although warlike or sacrificial themes had been mentioned by Eduard Seler,[11] Laurette Séjourné,[12] Hasso von Winning,[13] and others, Teotihuacan had come to be seen through "Tlaloc goggles." Even predatory or military subjects acquired benign interpretations. Figures with jaguar faces, claws, and weapons painted in red with no clear water associations in another patio at Tepantitla, although found before the "paradise of Tlaloc," were called the "Red Tlalocs" and were thus initiated into the same complex of ideas. In a book published in 1962, George Kubler could write rather authoritatively,

During its early history, Teotihuacan was not a city but a ceremonial centre for the periodic rituals of an agrarian calendar. The pyramids were built and used by farmers from widely dispersed villages. . . . The iconographic system at Teotihuacan allows a few inferences about intrinsic meaning. Representations of aggressive behavior are absent. The signs represent flowers, water, mountains, and other items of peaceful agrarian experience.[14]

Although Teotihuacan's religion and world view were defined on the basis of Aztec images, all "good" and peaceful qualities were attributed to Teotihuacan, while all "bad" and militaristic ones were reserved for the Aztecs. This fantasy was not unlike that of Séjourné, except that she *saw* the hearts, claws, and sacrificial knives but felt compelled to explain them away; others apparently did not *see* them at all.

Besides the interpretation of symbols as relating to the rain god Tlaloc, the supposition of an Aztec identity had other effects on Teotihuacan archaeology. The Aztecs were in the habit of enlarging pyramids by building a new shell over an earlier one; some structures consist of six to eight such layers one on top of another. Archaeologists knew of this Aztec construction technique at the end of the nineteenth century when they began excavating at Teotihuacan. Leopoldo Batres was the Mexican inspector of archaeological monuments, and he began to excavate the Pyramid of the Sun in 1905. He was supposed to restore it to commemorate the centenary of the outbreak of the Mexican Revolution. To complete the "restoration" quickly, he planned to remove the outer layer of rubble to reveal an earlier pyramid in mint condition underneath it. This approach has been much criticized by many archaeologists, especially Seler[15] and Manuel Gamio.[16] Apparently Batres removed several meters of material before he realized that there might not be an earlier pyramid inside. He quickly consolidated the shape as best he could with cement when rain began to wash away the loose fill. As later tunnels inside the pyramid showed, the entire gigantic structure had been built mostly in a single building campaign. Batres not only removed the facing stones and whatever cultural debris might have remained from Teotihuacan times that had been added to the surface of the pyramid, he also dumped the material on top of the surrounding mounds, thus confusing *their* archaeological context for future excavations. As for the Pyramid of the Sun, we will never know its original size. Later excavations have shown a very small inner structure and the possibility of a larger pyramid (indeed only somewhat smaller than the present one) in the interior. This pyramid may have had two shrines on top, according to René Millon.[17]

The designation of the two large pyramids as being dedicated to the sun and the moon is also of Aztec derivation. The Pyramid of the Sun, which faces west, may indeed have a solar significance. Whether the Pyramid of the Moon is associated with moon symbolism we do not know as yet. Its fill is so loose that whenever tunnels have been dug inside it they have collapsed.

Perhaps the most influential image of Aztec derivation, however, is that of Quetzalcoatl, the feathered serpent—one of the most complex and difficult figures in Mesoamerican mythology. In a brilliant study, Pedro Armillas analyzed the various aspects of the feathered serpent as early as 1947.[18] Like Armillas, I must examine the meaning of Quetzalcoatl for the Aztecs to try to understand the meaning of the feathered serpent at Teotihuacan.

In Nahuatl, the word *quetzalcoatl* means literally "quetzal bird–serpent." The reference to the splendid green feathers of the quetzal bird always means preciousness. The quetzal, now nearly extinct, is a bird of the Guatemalan highlands. Only male quetzals have the highly prized, long green tail feathers, and each male has only two. The Aztec rulers and elite wore quetzal feathers on headdresses and costumes. One surviving Aztec headdress, in Vienna, has more than two hundred quetzal feathers ornamented with gold. Quetzal feathers were valued not only because they were rare and imported, but also because of their green color. Green, the color of verdant nature in the rainy season, was the color of life and of well-being. An Aztec father praising his daughter would call her a "precious feather" or a "precious jade."[19] (By contrast, the Nahuatl word for gold meant "the excrement of the gods"–it was not an epithet for beauty.) Recently, Christian Feest has shown that the famous quetzal headdress in Vienna, known as Montezuma's crown, is rather ordinary and far from being a "royal" artifact and that the splendor of the truly royal objects we cannot even imagine.[20]

The symbolism of the serpent in Mesoamerica is the opposite of the evil spirit that tempted Eve in the Judeo-Christian tradition. Very likely the early Mesoamericans also respected the poison and bite of serpents: that quality would have given the serpent its power, invoked in ritual images for human protection. At Teotihuacan, the artists emphasized the rattles of the snake, so that the violent characteristics of the snake were always evident. But the aspect of the serpent that fascinated Mesoamericans was the serpent's ability to shed its skin. The ability to transform itself from an old to a young creature turned the serpent into a symbol of immortality. These serpents were therefore images of renewal and positive transformation. This is not unlike the meaning of dragons in China, where they are symbols of good luck and were associated with the emperor, rather than being cut to pieces by knights in shining armor or trod under the foot of the Virgin Mary, as in Western mythology.

A feathered green serpent could thus allude to a variety of ideas, including the renewal of nature in the rainy season, the verdant surface of the earth, and something both precious and potentially violent. So far, an Aztec and a Teotihuacan individual might have agreed.

The word for "feathered serpent," *quetzalcoatl*, could also be a name in Mesoamerica, and feathered serpents appear to be the name glyphs of personages in art. The most famous "Quetzalcoatl" is known to us from Aztec mythology. According to sixteenth-century colonial Aztec texts, Quetzalcoatl was the name of a ruler in Toltec times. This ruler was distinguished by being priestly and wise. Some accounts say that he did not believe in human sacrifices and sacrificed only birds and butterflies. This Quetzalcoatl was known by his birthdate, One Reed; the glyph One Reed

(Ce Acatl) accompanies his representation in Aztec art. According to legend, he was opposed by a more warlike faction at Tula led by Tezcatlipoca. (Tezcatlipoca is an Aztec deity of war, the night, and sorcery, with some feline aspects. The name means literally "smoking mirror" and suggests Tezcatlipoca's ability to see beyond the visible world.) Tezcatlipoca drove Quetzalcoatl and a handful of followers from Tula after Quetzalcoatl had committed a sin—he drank too much pulque and made love to the goddess of nature and love, Xochiquetzal (or "flower–quetzal bird"). According to some chroniclers, Quetzalcoatl built a funeral pyre when he reached the coast and then threw himself into it. According to others, he sailed off on a raft of serpents, saying that he would return on a date One Reed.

It so happened that the year 1519, when Hernán Cortés sailed up the coast of Mexico and began to look for the Aztecs' fabled ruler Motecuhzoma Xocoyotzin, was One Reed in the Aztec calendar. In trying to explain who these bearded strangers were, sailing in their wooden towers, Motecuhzoma Xocoyotzin and his advisors were very much afraid that they were the Toltecs, led by the returning Quetzalcoatl to reclaim their kingdom. By the time Cortés reached the capital, Motecuhzoma Xocoyotzin welcomed him as the returning Quetzalcoatl and in effect handed the city over to him. The Aztecs were all too aware that they were interlopers in the Valley of Mexico where the legitimate rulers were the Toltecs. Though they boasted of a mission in maintaining the cosmos in their bloody rituals as a "chosen people," at the same time their sense of inferiority in relation to the ancient kingdoms never left them.

Since the Europeans had interpreters, Cortés's mistress La Malinche and a soldier who had been shipwrecked in the Yucatan, the Spanish soon learned of and used the Quetzalcoatl myth for their own purposes, as they talked of the great king (Charles V) across the water who claimed the land of the Aztecs. The Spanish friars who arrived later to record the history and myths of the Aztecs, who had by then been totally conquered, were especially interested in Quetzalcoatl, because as a bearded man who fought against human sacrifice he seemed like a precursor of Christianity. Whereas some sixteenth-century writers decided that the Aztecs were the descendants of the lost tribes of Israel mentioned in the Old Testament, others concluded that Quetzalcoatl must have been the apostle St. Thomas, sent to the New World to convert them.

Was there ever such a person as Ce Acatl Quetzalcoatl of Tula? Although several scholars have tried to prove his existence, they have uncovered no irrefutable evidence.[21] All Toltec art seems to deal with war-

Figure 2.2. Drawing taken from an Aztec rock carving of Quetzalcoatl. Cerro de Malinche, Tula, Hidalgo. Aztec, 1486–1519. Drawing by J. Robertson.

fare and sacrifice, in which the Aztec portrayal of Quetzalcoatl would be out of place. The known representations of Quetzalcoatl—including a cliff relief at Tula showing a figure drawing blood from his ear with a feathered serpent behind him and the date One Reed—all seem to be Aztec in date.[22] Therefore, the story may even be an Aztec fabrication to account for the fall of Tula.

The French historian Jacques Lafaye suggests that much of the Quetzalcoatl story is a creation of the colonial period, made to account for the fall of the Aztec empire at the hands of the Spanish: Quetzalcoatl sounds suspiciously Christian with his antisacrifice bias. Lafaye suggests that the myth could have been created by the Aztecs to provide a supernatural and historical predestination for their defeat and could have been used by the

Spanish to provide a divine justification for the conquest.[23]

In the myth (outside of its historical dimensions), many of Quetzalcoatl's aspects refer to a divinity. His enemy at Tula is a god; the mistress of his downfall is a goddess; and his immolated heart becomes the planet Venus. From other sources, scholars know that Quetzalcoatl in some aspects was a creator god associated with the wind. Because the Quetzalcoatl story was told in such detail in the sixteenth century—the Spanish were fascinated by this figure—modern scholars have difficulty piecing together what the nature of the original deity might have been.

None of these aspects, however, has much to do with the feathered serpent. As the god of creation and wind, Quetzalcoatl is represented as a man with a duck mask. As the ruler of Tula, he is a man sometimes with a beard. He can be recognized only by the presence of the glyph One Reed and a feathered serpent near or behind him. The feathered serpent is not Quetzalcoatl but instead seems to function as an indication of a name. The Aztec sources do not clarify whether the symbolism of the feathered serpent is related to the deity or to the king of Tula, or whether it is purely a name, perhaps referring to a great dynasty, like the Hapsburgs of Europe (their long history and rule in multiple states may make them a particularly appropriate comparison).

At Teotihuacan, the excavations of the Ciudadela by Gamio revealed the Temple of the Feathered Serpent, where a feathered serpent head alternates with a grotesque head usually interpreted as that of Tlaloc. As soon as the feathered serpent image was found in the 1920s, it was associated with Quetzalcoatl. With the name "Quetzalcoatl" came all the associated ideas, such as the peaceful ruler of Tula, the creator god, and so forth. According to Séjourné, Quetzalcoatl was a ruler of Teotihuacan, which supported her theory that all the hearts represented were purely symbolic.[24]

I prefer the name "Temple of the Feathered Serpent," since it leaves out the complicated question of Quetzalcoatl. This feathered serpent is surrounded by shells, evocative of water and of marine places far away from Teotihuacan. The best explanation for the two heads is still, in my opinion, that proposed by Caso and Ignacio Bernal, who suggested that the feathered serpent represents the rainy season, while the scaly creature represents the dry season.[25] They refer to an Aztec hymn at a spring ritual:

> Oh, my god, thy water of precious stones has fallen;
> The tall cypress has changed into a quetzal bird.
> The fire-serpent has been changed into a plumed serpent.[26]

The myth of the peaceful city of Teotihuacan had been created out of many building blocks: the verdant land of Tlaloc, the pious ruler Quetzal-coatl, the evident lack of fortifications around the site, all were combined to support the image of a city without the military apparatus and accompanying human sacrifices characteristic of the Aztec empire. Still, murals found both in the 1890s and in the 1940s provide evidence of warfare at Teotihuacan. Murals at Atetelco show warriors holding weapons and priests holding sacrificial knives; clawed "Red Tlalocs" were visible at Tepantitla. Hasso von Winning noted an owl-and-weapon military symbol on other murals. Perhaps the most important evidence of warfare came from the excavations at Kaminaljuyu within present-day Guatemala City. There archaeologists from the Carnegie Institution of Washington, D.C., found several elite burials in which both Maya and Teotihuacan objects existed side by side. The building even had Teotihuacan-style moldings, which did not suggest brief or casual contact. In 1946 Alfred V. Kidder, Jesse Jennings, and Edwin Shook concluded that Kaminaljuyu was likely to have been a Teotihuacan colony.[27] Colonization could indicate trade or warfare, or both, and the evidence at Kaminaljuyu could have been a signal to abandon the idea of an "agrarian theocracy," but that did not happen until the 1960s.

To what can we attribute the blind spot of so many archaeologists and art historians? A similar situation has been demonstrated for the Maya

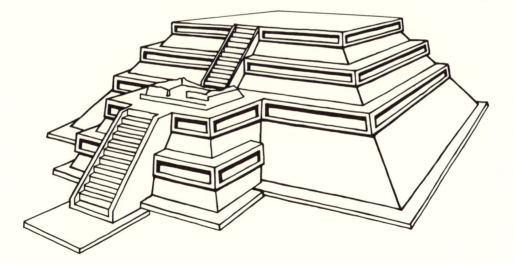

Figure 2.3. Kaminaljuyu building with Teotihuacan-style structure. Drawing by J. Robertson.

by Linda Schele and Mary Miller, who blame the naiveté of the leading Mayanist scholars, such as Eric Thompson and Sylvanus Morley.[28] The phenomenon is broad—it holds for not only a few leading scholars, but also lesser lights, such as Séjourné, and otherwise remarkably perceptive scholars, such as George Kubler.

It is not accidental that these "peaceful visions" were developed at the same time that the chronological divisions of the Mesoamerican past were codified into the Preclassic, Classic, and Postclassic periods. The Classic period, defined by the Maya, Oaxacan, Veracruz, and Teotihuacan civilizations, was placed in contrast to the militaristic peoples of the Postclassic period, such as the Aztecs. By definition, then, cultural florescence, great art, and a less bloodthirsty religion characterized the Classic period. The Postclassic cultures were not just bloody, but also less intellectual and less artistic.

The reason for this blindness to the negative aspects of the Classic period is probably wishful thinking. From the first, Westerners have been fascinated, indeed seduced, by Pre-Columbian cultures, only to come up against the entirely nonhumanistic custom of human sacrifice. This fascination afflicted even sixteenth-century friars like the Franciscan Bernardino de Sahagún. He wrote his great opus on the Aztecs, *The Florentine Codex*, in the hope that Aztec life and language could be completely documented, so that at the time of the millennium, when all life became Christian, the good aspects of the Aztecs could be taught again! The Franciscan clearly found many of the Aztecs more moral and ethical than the Spaniards. His work was labeled as subversive, and he was brought in front of the Inquisition. Sahagún thought that in some future time the good and bad aspects of the Aztecs could be separated.[29]

The scholars of the early twentieth century conjured a different magic trick. As the ruins and cultures of the Classic period were unfolding before their eyes and as the dates were pushed back to between A.D. 200 and A.D. 900, they heaped all the negative traits on the Postclassic cultures, especially the Aztecs, and applied all the positive ones to the Classic cultures. Westerners contemplating ancient America have a deep desire for a "good"—that is, "humanistic"—Pre-Columbian civilization that we can love with a clear conscience. The American past rivals in its art and architecture at least Egypt and Mesopotamia, if not quite Greece and Rome. That Mesoamerica was technologically inferior, lacking wheeled transport and metallurgy, did not seem too bad, since they seem to have done the impossible with simple stone and bone tools. In fact, their technological simplicity points up the miracle of their social organization and artistic will. The astronomical and mathematical knowledge of most Pre-Columbian cultures, the Maya preeminent among them, also make them intellectually the equals of the Old World.

Western observers can also explain away the inhumanity of the practice of human sacrifice. I once argued that Pre-Columbian warfare by the Aztecs had fewer casualties than Western warfare (to say nothing of nuclear warfare) because the Aztecs' aim was to take live victims to sacrifice later.[30] The difficulties of transport and the ceremonial context of much war in Mesoamerica limited the scale of the encounters and the number of people killed. The fact remains, however, that as Westerners we are willing to condone massive deaths in the name of a holy or righteous cause but must condemn as barbaric those forms of torture and killing that are designed to appease the gods. We belong to a culture in which the knight slays the evil dragon or the serpent, not one in which we make sacrifices to power symbolized by dragons and serpents. Our Judeo-Christian morality is based on the idea that man is the supreme creation, his life inviolable; Mesoamerican morality was based on the idea that man was only a part of the cosmos, that voluntarily or involuntarily he would be persuaded to give up his life for the community and the world as a whole. Imbued as we are in the twentieth century with the idea of "human rights" and self-fulfillment, we cannot admire an ethos of torture and self-sacrifice. Even at our most sympathetic, we can explain that ethos but certainly cannot approve of it or suggest that it be tried again—the mere idea is ridiculous. This is the gulf that will forever separate us from the Pre-Columbian past. We cannot admire a world in which political and cosmic values override individual ones to such an extent. And yet we cannot help but admire it.

The Aztec identity that Teotihuacan first acquired resulted in the indiscriminate identification of deities and rituals based on those of the Aztecs. It is my aim to show that except for the persona of Tlaloc, now called the Storm God at Teotihuacan because his actual name there remains unknown, Teotihuacan imagery cannot be identified directly from Aztec sources. This limitation does not mean that Aztec information is of no value in reconstructing Teotihuacan, however. Because we have textual sources, archaeology, and many works of art belonging to a culture that existed in the same region hundreds of years later, the Aztec information provides interesting parallels as well as cautionary tales of interpretive pitfalls we cannot do without. Though I will try to extricate the people of Teotihuacan from interpretations that treat them as though they were the

Figure 2.4. View of Teotihuacan before excavations. Frederick Starr Collection, 1895. National Museum of the American Indian, Smithsonian Institution.

same as the Aztecs, I will use Aztec references to throw light on similarities and differences. The art and culture of the Aztecs provides an essential sounding board in the reconstruction of Teotihuacan.

The peaceful aspect of Teotihuacan and of Classic period Mesoamerica emerged in contrast to and opposition to the Aztecs during the first half of the twentieth century. It has since been dealt a spectacular blow in the *Blood of Kings* exhibit in which Schele and Miller suggested that royal bloodletting and bloody sacrifices were central to Maya art and ritual and that in this respect the Maya were little different from the Aztecs. Recently, interpretations of the Maya have had considerable effect on Teotihuacan studies. The discovery that the Maya figures in art were historic named individuals (and advances in the deciphering of hieroglyphic writing) sent scholars to search for historic named persons, glyphs, writing, and numbers at Teotihuacan. The discovery of nearly a hundred young men dressed in military costume in the Temple of the Feathered Serpent

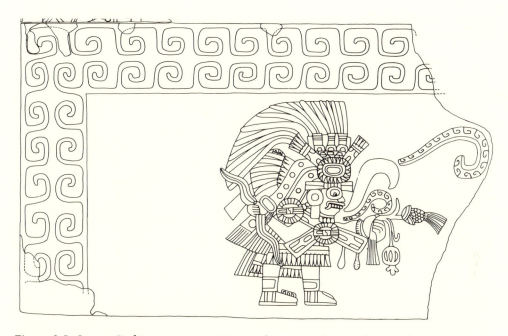

Figure 2.5. Storm God in procession. Drawn from mural at Techinantitla, Teotihuacan. A.D. 600–750. Drawing by Saburo Sugiyama, 1984. Copyright © 1984, by René Millon. (See page 136).

as sacrificial victims has resulted in the reinterpretation of Teotihuacan imagery as dealing with blood, war, and sacrifice. A reasonable perspective is as likely to be lost in the new view of the "blood of Teotihuacan" as in the old hypothesis of the "paradise of Tlaloc."

Mesoamerica, a geopolitical complex like Europe, shared many cultural features—from economic organization to religion, calendar, and artistic imagery—for more than a thousand years. At the same time, individual cultures were as different as England is from Italy or Poland from Spain. It is, of course, possible to focus on the similarities in Europe, such as Christianity, but the differences are also always evident. Because Teotihuacan has been studied too much in terms of its similarity to the Aztecs, and, more recently, to the Maya, I will be focusing on the ways in which Teotihuacan differs from the other Mesoamerican cultures.

III

The New Archaeology
and the State

THE "NEW ARCHAEOLOGY" WAS VERY CONVENIENT FOR ARCHAEOLOGISTS working in foreign countries such as Mexico or Peru, which generally preferred to excavate their ruins themselves. The "new archaeologists" did not seek to excavate the major public buildings; instead, they planned to make maps of the sites and analyze places in terms of the potsherds found on the surface. They dug occasional "test pits" but left the public buildings and tombs pretty much untouched. Therefore, these foreign archaeologists were unlikely to find the headline-grabbing tombs or works of art, which remained the concern of local archaeologists. But even if their work was unglamorous, the "new archaeologists" walked away with the intellectual glory—their research resulted in new information, and their ideas came to dominate the field in the end. They had discovered the alchemy that turned drab potsherds into information. In the 1960s the New Archaeology was still "new" and radical, though by 1990 it was not only close to becoming the norm everywhere but was also receiving severe criticism.[1]

The "Old Archaeology" was a hit-and-run affair even at its scientific best. Archaeologists excavated a chosen building, like the Castillo of Chichen Itza, looking for spectacular tombs or offerings. When they conducted the excavations well, they mapped and noted the location of all objects, then carefully stabilized or possibly restored the structure. Excavators hoped that the various finds in the different layers would indicate the different time periods in which the structure and artifacts had been constructed. By comparing similar finds in widely separated areas—such as Teotihuacan in Mexico and Kaminaljuyu in Guatemala—archaeologists could figure out which sites were contemporary. The Old Archaeology was especially concerned with chronology and history: if one knew when something was made, and the steps that led up to its completion, it had been understood and explained. In many ways the Old Archaeology was not unlike the looting of antiquities, practiced globally from time immemorial. The aim was to find splendid works of art and to uncover marvelous buildings. Only the meticulous recordkeeping of the affair separated the archaeologist from the garden-variety grave robber. (Nor were these two separate—archaeologists often received valuable information from local grave robbers as to the location and nature of finds, while many a paid shoveler-of-dirt on an excavation acquired a valuable archaeological education that became remunerative in grave-robbing once the expedition was over.)

In explaining finds, the Old Archaeology turned whenever possible to the available texts associated with the culture. The most spectacular example of that reliance on texts occurred in the 1870s when Heinrich Schliemann excavated Troy and related the seven levels he distinguished to the account of the city in the *Iliad* (his collaborator, Wilhelm Dorpfeld, later established nine levels in the excavation).[2] Such luck could not be expected everywhere but worked sometimes, even in Mesoamerica, as when Wigberto Jiménez Moreno identified the site of Tula in the modern state of Hidalgo with the Toltecs (A.D. 900–1200) and the city called "Tollan" in the Aztec chronicles.[3]

By contrast, archaeologists excavating Native American sites in the United States had neither spectacular temples nor related texts. Their finds were often arrowheads, potsherds, and the postholes of houses. The very meagerness of the finds led to the development of sophisticated techniques of analysis. For example, archaeologists learned stone-chipping techniques, and with that experience they could distinguish stone chips made in the process of creating a blade from naturally occurring bits of stone. If many chips, or flakes, from knapped blades were found together, the place might have been a working area or workshop in the manufacture of blades. Entirely on the basis of artifact assemblages, archaeologists could suggest that some households were blade makers, while others were potters.

However, this kind of analysis could not be focused on a single building or set of finds. Clearly if the remains of a "village" were to be understood, all of its houses had to be mapped, and the contents of all of them had to be compared. This approach resulted not in the creation of history but in the reconstruction of the social and economic structure of the community: the recognition of status differences in the residences and the objects pertaining to them, occupational differentiation, differences in burial practices. The New Archaeology chose to reconstruct the life of its ancient peoples from the top of the social pyramid to the very bottom. Moreover, it has done so not just without texts, but also using the material evidence as a check on the accuracy of the available texts.[4]

The New Archaeology is remarkably inventive in teasing social and economic information from modest material things. At Teotihuacan, for example, Warren Barbour noticed well-preserved thumbprints in clay figurines, the inadvertent signatures of the artists. Because male and female patterns in thumbprints are consistently different, he has been trying to determine whether the figurine makers were male or female. In the early history of the city they appear to have been female, while later they were male, a distinction that affects the reconstruction of both the division of labor in the family and craft patterns.[5] The study of the bones found in the burials of the apartment compounds has shown that the men were biologically closer to one another than were the women. This physiological information has led Michael Spence to conclude that the Teotihuacan apartment compounds belonged to males related to one another who brought in the wives they married from other compounds, a feature usually termed "patrilocal residence."[6] This type of residence and marriage pattern indicates where the strengths and weaknesses of the Teotihuacan social system would have lain. This kind of material evidence is often superior to that of texts, because the information is explicit and, because it comes directly from the evidence, has not been described or analyzed by anyone to prove a point until the archaeologist comes to analyze it and brings his or her own biases.

In situations where both texts and detailed material evidence are available, not surprisingly, inconsistencies seem to emerge. In the case of the Aztecs, for example, history was at first based on the texts, which put the founding of Tenochtitlan, the Aztec capital, at A.D. 1325. Excavations, however, revealed earlier "Aztec" occupations, as well as floods, before A.D. 1325.[7] The texts, therefore, either are lying, are telling an "official" history that disregards the earlier occupation, or are silent on this matter for other reasons. As factual evidence, the physical remains are primary, in that they are the result of what people actually did: most people do not "falsify" obsidian debris. By contrast, the texts are secondary: whatever history they tell, they have a particular aim in mind. They may aggrandize one people over others (for example, the Aztecs openly claimed to have rewritten history when they came to power) or may be created in smaller matters to justify land disputes or to protect a family or an individual. Almost always, historical texts are partisan.

One strand of the New Archaeology focused on the systemic understanding of ancient sites by the creation of maps of the whole city, or even a valley or geographic region, so one could understand how big a site was, how many villages were related to cities, or who among the inhabitants did what and had what at any given time level. The development of settlement surveys made this type of mapping possible, since obviously archaeologists could not dig and clear as big a site as Teotihuacan. The "new archaeologists" found, however, that if they collect cultural debris—potsherds, stone blades, bones, and such—on the surface without excavation, statistically the artifact assemblages reflect accurately the nature of what is underneath, both in periods and occupation. These surveys require not "shovelers" but well-trained graduate students to examine every square foot of an area.

In this manner, René Millon and his associates discovered that most of the population of Teotihuacan had lived in apartment compounds built on a grid plan, and Millon estimated that approximately two thousand of these compounds existed. The investigators discerned many of the edges of the outside walls in the survey. They were also astonished by the amount of obsidian debris and discovered several hundred workshops, some in the vicinity of the great pyramids. In this manner the great architectural monuments such as the Pyramids of the Sun and the Moon and the Temple of the Feathered Serpent were set in the context of a great city with apartment compounds and evident craft specialization, as first suggested by Pedro Armillas.[8] The New Archaeology was creating a setting in which the structures cleared by the Old Archaeology could be understood.

Perhaps one of the earliest of these "settlement surveys" was done in the Viru Valley in Peru under the direction of Gordon Willey of Harvard University beginning in the 1940s.[9] In the 1960s, settlement surveys mushroomed: besides the Teotihuacan Mapping Project there was the Tikal project in Guatemala and the Monte Alban project in Oaxaca, to name only a few of the largest.[10] The most ambitious of these was the Basin of Mexico project, directed by William Sanders, Jeffrey Parsons, and Robert Santley.[11] They took the Basin of Mexico, including Mexico City (the ancient Aztec capital Tenochtitlan-Tlatelolco) and Teotihuacan and made a series of chronological maps from 2000 B.C. to A.D. 1500. This survey set Teotihuacan, as a city, in the context of the entire Basin of Mexico. Modern observers now have an idea of how many hamlets, villages, or major cities existed at any given time and where they were geographically. A study of the ecological setting allowed for interpretations of the location of settlements on the basis of soil conditions, climate, and natural resources.

One aim of these ingenious studies was to reconstruct the life of an ancient place. But the New Archaeology had a greater ambition than that. The "new archaeologists" wished to gather data to explain why people created civilizations—what made them give up hunting and gathering, or a simple village life, for pyramids and apartment compounds and awesome piles of earth and rock? This was by no means a new question. Various theories of human cultural evolution were devised starting in the eighteenth century and culminating in the evolutionist theories of the nineteenth century by economists such as Karl Marx and Friedrich Engels and by various anthropologists. Imbued with the notion of progress, they suggested various stages on the road from the life of early humans to capitalism—and beyond, in the case of Marx and Engels.

In the late 1950s and 1960s, these evolutionary theories enjoyed a major revival. Various authors suggested that this process could best be analyzed in four types of social integration, which were in some times and places also stages of evolution: the band, the tribe, the chiefdom, and the state.[12] The earliest form of human society are presumed to have lived in small family groups, called bands, and to have survived by hunting and collecting foodstuffs. Because they were nomadic, they had no permanent architecture or much in the way of material things. Also, few differences in status or occupation distinguished them. Such societies are seen as egalitarian. (This lifestyle is what intellectuals of the nineteenth century imagined as "primitive communism.")

So-called tribes (the word is now considered derogatory, but no substitute is available) are now thought of as independent village cultures with some kind of agriculture—millet, manioc, and the like—supplementing hunting. In these sedentary village societies, people are still family-related,

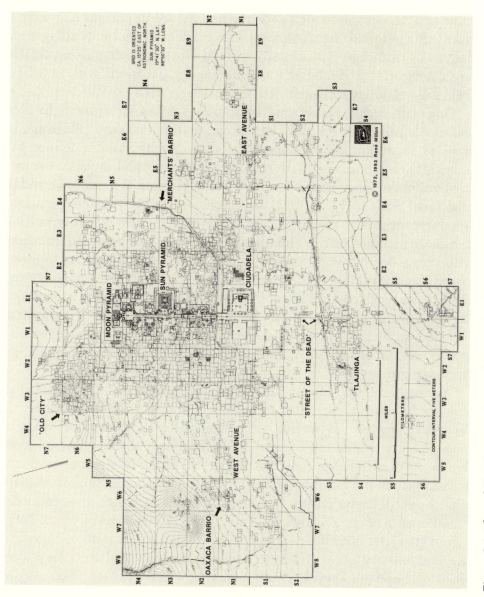
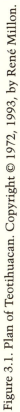

Figure 3.1. Plan of Teotihuacan. Copyright © 1972, 1993, by René Millon.

but various "secret" initiation societies may cut across family lines. Because villages are larger than bands, social cohesion is a greater problem. Various ceremonies in which artworks (such as masks, ancestor figures, spirit images, decorated men's society houses) are important help knit society into a political and ideological whole. Such autonomous villages may frequently exchange gifts ritually or feud with their neighbors, creating larger networks. Although status differences exist in villages, hereditary rank, classes, or great inequalities in wealth do not.

One of the major theoretical contributions of this literature in the 1960s was the definition of the chiefdom, separate from both the village and the state, as an important developmental stage. A chiefdom is defined by a hereditary rank structure with the chief at its apex and the rest of society in a pyramid of lesser status levels. The chief is both the symbolic and the functional heart of the political unit. Symbolically he may be essential to rituals for the gods or the ancestors, and semidivine power may be invested in him. In practical terms, chiefdoms often derive their wealth from trade with neighbors and with faraway places. Most of this trade is in rare or exotic things: ivory, coral, jade, grizzly-bear teeth, shells, amber. Some of these items reach persons lower in the social pyramid, but most remain in the hands of the upper echelon. Chiefdoms also have artists making beautiful and exotic things both as insignia for the ruler and as items of trade or gifts: elaborate textiles, gold masks, carved shell jewelry, ceramic and stone sculptures.

Although the splendor of chiefdoms may be very real, the power of the chief usually is not. The chief rules by virtue of consensus—he has no independent powers and in effect cannot make his own policy or undertake projects his people do not want to do. Archaeologically, chiefdoms are visible in the occasional presence of plazas and mounds, stone monuments, and sculptures, but rarely colossal architecture. Examples include the large stone heads of Easter Island, the megaliths of Stonehenge, the ceremonial paraphernalia of the Ashanti of Ghana, the jade pendants of Costa Rica.

In states, the ruler has nearly absolute power in the form of courts, police, and military forces. The ruler can collect tribute and use it for projects whether the people approve or not. One characteristic of states is that great building projects such as the pyramids of Egypt and the road system of the Inca are undertaken both to deploy and to advertise this power. States usually exhibit abundant evidence for occupational specialization, as well as scientific and recording systems. The geometric, mathematical, and astronomical knowledge of ancient states is legendary. In many, some kind of writing system records histories, myths, or economic transactions. It is the "state" that is synonymous with the usual concept of "civilization." In this sense the term *civilization* suggests that these cultures are the direct precursors of modern life.

Even today many groups of people can be said to live in a band, village, or chiefdom type of society. But no cultures are comparable to ancient states. Only six "pristine" ancient states existed: Egypt, Mesopotamia, India, China, Mesoamerica, and Peru. The last ancient states were destroyed by European conquest. Therefore, we know the pristine state mainly from archaeology and ancient texts.

What made ancient people—probably in a large chiefdom—willing to create great social inequalities and to become the builders of gigantic monuments in these ancient states? How did the rulers convince people to come together in state-sponsored projects and to stay without rebelling or going elsewhere? The modern nation-state is a descendant of these "pristine" states, so when we ask these questions we are asking ultimately about the origins of the states in which we now live. We do not find the elite's desire for power and control for their own advantage mysterious, but the willingness of others playing the role of the poor, of the "commoners" in a ranked society at first seems puzzling. However, the institutionalization and acceptance of human sacrifice is similar, in some ways, to the acceptance of low income and low status, to which modern society has become accustomed.

One theoretical explanation of the rise of the state was put forth by Karl Wittfogel on the basis of ancient China and Egypt. He argued that irrigation systems necessitate managerial control in the hands of an elite and that the projects of the Yangtze and Nile Rivers resulted in the creation of the state. Scholars have argued whether this was a relatively benign social contract in which the elite performed a necessary organizational task for society as a whole (since everyone benefited from the higher agricultural production) or whether it was a coercive situation in which commoners had no choice but to submit to absolute rulers. Wittfogel believed in the latter interpretation and entitled his book *Oriental Despotism: A Comparative Study of Total Power.*[13] This "hydraulic hypothesis" may also explain the situation in Mesopotamia (the Tigris and Euphrates Rivers) and the many small river valleys of Peru. Wittfogel's idea of centralization has been seen as characterizing the ancient states of most of the world and to have ended only with the European development of capitalism.

Robert Carneiro proposed another theory which is currently more popular.[14] He suggested that all social stratification in both chiefdoms and states might be due to "circumscription." As used by Carneiro, "circumscription" means that if the natural or social environment is open and homogeneous (as in large tropical forests), if a group gets to be too large or if members of the group start quarreling, people may separate from the group and move to new places. In these situations, hierarchic organizations are unnecessary. If, by contrast, an area is surrounded by obstacles (such as deserts or other dense populations) and therefore moving away is not a viable alternative, society faces crises by reorganizing itself along hierarchic lines. Hierarchy is efficient in that it results in centralized control, the organized allocation of tasks, and occupational specialization. Conquest and the extraction of tribute or taxation is as much a part of the Carneiro as of the Wittfogel model. The circumscription theory works well to explain many ancient cultures that did emerge in arable lands surrounded by deserts. A paradox lies at the heart of every hierarchic society: the upper level of society works to create food and a worthwhile life for the entire society, but in the process, a wide gap is created between the upper and the lower level. If people cannot move away, they may have no choice but to go along with a bad bargain. The circumscription theory therefore underscores that force is involved. Nearly all scholars involved with the theory of the rise of the early state suggest that military conquest or some element of force was used to create states.[15]

Once Teotihuacan was mapped as the first major "state" in Mesoamerica, the "new archaeologists" asked how it had emerged as a state. William Sanders and Barbara Price argued that the process was very similar to that of the rest of the world.[16] The Americas were populated by people migrating from Asia around 40,000 B.P. as hunter-gatherers moving in small, nomadic bands. Around 8000 B.C. most of the great mastodons and sloths hunted by these early groups died out. People began to explore the seeds, plants, and smaller animals of their local areas. In adapting themselves to local conditions, they began the process of domesticating plants and animals.

Between about 3000 B.C. and 2000 B.C., large areas of Mesoamerica were occupied by settled villages ("tribes") practicing maize agriculture and making pottery vessels. The interest of Mesoamericans in ritual is evident in the clay masks and figurines that are often found in their trash and burials.

Sanders and Price saw the chiefdom stage illustrated by the Olmec and their contemporaries. In Mesoamerica there is some evidence of flood-water irrigation and the centralization of power first for the Olmecs along the Cotzacoalcos River. The Olmec rulers persuaded people to build earth mounds and to move colossal boulders in which their "portraits" were carved. Long-distance trade is evident in the presence of greenstone, hematite, and jade used for Olmec insignia and mirrors. Sanders and Price also saw the Maya cities of the tropical forest as no more than especially splendid chiefdoms. They argued that the greatest Maya site recently mapped, Tikal, might have had a population of no more than 40,000 and that the population of Tikal had been widely dispersed. The emphasis on art and ceremony was, to them, quite consistent with a chiefdom.

For Sanders and Price, the only place in Mesoamerica where states developed was the Basin of Mexico, where Teotihuacan, Tula, Tenochtitlan, and even modern Mexico City are all located. The Basin of Mexico is in some ways an ideally circumscribed place according to the requirements of the "circumscription theory." In ancient times a large and shallow lake was surrounded by rich valley land, especially on the southwestern side. The basin is further circumscribed by a series of tall mountains and volcanoes. Moreover, the largest contiguous area of flat arable land in all of Mesoamerica is in the Basin of Mexico, and this area was and is the seat of political power in the region. However, because this is a high plateau, the climate is cold and arid, and agriculture with irrigation made a much larger concentration of population possible. Therefore, in early times, when the people who lived in the warmer and wetter Gulf areas (the Olmec) were erecting mounds and carving jade, the Basin of Mexico largely contained villages and modest chiefdoms without great public architecture.

Evidence of irrigation at Teotihuacan and the presence of a high water table and many springs indicated to Sanders that Teotihuacan fit the idea of an original "hydraulic" state. René Millon, however, has pointed out that the San Juan River is but a small brook next to impressive rivers like the Nile and that Teotihuacan could not have had nearly as great an agricultural abundance as the ancient Egyptians had. Nevertheless, in Millon's view, Teotihuacan was a state, even if not a "hydraulic" one. He created the alternative concept of Teotihuacan as a great "market-pilgrimage" center.[17]

Unlike the "hydraulic" and "circumscription" theories, in which an existing population is reorganized due to external circumstances, Millon's premise was that Teotihuacan was a great magnet pulling people in. This interpretation of the "market" component emerged as a result of the mapping of the city. Across from the Temple of the Feathered Serpent archaeologists identified what appeared to have been a vast walled but empty plaza. Mapping also showed that besides a north-south Avenue, there was an east-west avenue that created a special center out of the temple and this open area (Chapter 8). Referring to the various sixteenth-century accounts of the Aztec capital Tenochtitlan, where a great market was next to the central temple, Millon felt that the plaza at Teotihuacan might have been a market, and he termed it the "Great Compound."

Indeed, Mesoamerica was (at the time of the Spanish conquest and before) very much a market civilization. Because altitudes vary greatly in a small area, natural resources vary also, making exchange necessary and profitable. Cacao beans, used as currency during Aztec times, require a hot and moist climate and cannot be grown in the Basin of Mexico. The beans were thus imported from the lowlands of Veracruz or Guatemala—perhaps even from Kaminaljuyu in Guatemala, which Sanders interpreted as an outpost of Teotihuacan merchants involved in long-distance commerce.[18] Besides cacao, quetzal feathers and other rare tropical goods may have been obtained in Kaminaljuyu. More recently, archaeologists have found a Teotihuacan settlement in Matacapan, Veracruz.[19] Cotton, like cacao used as currency by the Aztecs, can be grown only in the warm lowlands and had to be imported to Teotihuacan. Teotihuacan, judging by its art, also prized marine shells and feathers unavailable in the highlands. Certainly merchants must have been an important group within the city.

Sanders has argued that besides ordinary short-distance merchants, Teotihuacan also had long-distance merchants, like the Aztec *pochteca*. The *pochteca* were wealthy and semi-independent; they traveled and traded on their own but were also used for state purposes by the Aztec rulers as ambassadors and even spies. Whether the Teotihuacan traders were like the *pochteca* we do not know, but evidently long-distance traders were active. It is clear that they acquired such luxury items as cacao, cloth, quetzal feathers, and greenstone. It is less clear what they traded in exchange. For a while studies concentrated on the obsidian found in abundance at the site of Teotihuacan.[20] A more common gray obsidian comes from nearby Otumba, and a finer green obsidian from near Tula. The gray and, more especially, the green obsidian from these sources are found in many parts of Mesoamerica, and archaeologists once thought that

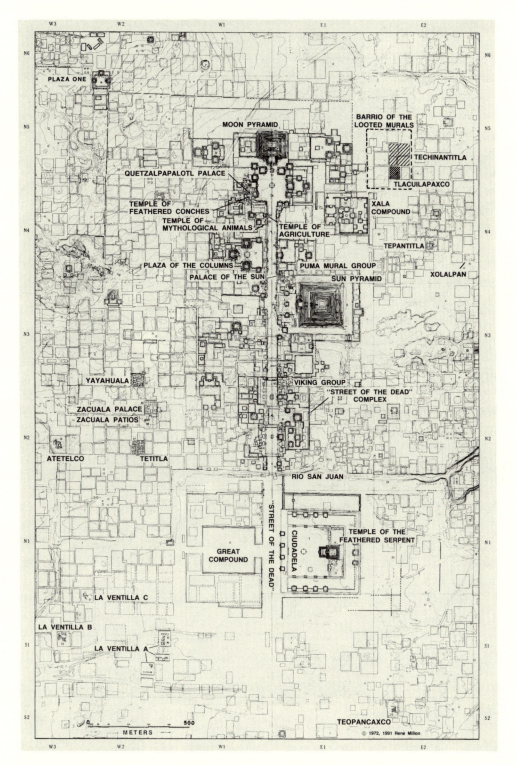

Figure 3.2. Plan of the center of Teotihuacan. Copyright © 1972, 1991, by René Millon.

Teotihuacan manufactured obsidian objects for export and had an "obsidian monopoly." The transportation of the heavy, glasslike obsidian over long distances makes this theory problematic except as applied to small, ceremonial quantities rather than large-scale utilitarian ones. Moreover, archaeologists now believe that many of the so-called obsidian workshops actually were something else—perhaps sites of manufacture of other craft products.[21] Craft production, including the manufacture of obsidian objects, could still have been of the greatest significance in the economy of Teotihuacan.

Teotihuacan merchants did carry one of the prestige potteries of their time, the Thin Orange wares. These ceramic wares were made not at Teotihuacan but in Puebla; however, Teotihuacan merchants carried them to Teotihuacan and elsewhere.[22] They are frequent in tombs, thus indicating their high value.

Though much can be read out of material remains, it must be remembered that once a great many perishable things existed that do not survive archaeologically. The Aztec tribute books list many items that would seldom appear archaeologically: cloth, foodstuffs (ranging from chili peppers to honey), feathers, and down, as well as military garb and shields ornamented with feathers. Undoubtedly perishable goods were also important at Teotihuacan.

According to Millon, Teotihuacan market activities were associated with Teotihuacan as a pilgrimage center. It is not hard to imagine that other Mesoamericans, like modern tourists, flocked to the city of Teotihuacan. The Aztecs had pilgrimage temples and cities, the one at Cholula (often called Tollan) being one of them. Motecuhzoma Xocoyotzin himself made pilgrimages to Teotihuacan. It would have made sense, certainly to an Aztec, to have market and temple together as they still are in many Indian communities in Mexico and Guatemala.

However, archaeologists have little hard evidence either for the Great Compound as "market" or for the temples as "pilgrimage centers."[23] Most evidence about Teotihuacan as a trading center comes from outside Teotihuacan. No great quantity or quality of foreign objects has ever been found at Teotihuacan (despite the discovery of a merchant's barrio by Evelyn Rattray).[24] More extensive excavation of the Great Compound may determine more clearly its use.

Recently Millon, less interested in "hydraulic theory" and more in the unique situation of Teotihuacan, has suggested an ideological rather than

Figure 3.3. Obsidian blades. From Cuauhtitlan. Largest, 15.5 cm (6 in.); smallest, ca. 2 cm (1 in.). The Saint Louis Art Museum, Acc. 135: 1980.1–58, Cat. 155.

an economic explanation for the origin of Teotihuacan. His theory tries to account for some interesting changes in settlement patterns identified by Sanders, Parsons, and Santley in 1979.[25] The maps for the Basin of Mexico show that the best lands and the early agricultural centers in the area (from 1000 B.C. on) were in the southwest of the basin (the Aztec capital Tenochtitlan was also in this area). The major center in this early period was Cuicuilco, with the largest pyramid of its time, built in a round, stepped configuration. Teotihuacan, in a small valley to the northeast, had mainly villages without great public architecture. Cuicuilco was, however, shaken by the eruption of the volcano Xitle, which covered much of its center—including the round pyramid—with more than a meter of lava. Although Cuicuilco did not immediately disappear, as Teotihuacan began to grow, eventually the earlier center declined. The basin maps showed another striking development: in the days of Cuicuilco, circa 300–100 B.C., the area also had a number of widely spaced hamlets and villages and small towns. By the beginning of the first phase of Teotihuacan, the Tzacualli phase (at A.D. 1), most of the basin was depopulated, the hamlets and villages were abandoned, and nearly everyone lived in the city of Teotihuacan, the population of which has been estimated at 90,000. Throughout most of the life of Teotihuacan no settlement of any great size existed outside the city. People began to move out during the later phases of Teotihuacan, when two settlements, Atzcapotzalco and San Miguel Amantla, became small towns. After the fall of Teotihuacan, during the hegemony of the Toltecs and Aztecs, the settlement pattern was more similar to that in the era of Cuicuilco, consisting of a capital and smaller centers, villages, and hamlets scattered throughout the area. This was probably the most practical and "natural" population settlement in the Valley of Mexico. These towns and villages all had markets to trade their various resources with one another. In its settlement pattern, therefore, Teotihuacan was unique.

Because of the earlier and later settlement patterns, Sanders saw the unusual Teotihuacan pattern of one huge city as something created and enforced by a ruling elite. To him it was similar to the Spanish practice of forcing the conquered Native American peoples from isolated hamlets into towns, making it easier to proselytize and collect tribute from them. Thus Sanders saw the beginning of Teotihuacan's dominance as having occurred through conquest and forced resettlement. In his view an all-powerful state had created irrigation works, had sent out long-distance trading parties, and had ruled with unquestioned authority.[26]

Millon's "ideological" explanation for the rise of Teotihuacan is based partly on the fact that the agricultural base around the San Juan River is too meager for Teotihuacan to have arisen as a hydraulic state. His "market-pilgrimage" idea may explain the state's persistence but not its origins. Two aspects of the Tzacualli phase (A.D. 1–A.D. 150) he found striking: the depopulation of the basin and the great and sudden growth of the city coeval with the building of the Pyramid of the Sun and much of the Pyramid of the Moon, the laying out of the north-south Avenue, and the general setting up of the temples of the site. He suggests that the people were brought in to build the pyramids through some powerful religious myth and that in the process they literally built the city, as their temporary shelters were eventually made more permanent. The monuments themselves were thus part of the dynamic that resulted in the city.[27] Most recently, Millon theorized that Teotihuacan was forcibly settled under the rule of a series of charismatic early leaders, subsequently buried in the Pyramids of the Sun and the Moon. He suggested that they created a new religion and claimed that both time and a new era began at Teotihuacan.[28]

Like Sanders, Millon emphasizes an all-powerful state that controlled the lives of the people of the entire Basin of Mexico, more than ever before or after. Although these scholars do not suggest that slaves were whipped, they suggest that the existing situations and circumstances allowed people no other choice than to submit to the rulers. Sanders's theory is ecological while Millon's is more ideological, but both see Teotihuacan as a place of absolute centralized power.

There is no doubt that Teotihuacan was a state, and in fact the first urban state in Mesoamerica. It fulfills the criteria of a state in terms of intensive agriculture, long-distance trade contacts, militarism, division into social classes, specialization, and a large urban population. It also has some features that are unique in the Mesoamerican context. First, the population was concentrated in one city rather than in the hierarchy of villages, towns, and a capital that was characteristic of the Maya and Aztec. Second, the people of the city all lived in multifamily apartments that were unknown before or after in Mesoamerica. The New Archaeology accounted well for Teotihuacan as a state, but Mesoamericanists are still debating Teotihuacan's unique features.

IV

The View from the
Apartment Compound

FROM THE TIME THEY WERE FIRST FOUND IN THE NINETEENTH CENTURY until the 1950s, the Teotihuacan apartment compounds were considered "palaces."[1] In comparison to the known dwellings of commoners, both Pre-Columbian and modern, they are spacious and well-made, not unlike the palaces of the Maya and in Monte Alban. Large central patios with altars are frequently located in their middle. Temples on one side of the central court and spacious porches on the other sides suggest use as quarters for the reception of guests, for administrators, for rituals and feasting. Mural paintings on many walls remind one of such remains all over the world from Knossos and Mycenae to China and India. The apartment compounds with their painted walls are especially evocative of the Roman ruins of Pompeii, in which the daily life of the Romans is made vivid for the visitor.

Until the middle of the twentieth century observers assumed that few such "palaces" were present at Teotihuacan. Excavations by Laurette Séjourné[2] and by the Swedish archaeologist Sigvald Linné[3] brought to light many things buried with the dead under the floors: pottery vessels, figurines, even dismantled incense burners. Although both Séjourné and Linné thought of the buildings as "palaces," neither wondered why more expensive materials, such as greenstone, were not found. This absence of luxury items was especially interesting since hundreds, perhaps thousands of Teotihuacan masks in a variety of sizes and types of stone had been collected since the late nineteenth century and were generally believed to be attached to "funerary bundles." But except for the fragment of a very small mask found by Linné, the "palaces" seemed not to be the source of the famous masks.

It was the mapping project led by René Millon that supported Pedro Armillas's observation that the "palaces" were actually the homes of most of the residents of Teotihuacan and that they were multifamily units housing sixty to one hundred people. Millon renamed them "apartment compounds." Millon and George Cowgill estimate that more than two thousand apartment compounds existed at Teotihuacan.

While writing my dissertation on the murals of Tepantitla, I spent many hours in the cool quiet of the apartment-compound patios and porches. Most tourists are herded to climb the pyramids, and the noise of their exhausted cries of having made it to the top would be audible to me from a distance. Most tourists did not have the time or inclination to bother with fragmentary paintings, so usually I was alone with the guards. Though the guards checked on me periodically, they often wandered to other parts of the compounds and left me the sole occupant. Some compounds, like Atetelco, looked in the noonday heat as if their owners were merely out for the day, the walls and roofs under renovation but in good enough condition to allow me to imagine everyone returning by nightfall. I imagined a listing for the Tepantitla apartment in the real estate section of the *Teotihuacan Times*: "Finely painted compound, twelve rooms, spacious patio, excellent view of the Pyramid of the Sun."

I noted the knobs at the doorways to which mats or curtains had probably been fastened, the pottery vessel built into one floor, the drains that functioned during the summer downpours. Lacking windows, the interior rooms were dark. I imagined mats and blankets on the floor, functional and personal objects in boxes or hanging in nets from the rafters. Test pits from the mapping project showed that some rooms were kitchens, with layers of ash for the fireplaces and much broken crockery.[4] I spent my time sketching and observing the murals in the cool shade of the porches, and I could imagine Teotihuacan elders discussing household and city issues on some porches, mothers nursing babies on others, children being shooed from the courtyards to the alleys.

The apartment compounds were not merely *livable*; many were *splendid*. One could easily imagine living in them, even coming from a twentieth-century culture. Moreover, even Tlamimilolpa, an apartment compound excavated by Linné, which is often considered "slumlike" because of its labyrinthine arrangement of small rooms without a clear

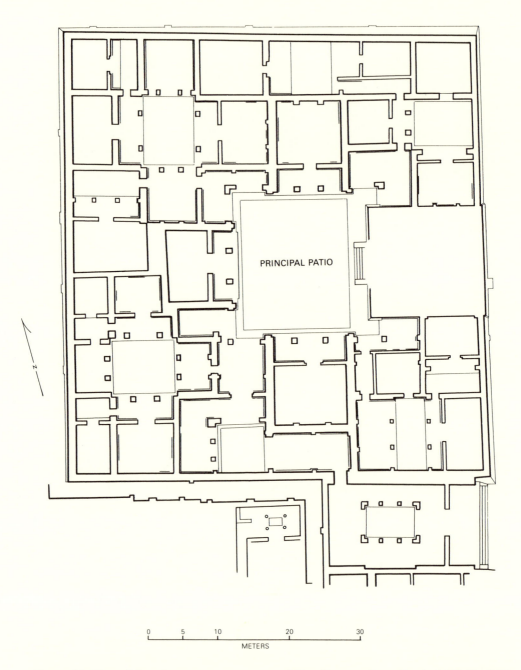

PRINCIPAL PATIO

| 0 | 5 | 10 | 20 | 30 |
METERS

Figure 4.1. Plan of Zacuala apartment compound, Teotihuacan. From Berrin 1988, fig. 3.11, copyright © 1988, by René Millon.

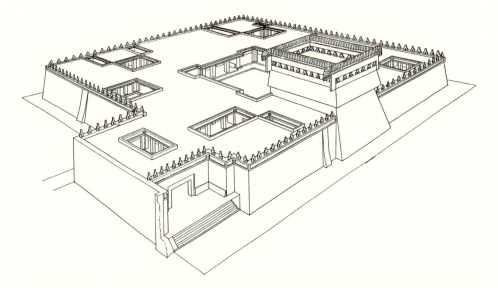

Figure 4.2. Elevation of Zacuala apartment compound, Teotihuacan. From Séjourné 1966b, fig. 23, pp. 80–81.

central patio, had mural painting fragments that were no different in style and conceptions from those in other compounds.[5] In all cases the apartment compounds are a far cry from the squalid houses in which most modern and Pre-Columbian peasants lived—one-room thatched structures built on a stone foundation with an earthen yard for children, animals, tools, and the overflow of things from the house.

In the 1970s, although I had a very strong sense of the nature of the apartment compounds, I did not know quite what to make of them in view of Teotihuacan's structure as a city. But I think I was imprinted with a "view from the apartment compound" that eventually led me to ask different questions about Teotihuacan many years later. I imagined the two thousand headmen of the compounds forming an advisory, legislative, or consulting body that met with or was consulted by the priest-rulers for political and economic purposes (or if not the priest-rulers directly, then through the ward leaders, since Millon had tentatively divided Teotihuacan into wards as well).[6] I was beginning to imagine a city organized very differently from the rest of Mesoamerica, especially the Maya, with its feudal kings and nobility living in palaces and the peasants in small, perishable houses. As William Sanders has pointed out, Teotihuacan might have had a prosperous middle class like that of ancient Rome. The similar plans of the apartment compounds suggested that they might have been

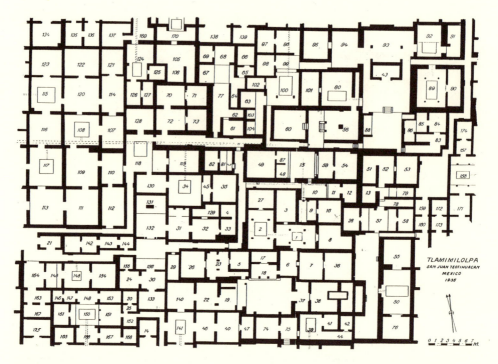

Figure 4.3. Tlamimilolpa plan. From Linné 1942, pl. 1, © The National Museum of Ethnography.

corporate social organizations with a collective ideology.

We all create our theories out of the data we find most striking, and a few of these become "clothes hangers" for whole "outfits" of ideas. My "clothes hangers" in this redefinition were as follows:

1. the apartment compounds
2. the lack of representation of individual rulers in Teotihuacan art
3. the representation of the elite as anonymous groups in military or ritual dress in ceremonial contexts
4. the creation of works of art assembled out of mass-produced pieces as in incense burners, host-figures, and figurines, which paradoxically showed both standardization and individualization
5. a major female deity

I began to see the apartment compounds as representations and embodiments of civic wealth and power. They were not built immediately in the history of Teotihuacan—at first people lived in impermanent constructions while the Pyramids of the Sun and Moon and the Temple of the Feathered Serpent were being built. They were first built during the Tlamimilolpa phase, which began about A.D. 200. From the time of this original building until the collapse of the city in A.D. 750 (more than five hundred years), the apartment compounds appear to have been continuously inhabited. Although new floors were laid, some walls were changed, and plaster was renewed, the basic plan remained pretty much unchanged.

Curiously, moreover, after the people of the city shifted their efforts to building housing for the community, they undertook no colossal architectural project like the Pyramids of the Sun and the Moon or the Temple of the Feathered Serpent. That shift in emphasis does not mean that they built no ceremonial architecture for five hundred years—merely that it is of a different character. For example, many of the temples around the Pyramid of the Moon and along the Avenue were rebuilt during this period, in a homogeneous architectural form. Each platform body was divided into a lower sloped panel (*talud*) and an upper rectangular panel with a sunken interior (*tablero*), which gives Teotihuacan its unique architectural char-

Figure 4.4. Apartment-compound central platform at Yayahuala, Teotihuacan. Pasztory photo.

acter. This rebuilding is pervasive throughout the city, rather than being concentrated on one massive structure.

George Cowgill also suggested that at this time the administrative center of the city was shifted from the Temple of the Feathered Serpent and the Ciudadela to a new Street of the Dead Complex.[7] The Street of the Dead Complex is a walled area carved out of already existing spaces including room complexes (like the apartment compounds, only on a more lavish scale, now called the Viking Group and the Superposed Structures —Leopoldo Batres's "Toltec palace") and several three-temple complexes facing each other across the Avenue. The area is 350 meters square, that is, only a little smaller than the Ciudadela. The location of the Street of the Dead Complex is strategic—it lies between the Ciudadela and the Pyramid of the Sun, and here the Avenue is divided by several transverse steps blocking easy passage at the very center of the city.

The significance of the Street of the Dead Complex is closely tied to the three-temple complexes within it, indicating a partial ritual function for the complex. The three-temple complexes are something of a mystery. Linda Manzanilla thinks that they were ward temples.[8] They consist of a

Figure 4.5. Apartment-compound central platform at Tetitla, Teotihuacan. Pasztory photo.

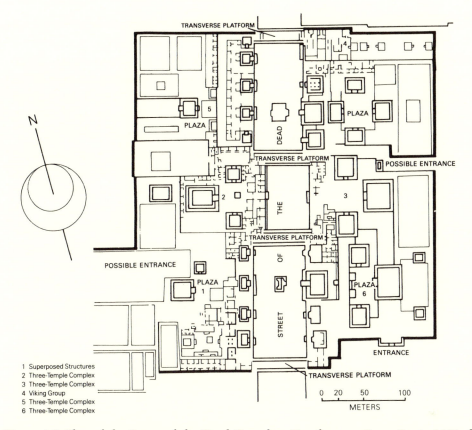

Figure 4.6. Plan of the Street of the Dead Complex, Teotihuacan. From Berrin 1988, fig. 3.13, copyright © 1988, by René Millon.

large central pyramid, flanked by two smaller pyramids around a square court. The Pyramids of the Sun and Moon are actually three-temple complexes, but their flanking temples are so small that the larger pyramids are thought of as individual structures. About twenty of these three-temple complexes have been identified, and many of them were built in the early years of Teotihuacan. Many are in the northwestern village of Oztoyahualco, from whence the city of Teotihuacan expanded. The three-temple complexes therefore may signify antiquity: the early years and ritual practices of Teotihuacan. In addition, because there are about twenty of them they either indicate divisions into parishes (like churches in Rome) or some kind of sociopolitical groupings subdividing the city. Moreover, because they vary greatly in size and centrality of location, these parishes or divisions appear to have been hierarchical and not of equal importance. The three-temple complexes indicate dispersed rather than concentrated power, whether they expressed local power or the local tentacles of centralized power.

The presence of two three-temple complexes in the Street of the Dead Complex suggests a veneration of ancient cult practices and the creation of an administrative center out of what already existed in the city, not a radically new structure in a different place or on a different plan. The Street of the Dead Complex thus appears to be an affirmation of what the people of Teotihuacan perhaps felt was *traditional* about their city, and not the creation of a new, innovative, or striking architectural vision of itself. (One could argue that the complex was rebuilt as it was due to scarce resources, but that premise is unlikely in view of the fact that resources were lavished on the apartment compounds contemporaneously.) In that sense, the political-religious governing power of Teotihuacan is visually underplayed from A.D. 200 to A.D. 750.[9] The Street of the Dead Complex may have been dramatic and central in the time that Teotihuacan flourished, but it is invisible as an architectural monument from the rest of the city of Teotihuacan as a ruin.

Instead, the architectural emphasis was placed on the organization and control of the community as a whole, divided into the apartment compounds. The very idea of the apartment compound seems to me to be, in miniature, a version of the Ciudadela and the Temple of the Feathered Serpent (Chapter 8). The high wall, single entrance, central patio, central shrine, and apartments all have their parallels. Most apartment compounds have a temple facing west, like the Temple of the Feathered Serpent. In that sense, the early excavators of Teotihuacan were right—the apartments are miniature palaces: palaces for the people.

The sheer expense of time and wealth that went into the building of the apartment compounds suggests major concern with the population. It suggests a relatively high standard of living as well as some say in the running of the city for perhaps a remarkably large segment of the city. Millon argued recently that the apartments were built by a decision of the higher authorities and that materials may have even been handed out to apartment builders along with strict instructions to fit their structures into the alignment of the city.[10] Sanders suggests that the purpose of this "urban renewal" was taxation, census taking, and administrative control. Whether the order came from the temples or whether the idea was local, such investment in public housing is remarkable. The situation argues for the economic and political power of the population, especially if "the people" had to be "controlled."

Figure 4.7. Aerial view of the Ciudadela, Teotihuacan. CNCA-INAH-MEX. CIA Mexicana Aerofoto.

After about A.D. 200 at the start of the Tlamimilolpa phase, Teotihuacan appears to have celebrated collective values and to have avoided or played down themes of dynastic and elite power in imagery. This hypothesis is illustrated by the fact that no rulers are represented in Teotihuacan art, in contrast to earlier Olmec and contemporary Maya and Monte Alban art. Even the Aztecs, much of whose art was religious, represented their rulers in cliff sculptures at Chapultepec and on dozens of major monuments accompanied by their name glyphs. Elite figures are represented in the murals of Teotihuacan from the Xolalpan through the Metepec phase (A.D. 350–750), but they are always in groups, in profile, dressed in identical costumes, as though they were a "committee," or a "senate," for which their individuality was not essential. In only one example do they appear to be named, and even that is uncertain. No portraiture has been found. Because of the usual Mesoamerican tradition, which is just the opposite— royal portraiture begins with the Olmec colossal heads—this absence of portraiture is unlikely to be chance. The leaders of Teotihuacan were therefore consciously playing down their individuality and not advertising their dynastic legitimacy in art.[11]

These elite figures, moreover, are always performing acts of service— pouring libations, singing, or performing sacrifices. Sometimes they proceed in profile toward a frontal deity or emblem, like worshippers. Even when the central deity or emblem is missing, the implication is that their

Figure 4.8. Tepantitla mural of Sowing Priests. From A. Miller 1973, p. 172b. Courtesy of Dumbarton Oaks Research Library and Collections, Washington, D.C.

acts are in relation to a higher being. This distinction is not unlike that between the arts of Egypt and Mesopotamia. In Egypt, as among the Maya, rulers are godlike beings, and life and art focus on them. In Mesopotamia, by contrast, rulers are often shown as supplicants to much larger and more powerful deities. On the stela of Hammurabi, for example, the Babylonian king presents his laws, standing in profile in front of a much larger, seated, and partly frontal deity. At Teotihuacan, this self-effacement is much more extreme.

This pattern of representation does not mean that Teotihuacan did not have differences in wealth and status, and hierarchy is very clear in all areas and activities. The elite are richly dressed with garments bordered in feathers and with big headdresses quite similar to those of the gods. They are much larger and fancier than the ordinary mortals sometimes shown in murals and represented in the figurines. The three-temple complexes also were unequal, varying in size and location. The mapping project has shown that Teotihuacan had poorer living sections in the south of the city, below the Ciudadela. The analysis of apartment-compound burials has shown that some families were quite wealthy, while others were like "poor relations."[12] Millon emphasized the great differential in the size and quality of apartment compounds, indicating the existence of quite a number of status levels from the very poor to the very rich.[13] As many as two-thirds of the apartment compounds may have been inhabited by the poor. Thus abundant evidence suggests that hierarchy and a large gradient of status was built into the structure of the city. Mural painting may have been one of the differences visible architecturally between the poorer and richer apartment compounds. This supposition is difficult as yet to determine, because only three apartment compounds have been fully excavated and thirteen partially excavated. Because a number of apartment compounds were excavated precisely because of the accidental find of mural paintings, it is hard to know the extent of the wealthy segment of Teotihuacan.

Nevertheless, an equivalent body of evidence indicates that even if Teotihuacan did not have an egalitarian social and political structure, some kind of a collective ideology had to have been at its base. In principle, this structure is not unlike that of the United States, where great distinctions of wealth and status exist but most people insist that they are "middle class" and theoretically all have the same "equality of opportunity." The parallels continue with the strong United States sentiment against monarchy and for a type of democratic government based on popular election. This ideology of equality is not shaken by the fact that most politicians who succeed in these elections are wealthy and may even come from "blue-blood" families. Characteristically, however, many politicians seek to speak and behave like ordinary folk, even using regional accents, thus reassuring the electorate that the system is "democratic" and not "aristocratic." Moreover, voters in the United States also elect some remarkably ordinary men (to the great consternation of states with more hierarchic traditions such as Europe) because symbolically they are men "of the people." Great images of them are unthinkable while they live, although we make images of the ones we felt were great in the past. Many of those, too, like Abraham Lincoln, fought for democratic values and thus were part of the ideology of equality. Some of Ronald Reagan's contradictory power and popularity lay in the fact that he adopted a policy favoring the rich while sounding like an ordinary working citizen, a retired actor—no upper-class manners, no superior education. The rest of the world is dismayed by or laughs at the way people in the United States select presidents, but the people are largely content with the process. Its purpose is partly symbolic internal integration and not primarily foreign relations, because the problems of internal integration of a large and diverse country are greater than its problems of foreign relations. Foreign relations are more crucial to small countries.

My first inkling that the art of Teotihuacan was concerned with collective ideas was suggested by the analysis of the composite clay incense burners.[14] These incense burners appear to have been invented during the Tlamimilolpa phase when the apartment compounds were first built. Archaeological evidence suggests that they were used on the central shrines of the compounds.[15] However, when an important person died, an incense burner was disassembled and placed in his grave. Linné found one such burial at Tlamimilolpa built into one of the lowest walls. Unlike the others, who had few grave goods, this person was buried with more than a thousand objects of various sorts.[16] Since then archaeologists have found other early lavish burials, suggesting the possibility that these individuals may have been the "founders" or original builders of the compounds. These censers are thus intimately related to the apartment compounds and their ideology. Recently, Mexican excavators found an incense-burner workshop in a sector north of the Ciudadela, leading to the suggestion that the state may have been involved in making or distributing incense burners. However, too little is known of the occupation pattern of the rest of the city to be certain who made the incense burners and how these objects were acquired by the apartment compound dwellers.

These incense burners, technically called composite ceramic incense burners, are built from flat frames of clay that suggest a theatrical stage framed by a proscenium. The entire image is a facade that hides the practical side of burning incense. The incense is burned in a flowerpot-shaped vessel placed on another inverted "flowerpot." A chimney is attached to the cover on the back, and the smoke comes out at the top. The "stage" is created by flat frames of clay laid parallel to each other on the cover, leaving an opening in the center, where a mask is attached to the chimney. Small, mass-produced ornaments, called *adornos*, cover the frames and sometimes the sides of the vessels. The mask may represent a spirit, but this spirit is remote within the shadow of the proscenium. A nose ornament usually covers the spirit's mouth so that it appears not only distant, but mute. Why were the mass-produced *adornos* attached, and why were they often glued on later? Why were the censers frequently disassembled?

Mass production seems to suggest something cheap and standardized, something to which everyone can have access. This quality has often made Teotihuacan art less than desirable with collectors. Yet standardization can also have the positive values of something commonly shared, where no one person has a better version than another. It is thus a very visible symbol of the value of collectivity. In their structure, these clay incense burners reveal further aspects of Teotihuacan ideology. Despite the mass production of the *adornos*, no two of these incense burners appear to have been alike. Thus, individual choice may have dictated the actual assembly of one. Incense burners could have been refurbished for different events or rituals. The incense burners demonstrate not only a concern for communal values, but also evidence for individual choice in Teotihuacan ritual activity.[17]

As striking as the apartment compounds is the discovery that the major deity of Teotihuacan coeval with them was a goddess. She is frequently painted on the apartment-compound walls and may be the being represented on the incense-burner masks. The known colossal statues of Teotihuacan represent her. I wondered whether there is a correlation between the city's not commemorating male dynastic rulers and elevating a female deity into paramount importance.[18] Anthropological studies of female images suggest that these images are selected when they are cosmically important or when particularly idealistic and inclusive concepts need to be embodied. Male images tend to stand for more specific powers. In an article entitled "Female Is to Nature as Male Is to Culture," Sherry Ortner noted the cross-culturally held idea that women symbolize the forces of nature while men are related to culture.[19] It thus seemed to me that Teotihuacan appealed to nature (symbolized by a feminine deity) rather than to dynastic rulership in forging a myth and ideology for its population.

Together, these features—the lack of dramatic civic-temple building in the later centuries of Teotihuacan, the presence of the apartment compounds, the avoidance of the representation of individual rulers, the emphasis on anonymous elites performing rituals, the making of symbolic objects such as incense burners whose structure reflects collective symbolism as well as individual choice, and the existence of a major female deity—form a remarkable set of data to try to explain both culturally and artistically.

Reconstructing the socioeconomic spheres of Teotihuacan has not been too difficult. The people who lived in the apartment compounds at the lower level of the social scale were agriculturists and artisans, whereas the wealthy may have had priestly, military, administrative, and commercial functions. This much detail can be read out of archaeological excavations and art.

For the rulership of the city there is less direct evidence. The monumental architecture and the organization of the city suggest strong central power, but no one knows in what form that power existed. If Teotihuacan had a ruling dynasty, it was remarkable in not making images of itself. If rulers were selected out of certain lineages or from certain titled individuals, a practice in some Aztec towns, this situation would be highly interesting in connection with the archaic state. No evidence confirms either a ruling dynasty or a selection process.

The apartment compounds and their arts suggest that the people of Teotihuacan had a complex relationship with the ruling powers of the city. A wealthy middle class may have had some say in the running of the city. The leaders of the apartment compounds were perhaps high enough in status to be called in for some decisions by the elite. The Aztec ruler is said to have met every day with the heads of the wards or *calpulli* of the capital: this access to the ruler could also have been true at Teotihuacan.

Whatever the mechanism, the families in the apartment compounds seem to have exerted some kinds of checks and balances on the activities of the elite. These families were complex, ranging from rich to poor, sixty to one hundred people living in close proximity that must have required much organization and tact in their daily contacts. Teotihuacan from A.D. 200 to A.D. 750 seems to have been more sensitive to problems of integration or organizational structure than any other Mesoamerican culture, from what is visible in the nature and structure of its art.

Of the subtleties of Teotihuacan political organization, observers can have only a very vague idea. Judging by the emphasis on organization in the city and apartment compounds, I imagine that the political structure of Teotihuacan was dense, complex, and subtle. With various changes, it lasted more than eight hundred years. Yet it was so unusual, or the result of such special circumstances, that nothing like it was ever built again in Mesoamerica.

V

Mixed Messages

The Challenge of Interpretation

COULD A VISITOR FROM OUTER SPACE GUESS JUST BY LOOKING AT IT THAT one of Jackson Pollock's drip paintings is entitled *Autumn Rhythms?* Could anyone deduce that fact successfully from an understanding of all other twentieth-century art? Knowledge of contemporary art might indicate that the painting very likely had a title. A more exhaustive study might indicate that certain types of titles predominate. But would we not have as many titles as interpreters?

Teotihuacan art was structured so as to give multiple meanings, and it has provided scholars with "evidence" for contradictory interpretations. Like the witnesses to a crime, each author sees a different-colored jacket or perhaps no jacket at all on the perpetrator. Though I have been inspired by and have taken facts and ideas from all writers on Teotihuacan art, my aim is not to try to reconcile all the various accounts, since I doubt that any such "synthesis" would be any truer than each of the individual narratives. The Teotihuacan image system as a whole poses particular problems and scholars have devised various strategies to interpret it. My approach, which is largely structural and semiotic, may not be truer, but it reveals aspects of Teotihuacan not evident in other interpretations.

The strongly multivalent character of Teotihuacan art is a feature that it shares with Olmec, Maya, and Aztec art. Teotihuacan art is more difficult only because the contexts are less naturalistic and narrative. The problem of multivalence, or mixed messages, can be illustrated by the problem of defining individual deities. When the Spanish friars began the process of recording Aztec religion, they compared it to the polytheistic religion of Classical antiquity and tried to conceptualize relatively discrete individual personalities. Thus, the sixteenth-century texts and drawings describe each of the gods in detail. The division of the ritual calendar into twenty weeks each presided over by a deity and illustrated as such in the codices encouraged such a view. Each deity had its temple, priests, and cult rituals. The trouble is, the amount of inconsistency in and ambiguity between the representations of the various gods is very great. The Aztec gods did not have, for the most part, clear personalities and characters, and their interactions in myth were not humanistic and psychological. They shared each other's characteristics rather freely, mixing up water and fire, fertility and war, sometimes even male and female. The surviving illustrations are even worse; the costumes and insignia of the gods seem to migrate rather freely from one god to another, making iconographic divisions difficult. This ambiguity has led to interpretations in which the gods "cluster," so much so that various investigators, such as Cecelia Klein and H. B. Nicholson,[1] have found that lines could not be drawn clearly between the various female goddesses at all. Some time ago Bodo Spranz[2] concluded that all the "deities" of the Mixteca-Puebla codices, largely equivalent to the Aztec gods, were not discrete entities but assortments of supernatural features symbolized by costume elements put together for specific purposes. David Joralemon's studies of Olmec iconography revealed a similar problem—although the images could be segregated into about ten separate "deities," they shared enough features so they could all be considered aspects of one.[3]

Sanders suggests that a

better way of examining this question, rather than looking purely at the artistic representations of religious beings is to look at the behavior of religious groups, and the organization of religious behavior is much more important than concepts in religion, in determining whether there is a discreteness of ritual symbols like gods. For example, if you have separate temples, dedicated to separate gods, separate orders of priests attending those temples; and if these temples hold estates . . . to support themselves; and if each temple had its own school, then regardless as to whether the gods being worshipped in those temples had shared iconographic elements, they are separate deities. In the case of the Aztecs we even have certain craft groups worshipping particular deities.[4]

According to this view the insiders of a culture determine their supernaturals on the basis of function rather than on the basis of visual features striking to an outsider. This method of distinguishing one from another is compared to the worship of different Christian Madonnas, all of whom are special and individualized in ways not clear from their visual iconography alone. The lack of observers and textual sources on Teotihuacan make such interpretations even more difficult. We have an abundance of temples but no information even on the organization of the priesthood and in what ways it was the same as or separate from the bureaucracy. Although craft-working areas have come to light—of obsidian blade makers, potters, masons—no images are specific to each. Modern scholars therefore have to rely to a large extent on visual analysis.

The nature of Mesoamerican and Teotihuacan iconography is twofold. On the one hand there is a strong insistence on small features, details, and attributes that suggest an emphasis on difference, separation, and the making of minute distinctions. Evidently such minor nuances mattered a great deal. These differences encourage modern interpreters to get out their sketchbooks and their computers and try to segregate individual entities. On the other hand there is an equally strong insistence on the sharing of these details among figures that otherwise might appear to be distinct. This sharing suggests networks of relationship whose complexity is elusive. These similarities encourage modern interpreters to get out their sketchbooks and their computers and try to chart the interactions. The trouble is, both the initial separation of images and the subsequent charting of relationships are a little like seeing figures in clouds or rocks: what to one person looks like a rearing horse is to another a face in profile.

The first scholar to tackle this Mesoamerican system methodically was Eduard Seler, and his work was both brilliant and problematic:[5] brilliant because he developed the first coherent interpretation of the iconography of sixteenth-century codices, and problematic because not only did he not come to terms with the problems presented by the system of mixed messages, but his method is still the unquestioned canonical approach of most of those who write on Mesoamerican iconography.

To create his classification of deities and attributes, Seler relied on two strategies: the substitution of one motif for another and the principle of association. Thus, "water" could be signified by water, a water-creature like a frog, or green precious things like jade and feathers. So far this approach is in line with Mesoamerican thinking. An Aztec father would have called his daughter a "green stone" or a "feather" to signify "preciousness," which was also the epithet of "water."[6]

However, in Seler's interpretation the metaphor did not exist only in one context but was transferable. Thus, if the next context showed a "jade," that symbol would automatically signify not just "jade" but also "water." The nature of Seler's system is such that "jade" and "feather" could also turn up in contexts with sacrifice and blood, in which case "water" would have to be equated with "blood." Potentially, these chains of metaphors are endless and will, in the manner of some computer games, eventually saturate the entire field, so that "blood" and "water" are everywhere. If one thing equals everything, then it also equals nothing—and no real interpretation has been made. To avoid this potential problem, Seler and his followers have begun and ended each chain of metaphors arbitrarily, where they intuitively feel that it ought to begin and end to preserve boundaries. Scholars all indulge in this type of limitation to a certain extent, because analysis cannot exist without boundaries. I too will make up my own metaphorical boundaries, but I will also emphasize their fictitious and artificial character.

The second strategy of Selerian interpretation is association. If a given motif is found prominently on a certain type of figure, it is assumed to be this god's attribute and to represent this god, *pars pro toto*, elsewhere. Or, more perniciously, the attribute acquires the nature or quality of the context, for example, "water" so that whenever it occurs next, it is interpreted as a "water" symbol. The statement that a certain feature is "associated with" a certain figure or theme signifies the weakest possible relationship. Here again the problem is the arbitrary way in which these associations are determined out of a matrix in which everything is more or less associated. Because Seler correctly noticed the multivalent thought and image system of Mesoamericans, he did not see the extent to which he was manipulating the system to come up with a classification that meant something to him and to us Westerners. His classificatory system is surprisingly close to the Classical paradigm of individual deities and clear spheres of action. It is also close to other nineteenth-century systems of classification in the sciences based on the identification of key characteristics and interrelationships. Seler was thus a part of the great classificatory approach of the nineteenth century, brought over from the natural sciences into the social sciences and humanities.

I find it strange that iconographers dealing with Pre-Columbian art have not looked at other multivalent systems and how these systems were manipulated in their own times. The Middle Ages come to my mind in contrast to the Classical past, since during the Middle Ages multivalent concordances and complications were eagerly sought everywhere,

especially between the Old and New Testaments. Scholars dealing with
Medieval subjects have been remarkably inventive in avoiding old classificatory analyses and finding new types of interpretations. They seem to
me to be more sophisticated in dealing with the chains of substitutional
metaphors that flourished both verbally and visually in Medieval times,
as in Pre-Columbian times. For example, Barbara Newman analyzed how
the Virgin Mary was often equated with the Church, while the Church was
described as the Bride of Christ, which made Mary, the mother of Christ,
also his bride. Many manuscripts deal with this issue and represent Mary
and Christ as bride and groom.[7] Are we to assume from this association
that whenever an image of the Virgin Mary was made she was also intended to be the Bride of Christ, as the substitution theory would have it?
The answer is both "yes" and "no." Probably all the various connotations
of Mary hovered about any one image and could potentially be applied,
but a given image had a certain aspect of Mary as its original intention and
conventional and functional meaning. In the case of the Middle Ages it is
easier to know where to make the cuts and where to focus on the interrelationships because of the presence of texts, although there too the beauty
(and frustration) of the system lies in its ambiguity.

In Teotihuacan studies, besides using the Selerian system of substitutions and associations, scholars have traditionally interpreted images by
referring to Aztec texts, on the assumption that the cultures were similar.
Both of these approaches are valid to some extent. Teotihuacan shares a lot
with Mesoamerica and the Aztecs—but widening the field merely means
creating an even larger area in which to hunt for substitutions and associations, thus making any theory or argument possible. Monni Adams once
compared this approach to "daisy picking"—you are in a field of daisies and
you pick a bouquet out of the flowers you like, the ones near to you, until
you decide you have enough, without a more logical principle of organization.[8] Tacking on to these "bouquets" an interpretation from Aztec myth
is, to stay with a botanical metaphor, "gilding the lily." These interpretations are not necessarily wrong, but many others, similar or contradictory,
can be concocted out of the same field of evidence. Such analyses verify
the multivalent nature of the system but do not explain it.

In the Selerian system one interprets fully and in detail; the names and
traits of deities, the specific meanings of symbols, the related histories,
myths, and rituals are described as in ethnographic fieldwork. These interpretations are certainly possible, but not necessarily correct. Because their
chance of being correct is small, the specificity of these interpretations is

a form of overinterpretation. By overinterpretation, I mean going beyond what the evidence allows one to infer reasonably. These interpretations are presented pretty much as facts and not as hypotheses.

In the study of Teotihuacan, a few scholars, including George Kubler, James Langley, and myself,[9] have attempted to circumvent the Selerian approach. All of us have come out of a Selerian system and retain various vestiges of it. All of our attempts are in different ways structural and semiotic. By structural I do not mean the structuralism of Claude Lévi-Strauss but a preoccupation with structure and system. By semiotics I mean both the notion that signs in art operate similarly to words in language and that the structure and relationship of signs have inherent meanings independent of the specific cultural meanings assigned to them.[10] In this approach one underinterprets in not trying to reconstruct the specificity of historical or religious meaning. I am satisfied with general levels of meaning. For example, I can see the importance of the calendar and astronomy at Teotihuacan, but I hesitate to theorize specifically that the Teotihuacans believed that time began with their era, as René Millon suggests.[11]

This approach is conservative on the one hand because it refrains from making specific identifications, but it is radical on the other hand because it looks for meaning in the structure of the overall system. The Selerian "bouquet" was in its unsystemic "chains" comparable to the historical Old Archaeology. The structural/semiotic approach has the advantage of being systematic and is comparable to the holistic, processual New Archaeology. Structural/semiotic studies can be compared to settlement pattern surveys—analysts may not know the names of villages, towns, or temples but can nevertheless reconstruct their interrelationships. It is possible, if one wishes, to hypothesize identities and histories based on these relationships, but these have to be frankly admitted as being only hypotheses, best guesses, and (strictly speaking) beyond what the evidence can support. As long as scholars do not pretend that they are facts, we have a use and a need for such interpretive hypotheses: we cannot tell our stories without them.

In the structural/semiotic approach, the entire image system is analyzed in terms of its constituent parts and its clusters, and the focus is not on identification but on the principles of patterning. The result of such an investigation is not a myth or ritual but a mind-set or world view. To claim the ability to re-create mind-set and world view out of principles of organization is the radical and hypothetical aspect of my approach. Its weakness is that it assumes universal psychological meanings associated with forms that are, despite attempts such as Gestalt theory, unproven.

But the general nature of these interpretations makes them clearly approximations (i.e., literature) rather than the precise identifications assumed to be true in the Selerian approach (i.e., science).

Kubler, Langley, and I have written on Teotihuacan art combining Selerian identifications with structural/semiotic interpretations. In a short, impressionistic, but profound study Kubler analyzed Teotihuacan images as the grammar of a language consisting mostly of nouns and adjectives. However, subsequently he divided its themes into a watery rain god, a fiery butterfly, and a military owl-and-weapon symbol cluster following traditional Selerian classifications worked out in large part by Hasso von Winning and Alfonso Caso.[12] His innovation consisted of not giving his clusters specific names derived from the Aztecs. Langley's valuable computer study of signs and clusters is the first large-scale and systematic study of Teotihuacan signs, and he has succeeded in demolishing the idea that definite personages and qualities exist: "the notion of a clear-cut distinction between two entities is less valid than that of a single multidimensional figure whose characteristics and depiction vary with the circumstances and the role he is called on to play,"[13] he wrote in criticism of my early classificatory attempt to divide the storm gods into two groups. Langley showed that when more storm god images are examined than what I once divided into Tlaloc A and B, the clear differences between these figures disappear (Chapter 7).[14] Though Langley generally refrains from overinterpretation, he tends to use Selerian methods of analysis in substitution and association. Moreover, he returns to the Kublerian distinction between fertility, fire, and military themes. Inconsistently, however, he assigns many symbols, such as butterflies, on different pages either to fire, water, or war. His data are correct, but his theory cannot deal with such multivalence.

In the 1970s I considered my approach "contextual analysis," since I tried to take into account the entire field of images available to me prior to interpretation. I was always suspicious of substitutions but used associations freely. By focusing on context, I identified various aspects of the Storm God Tlaloc and a nature goddess I named Xochiquetzal using Aztec texts.[15] I eventually abandoned this approach as an intellectual dead end in the 1980s. A structural/semiotic point of view brought to light new questions of meaning—such as collective versus autocratic leadership, the role of the individual, the significance of a female supreme deity, and in general the relationship of art and society—that were not accessible through the old iconographic studies.

One of these new issues is the "fertility" versus "military" division that runs through all studies of Teotihuacan art. This division was inherited from the Aztecs, whose twin pyramid was dedicated to Tlaloc and Huitzilopochtli, and *presumably* represents a basic duality in Aztec thought. It would be worth examining how much of this division was Aztec and how much arose from the classificatory minds of the sixteenth-century Spanish writers. At any rate, the idea is of some antiquity and has a respectable history. The ability to classify something as "fertility" and something else as "war" has saved many an iconographic study.

I suspect that like the notion of individual gods, this duality of water/fertility versus war/sacrifice/fire is a Western attempt to create clear categories. In the early part of the twentieth century, until the 1960s, fertility themes were emphasized at Teotihuacan, though most scholars were aware of the existence of martial imagery as well. Since then emphasis has veered toward the themes of war and sacrifice in all Mesoamerican studies, including Teotihuacan.[16] Langley's wonderful study, though biased in favor of military themes, shows the extent to which images are intermixed. I have also noted some of these admixtures: the fertility goddess has hearts in her headdress; the tasseled headdress–wearing "generals" have shells in their speech scrolls; and compounds with major fertility-theme murals also have murals with martial or sacrificial themes. For example, at Tepantitla, there are the clawed "Red Tlalocs," at Tetitla birds with blood in their beaks, at the Palace of the Sun priests with sacrificial knives and hearts. By contrast, at Atetelco, where the major murals are military, the shrine in the Painted Patio has Storm God and water imagery, and the surrounding rooms have murals with figures on top of large conch shells. Techinantitla is no exception in its mix of fertility and military imagery. Since fertility and sacrifice/war imagery are mixed on individual figures and in the different rooms of apartment compounds, scholars cannot speak of a clear demarcation of these two themes. This lack of distinction is also illustrated by the images of richly dressed Teotihuacan elites, who are pretty much the same except for carrying spear throwers and darts, sacrificial knives, or incense bags. To conclude that a motif belongs either to war or to fertility is both problematic and not terribly meaningful.

This admixture also pertains to Aztec art, in which Tlalocs sometimes supplant the ambiguously gendered but vicious Earth Monsters on the base of sculptures. It is more meaningful to divide Aztec art between the art of the temple precinct of Tenochtitlan and that of rural areas—division by class and function, or by media, rather than by water and war.[17] (As Seler

showed, water is actually a part of the Aztec war sign, as in "fiery water.")
I am going to assume that for Teotihuacan the concepts water, nature, fertility, sacrifice, war, and fire could be separate for certain purposes but
were not distinct conceptually the way Westerners divide them and therefore are not always useful categories to force the material into. (We should
even ask why *we* make such a big distinction between these two.)

If one large mass of imagery emerges from this approach and is not di-
visible into fertility/war themes and into clear deities, what purpose can
it serve? I think analysts should experiment with different types of categories. One suggestion comes to me from the Postclassic religious codices,
such as the Codex Borgia, that are, like the art of Teotihuacan, nonnarra-
tive. Clearly in the Codex Borgia the attributes of the figures are important,
including the minor details that differentiate figures from those of other
codices. This pattern of variation indicates that a high degree of specificity,
also true of the Teotihuacan images as pointed out by Langley, was probably characteristic of most Pre-Columbian art. Such specificity is usually
lost in the traditional Selerian studies, which seek generalizations based
on a lowest common denominator. Mesoamericanists need to resurrect the
specificity of figures and to reestablish the importance of each. In Mexican
Christianity, for example, there are many Virgins—Virgins of Guadalupe,
of los Remedios, of the Rosary, and so forth. Not only does each Virgin have
her own variant Virgin iconography, she is often dressed differently at different times of the year. This level of variation may never be recapturable
through analysis, but scholars need to recognize that such specificity was
probably present at Teotihuacan.

The purpose of the multivalent images in the Mixtec Codex may
not have been the presentation of a single meaning or interpretation but
the presentation of potential for various interpretations—not unlike the
Western tradition of scientific illustration in which a plant is shown simultaneously with leaves, roots, flowers, fruits, and seeds, even though these
plant parts may never occur at the same time. The same image could have
been interpreted differently at different times, thus making maximum use
of the multivalent potentials of the various details. Moreover, book and
mural paintings need not have been exactly alike. The recent discovery of
a Mixteca-Puebla-style mural at Ocotelulco demonstrates both the similarities and the differences.[18] The mural is larger in scale, simpler, and
more decorative than the codices, and it leaves out much of the fine-scale
detail and attributes. If we imagine that books at Teotihuacan might have
been more complex than murals and included more glyphs, that premise

helps put our analysis into perspective. We may not even be dealing with the image system at its fullest and most complex.

If the potential of a structural/semiotic analysis is the discovery of a world view or a mind-set, a generalized approximation of history and religion, how is such an interpretation arrived at? One excellent example might be the importance of frames, borders, and medallions noted by Kubler, Langley, and myself as characteristic of Teotihuacan art. Assuming universally implicit meanings for the sake of a hypothesis, I have suggested that the insistence on frames might indicate the importance of making boundaries between things and the necessity of separation in Teotihuacan thought.[19] Going even this far may be beyond what the evidence can support, but I argue that this is a potentially fruitful direction in which to make hypotheses and is therefore worth the risk.

Before I can interpret borders and frames any further, I must deal with the difficult question of whether art reflects society as a mirror, represents an ideal different from and perhaps even contradictory to reality, or somehow combines both ideas. A historic example may be helpful here—though the images of the Parthenon glorify the victory of democratic Athens over the evil Persian empire, it was built by Athens in a time of imperial expansion with money illegally taken from the Delian league of Greek city-states, money that was intended for mutual defense and not for the glorification of the Athenian state. In the Parthenon is the celebration of democracy a reality or an ideal?

In the case of the borders at Teotihuacan similar questions arise. Do borders mirror clear divisions in other realms such as society or religion, or are they an ideal of a neatly divided artistic realm that was the opposite of reality? In my slowly evolving study of Teotihuacan I began with the assumption that art reflects culture and put together a world view of Teotihuacan where perhaps I often mistook the ideal for the real. More recently I have become sensitive to the possibility of a reality very much in contrast to the ideal. Information from archaeology is vital in this process of interpretation, because it can point out areas of contradiction. For example, archaeological evidence indicates that Teotihuacan was a heterogeneous city, whereas a great deal of its image system, like the overall layout of the apartment compounds, emphasizes standardization. Therefore, standardization at Teotihuacan may have functioned on the level of the ideal in creating the appearance of a more homogeneous society than was actually the case.[20]

A pivotal assumption in the structural/semiotic interpretation of art is that art is always made to fulfill a vital social function. I do not believe that people make works of art out of an "aesthetic" instinct outside of a social context. I think all art is made for a purpose—social, religious, political, and so forth, even including what is called "art for art's sake" in the West or in the Orient. (Anything made to be collected, to be displayed, bought, and sold has complex social purposes.) Art is made because it fulfills a purpose just as clearly as a pot is made to hold water. This purpose, stated in general terms, is to deal with problems on a symbolic level that cannot be dealt with on a practical level. Very often art is an idealized solution to intractable contradictions; a distraction from difficulties; an exhortation, threat, or seduction for culturally sanctioned behavior. (Much of modern art, coming not from the center of society but from the margins, is a critique of culturally sanctioned behavior, which just makes it an inversion of what it is in traditional societies.) Therefore, the art of a culture should tell us a great deal about the problems and issues that preoccupied it.

How can one test whether such an interpretation is correct? Like the Selerian chain, my structural/semiotic approach is also ultimately intuitive and subjective. Scholars of the past all write fiction: to be precise, historical romances. The advantage I see in the structural/semiotic approach is that together with the finds of the wonderfully creative New Archaeology, it allows for the writing of different types of stories about ancient cultures. In my "intuitive" view of Teotihuacan, the Pyramid of the Sun is dedicated to the Goddess and the Pyramid of the Moon to the Storm God. Millon and Janet Berlo have the opposite interpretation.[21] Because of the multivalence of symbols, evidence for each view exists; and of course, perhaps neither one is right. So we as scholars concoct our stories, assuming them to be the most reasonable given the current facts, assuming that our explanations are of the greatest elegance and simplicity. All the while Teotihuacan remains scientifically inscrutable.

VI

The Pyramid of the
Sun and the Goddess

IN 1968 WORKMEN CONSOLIDATING THE PYRAMID OF THE SUN NOTICED AIR
rising between the attached *adosada* platform and the pyramid and discovered that a long tunnel-like cave went from the entrance to the center. The
cave had been closed up during the Tlamimilolpa phase (A.D. 200–400), perhaps for fear of a collapse. Nothing spectacular was inside—bits of broken
Veracruz-style mirrors and evidence of some burning, of some flowing water. But the existence of the cave immediately suggested that the Pyramid
of the Sun might have been built over a sacred natural location.[1]

It has long been known that the Teotihuacan area is full of caves. In
1906 Porfirio Díaz had lunch in a restaurant in a cave called La Gruta that
still provides fare for tourists, not far to the east of the Pyramid of the Sun.
In the 1980s Linda Manzanilla explored the terrain with remote sensing
equipment and found that the entire site is full of caves and tunnels. She
found, for example, that the tunnel underlying the Pyramid of the Sun
continues both in front of and behind the pyramid, as part of a larger system. She also found a strong correlation between caves and three-temple
complexes, most of which had been built near caves.[2] Indeed, in one Aztec
glyph, Teotihuacan is represented by two pyramids and a cave. Evidently,
then, it was a city famous for its caverns and tunnels. The cave under
the Pyramid of the Sun has become significant in the interpretation of its
meaning and the possible deities to whom it was dedicated.

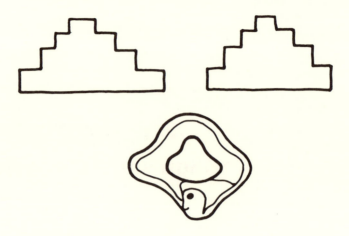

Figure 6.1. Pyramids and cave glyph. The Aztec place glyph for Teotihuacan from the Codex Xolotl showing two pyramids over a cave. From Benson, fig. 20, p. 21. Courtesy of Dumbarton Oaks Research Library and Collections, Washington, D.C.

No known textual sources reveal.to which deities the Pyramids of the Sun and the Moon were dedicated. Because the Aztecs placed one of their creation myths—in which the sun and moon were created at the beginning of the present era—at the site of Teotihuacan, they named the massive structures the Pyramids of the Sun and the Moon. The Spanish, eager to simplify Indian religion to "sun and moon" worship, continued the myth. To attempt an identification for the Pyramid of the Sun, one must consider Aztec practice and what scholars know from the excavations of the Aztec main temple, the Templo Mayor. The abundant sixteenth-century texts and recent archaeology indicate how difficult the question is.

The main Aztec temple was a twin-pyramid, dedicated to the rain god Tlaloc and the war god Huitzilopochtli. All sixteenth-century texts say so, and many refer to the statues of these deities in the temples on top. Those statues have long been destroyed, but many sculptures are among the nearly seven thousand objects uncovered in excavations directed by Eduardo Matos Moctezuma in the 1970s and 1980s in the interior of the pyramids.[3] Many images of Tlaloc exist in clay, onyx, and greenstone— but none of Huitzilopochtli. In fact, there are no identifiable images of Huitzilopochtli among the many hundreds of Aztec stone sculptures. (Although other characters in the Huitzilopochtli mythology were given sculptural form.) Thus, if it were up to archaeology alone, there would be no way to know that the other half of the temple was dedicated to Huitzilopochtli.

Moreover, many of the sculptures in the Aztec offerings of the Templo Mayor include an old man with two teeth projecting from a toothless gum, who may be an old creator god but is certainly neither Huitzilopochtli nor Tlaloc.[4] The conclusion scholars can draw from this pattern of representation is that the figures within a temple or in its offerings may, but do not necessarily, represent the deity of the temple. They may be there for other symbolic reasons. The archaeological identification of the gods to whom temples were dedicated is thus problematic. None of the temples of Mesoamerica built prior to the Postclassic period can be identified as being dedicated to a specific deity, nor are images that could be clearly deity cult images identifiable.

The second issue that the Aztec main temple excavations have illustrated is whether the pyramids were the burial places of rulers or whether they were dedicated to gods. This issue was raised in the mid twentieth century by the many finds of royal burials in the Maya area in pyramids. Sixteenth-century sources indicate that the Aztec rulers were usually cremated and that their ashes were often deposited in the Templo Mayor. The recent excavations of the main temple unearthed two fine orangeware vessels as well as an obsidian vessel (splendid enough to be the mortuary receptacle of royal remains) that contained ashes. Scholars have debated whether these vessels contained the remains of rulers such as Motecuhzoma Ilhuicamina or Axayacatl.[5] Although distinctions tend to be made between funerary temples and deity temples for ancient Mesoamerica the two appear to have been interrelated ideas at most times.

At Teotihuacan, as among the Aztec and Maya, people were usually buried not in separate cemeteries but under the floor of their houses. The cities were thus communities of both the living and the dead. Rulers and leading citizens were usually buried in the temples, since the temples were as much civic as sacred structures and in that sense were their "houses." Thus, a pyramid can easily contain the remains of one or more leaders of a community—a repository of the ancestors—and also be dedicated to supernaturals. I believe that this was the case at Teotihuacan.

In the Aztec example, the choice of the specific deities for the Templo Mayor is instructive. Huitzilopochtli was chosen as a civic deity. He was the patron god of the ruling Mexica ethnic group and dynasty; he had led his people on their migration and had promised them greatness. He was a private, ethnic war god. Other Aztec groups had private patron gods of their own. At the same time, to make them more universal, these patron gods had also cosmic aspects. Huitzilopochtli was thus the sun at midday, metaphorically seen also as a young warrior. In that very limited sense, then, one-half of the Aztec temple was dedicated to the sun.

The other half of the temple was dedicated to the rain god Tlaloc. This division suggests a dichotomy between the cult of war and the cult of agricultural fertility. However, the situation is more complex than that because one of the ostensible aims of war and sacrifice was the support of the cosmos and, certainly, agricultural fertility. Moreover, although Tlaloc (a Jupiterlike deity of storm and lightning) was one of the preeminent gods of agricultural fertility, he also had civic aspects. To the Aztecs he was the god par excellence of the defunct earlier civilization of the Toltecs, including Teotihuacan.[6] In raising a temple to Tlaloc the Aztecs were thus also venerating the ancient cultures of the Basin of Mexico.

Perhaps the term should be propitiating—hoping that old and new, Tlaloc and Huitzilopochtli, would coexist in the harmony of the empire. The choices of the Aztecs were based on their historical position in Mesoamerica. They were conquerors who came from an allegedly nomadic background to an area with over a thousand years of settled civilization and with ruins like Teotihuacan. The mere fact that they thought that Teotihuacan had been built by the gods indicates that they could not imagine such a place built by man and felt small in comparison. Their consciousness was therefore strongly historical—as the many archaistic sculptures and heirlooms collected in the Templo Mayor indicate. Political acts (such as marriage into Toltec dynastic lines), twin-pyramids, and eclectic monuments testify to the fact that the Aztecs were not only trying to synthesize the past and the present, but were also maintaining the differences between a constructed past and present. They could, after all, have presented their own view of life and the cosmos and let the past take care of itself.

Teotihuacan, however, emerged in a completely different situation. Preceding it were only small centers, the largest of which was Cuicuilco (destroyed by a volcanic eruption),[7] with stone architecture of a very modest scale dating to 400–200 B.C. Prior to that the basin had been inhabited since before 1000 B.C. but only by people living in villages of various sizes without significant monumental architecture or sculpture. At the time of Cuicuilco's prominence Teotihuacan was a provincial village in the northeast of the basin.

Archaeologists have not determined the sequence of economic, political, and psychological events. But by about 200 B.C. the Valley of Mexico had, besides the large center of Cuicuilco, many large and small villages as well as hamlets dotting the landscape. By 1 A.D. the situation changed drastically: the towns, villages, and hamlets became depopulated, and Teotihuacan swelled to a population of 90,000, the preeminent center in the valley. The Pyramid of the Sun was built and perhaps most of the Pyramid of the Moon as well. The north-south Avenue was laid out.[8]

How did these events come about, and what led Teotihuacan to initiate monument building and urban living on such a colossal scale? I believe that in contrast to the Aztecs (who looked back into history and traditions of greatness) the visionary individuals responsible for the early growth and plan of Teotihuacan looked to a future they hoped to create, one they convinced others they could create.

A particular crisis that might account in part for some of the special features of Teotihuacan is the volcanic eruption that covered Cuicuilco, which is dated to 50 B.C. The Basin of Mexico is ringed by volcanoes; eruptions and earthquakes were frequent and were perhaps in part responsible for a Mesoamerican view of the cosmos as hostile, powerful, and unpredictable. The significance of the eruption of Xitle that covered Cuicuilco is, however, specific and local. Even in Mexico only infrequently does a site or city lie directly in the path of a volcanic eruption, but at Cuicuilco the main pyramid is covered by several meters of lava.

A recent study of central Mexican volcanism by geologists[9] puts the eruption of Xitle into perspective. A volcanic belt runs across central Mexico with thousands of volcanoes. Hundreds exists in the Valley of Mexico alone, and many were responsible for the initial damming of rivers that created the Lake of Texcoco in its center in prehistoric times. A few of these volcanoes are poligenetic, that is, they are active for thousands of years. Popocatepetl and Ixtacihuatl near Puebla are examples of these. The eruption of such volcanoes is often tall and dramatic, as in the case of Vesuvius. Although all of these great volcanoes are "active" and periodically spew ash or some lava, in historic times none in Mexico has undergone a violent eruption. (Of course, as this is going to press, Popocatepetl may be erupting.) The volcanoes that have erupted with strong effect on communities and local ecologies are monogenetic—that is, they are created in their one explosion and are inactive subsequently. Instead of producing spectacular vertical eruptions, monogenetic volcanoes spew ash, but lava flows slowly, mainly from fissures at the base. The flow may last for many years. The volcano Paricutín, one of these monogenetic volcanoes in northern Mexico, was born February 20, 1943. It was active for nine years, covered the village of San Juan Parangaricutiro, and disrupted drainage. Paricutín emerged very near to where an older volcano, Jorullo, was formed in 1759. The buried village near Paricutín has remained an attraction to visitors and is listed in Mexican travel guides.

Geologists have determined that Xitle was a monogenetic volcano of the Paricutín type, in an area where there are many monogenetic volcanoes. The most recent explosion was that of Xitle, which in the past had been dated anywhere from 400 B.C. to 400 A.D. but is now dated to around 50 B.C.[10] The flow is estimated to have lasted ten years and covered 80 square kilometers known today as the Pedregal area of Mexico City. The thickness of this lava layer varies anywhere from a few meters to more than a hundred meters. Researchers have determined that "from the base of Xitli cone, the lava flowed northward, then turned eastward following the system of west-east river valleys. . . . The Xitli flow engulfed Cerro Zacatepetl and probably followed old river channels such as the Magdalena to the northeast and east. The flows subsequently merged again to spread in fan-like fashion near the lakeshore. Other minor flows descended directly from the volcano in a northeasterly direction, almost reaching the site of Cuicuilco."[11]

Geological studies indicate that the consequences of a monogenetic volcanic eruption are not just the occasional dramatic destruction of human habitations, but real changes in the ecology—in the river systems and in the vegetation. It is clear that Cuicuilco was built in the southwestern sector of Mexico that was ecologically the most favorable for agriculture. Rivers allowed for irrigation, and archaeologists have located irrigation canals in the area. Moreover, Cuicuilco was also close to Lake Texcoco and all of its resources.

Unfortunately, our archaeological information on Cuicuilco is quite limited.[12] Notes of early excavations were lost, and in any case much early excavation, relying on dynamite to get rid of the lava layer, was unprecise to say the least. Because the round pyramid and other structures seem to have been in a state of disrepair, anthropologists conjectured that the site might have been abandoned prior to the eruption of Xitle.[13] No geological evidence under the Xitle flow suggests an earlier eruption, but another monogenetic volcano, Chichinautzin, was also active in the area prior to Xitle and is believed to have had a similarly large flow and to have resulted in similar ecological changes. The Yololica volcano also erupted at about the same time as Xitle, and its lava flows are only a few kilometers from

Cuicuilco. Clearly, although Cuicuilco was built in a rich geological area for agriculture, it existed at a time of considerable monogenetic volcanic activity—which has not resumed since.

It is very hard to reconstruct ancient history on the basis of archaeology and geology, especially relying on radiocarbon dating. Many accepted "facts" of one decade change in the next, and new excavations rewrite history, sometimes completely. Whatever happened to Cuicuilco is hard to reconstruct. Possibly an earlier volcano disrupted the area and worried the population enough so that Cuicuilco declined or was partially abandoned even before Xitle made it a very inauspicious place. Certainly at one point (generally believed to be at the time of the change of Teotihuacan from a large village to an urban state) Xitle erupted, covering a part of the site, in a process that might have taken something like ten years. Though the country is dotted by volcanoes and people are used to earthquakes and periodic ash falls from the great poligenetic ones, eruptions that had such a direct effect on human life were extremely rare and must have been seen in ancient times as very significant.

The sudden appearance of a new volcano covering the major center of the Valley of Mexico with lava had to have had an enormous psychological impact that lived in memory for a very long time. Not all of Cuicuilco was destroyed, but the center was and its ruins could have been visited long after the eruption was over. Indeed, evidence of Teotihuacan visitors has been identified: a cache of two Teotihuacan-style stone figures found near the main pyramid of Cuicuilco may have been left by people making a ritual visit to the ruin.[14]

This destruction was likely to have been interpreted as the will, the anger, and the power of the gods. There would have been no way to know whether Xitle or another new volcano would erupt again.

The emergence of the Teotihuacan valley as the center of a new polity east of the lake and away from the volcanic zone has long been interpreted as a result of the Cuicuilco disaster. I believe that some of the other unique features of Teotihuacan may also have been results of the response to the eruption of Xitle. If Xitle rose up literally out of the ground in an unexpected place, no place in the valley was truly safe from such an event. I am suggesting that Teotihuacan was built as a symbolic "fortress" against the unpredictable powers of nature, that this notion accounts for its colossal size, concentrated settlement, and focus on the gods.

I suggest a scenario in which civic-religious leaders proposed a "new order" that would guard more effectively against such a catastrophe. A defensive ideology might have been very helpful in getting the population to move to Teotihuacan or to justify its forcible move. The pyramids may have been both propitiations of the gods and indications that humans could now rival the powers of the gods—could build their own volcanoes. The scale of the pyramids was perhaps assurance that the leaders and the community were so powerful that they had nothing to fear.

Did Teotihuacan continue Cuicuilco traditions or depart from them? This question is difficult to answer in view of the fragmentary nature of the information about Cuicuilco. Little clay censers representing old men were copied at Teotihuacan in stone versions, indicating the continuity of household and family ritual. Yet the orientation and layout of the centers are very different. Cuicuilco appears to have been oriented to the cardinal directions, judging by the east-west orientation of the stairway of the main pyramid and the other structures.[15] Teotihuacan was oriented quite differently, 15 degrees 25 minutes east of north, suggesting that it was based on new and different astronomical calculations. Teotihuacan seems to have chosen an astronomically derived order for itself that was consciously different from that of Cuicuilco and was very likely a part of its ideological "defense."

René Millon saw the beginning of Teotihuacan thus: an audacious ruler proposed that time began at Teotihuacan, at the site where the Pyramid of the Sun was later built, using astronomical observations. He conquered the people of the valley, resettled them at Teotihuacan, and organized them into huge building crews. He is buried in the interior of the Pyramid of the Sun. The conquests were continued by the next important ruler, who is buried in the Pyramid of the Moon. The monuments are thus monuments to autocratic rule, like the pyramids of Egypt.[16]

I accept Millon's idea of a "new era" as the foundation of Teotihuacan, but I have a different "story" to account for it. I agree that the city may well have been consolidated through conquest, which is true of most large chiefdoms and states. Ideology is almost always a part of a conquest. Great would-be world conquerors, like Napoléon Bonaparte, for example, did not win merely by superior force of arms and manpower but by promising superior new political conditions. Conquerors often claim to "free" their victims in some fashion. Ideology is essential both for the followers of the leader and for the conquered if they are to be assimilated into a new polity. Moreover, the leader too is most convincing if he believes to some extent in his own cause.

Most Mesoamerican warfare, even in the famous Aztec empire, was designed to gain tribute and not territory or population. Its ideological justification was the acquisition of victims for sacrifice to maintain the cosmic cycles of the universe. The conquered people shared this ideology. Conqueror and victim were often represented on monuments that dramatized and celebrated this situation of "eternal warfare." Historians have shown that the Aztecs did not have the practical resources—including roads and transportation facilities—to maintain a large territorial empire and to incorporate the conquered population permanently. The Aztec solution, punitive wars and sacrifices, followed from the problem of the instability of the empire. Such a pattern was probably characteristic of endemic Classic Maya warfare, sacrifice, and tribute collection as well.

The founders of Teotihuacan had, for their time, the novel concept of creating a large and unified political territory justified by social harmony rather than by conflict. They evidently wanted to concentrate the population of the Basin of Mexico in one center. While this goal may have had clear advantages in terms of social, political, and economic control, I imagine that the ideological justification was the creation of a place "free" from the unpredictable forces of the cosmos and based on models of order, harmony, and control rather than chance and conflict. Teotihuacan was going to outdo the gods through knowledge and organization.

All settlements in the basin need not have been conquered; some could have been persuaded to participate in the new community by privileges or threats. I suggest that the leaders of Teotihuacan presented themselves primarily as priests, rather than as the dynastic rulers common in Mesoamerica and perhaps also at Cuicuilco. I assume this from the lack of ruler representation and the lack of dates and inscriptions at Teotihuacan that are common in other Mesoamerican cultures associated with dynastic rulers. In my view, the founding leaders of Teotihuacan emphasized their knowledge of the will of the gods and their superior propitiating abilities, abasing themselves in the process. These early political-religious leaders may well have been buried in the great pyramids, but I doubt that the pyramids were dedicated to them.

The art of later periods indicates the Teotihuacan insistence that it was not governed by a dynastic family. Either Teotihuacan selected rulers from certain families and did not focus on primogeniture and descent, or if Teotihuacan had a ruling dynasty it chose not to dramatize its rulers. This anonymity could have been either because rulers were so much in control that they did not have to bother with ritual and artistic legitimation or because a low profile was their chosen strategy. Like the Inca, whose power is symbolized by great walls and not portraits, the rulers of Teotihuacan are portrayed in colossal architecture. The nature of Teotihuacan imagery makes me feel that the rulers chose to rule through the deities and the forces of nature that they represented, as a more effective approach than the cult of their own personality. Such "austerity" may have made them more impressive in the eyes of a heterogeneous population and hence was a superior form of legitimation.

Another attraction of Teotihuacan to outsiders might have been some promise of certain political rights and the retention of family or corporate grouping in residence and ritual. The rulers might have used the clan and lineage organization of the original town of Oztoyahualco in the northwest of the city as the model for the social organization and later residential layout of the city. As one indication of this pattern, the most numerous three-temple complexes are in Oztoyahualco. I imagine that arrangements were made for newcomers either to join the old groups or to form similar units of settlement themselves. At its inception, Teotihuacan must have been an ethnically diverse place, with the elite from Oztoyahualco. It must have been a rare feat of social engineering to organize a heterogeneous, rapidly expanding settlement in one crowded place into a cooperating whole. The great pyramids prove that in some fashion this unification was accomplished. Moreover, farmers were persuaded to live in the city and go quite some distance to their fields.

Ideology must have been a crucial tool in this organization, since voluntary participation is more cost-effective than force. Some scholars have suggested that the Olmec and Maya were "theater" states that used architecture, monuments, and ceremonies to create elite power. With its colossal pyramids, avenues, and plazas Teotihuacan is the greatest "ritual theater" in all of Mesoamerica, with both "performers" and "audience" living in the "theater" at all times. The architectural scale of the city literally competes with nature and was perhaps meant to be intimidating both to men and to the gods.

Millon sees a far greater role of force and centralized control at Teotihuacan than I do. I imagine force playing a role, but primarily through the creation of a psychological atmosphere of fear attributed to the demonstrably hostile outside forces. The rulers would then have offered "protection" and were not themselves the threat. I also think that in exchange for control, the population of Teotihuacan enjoyed certain very real benefits. Perhaps coming from a totalitarian country I have a cynical view of what centralized power can accomplish with an apathetic and alienated population. The communist governments are also good examples of power not respected because they preached equality for everyone while indulging in luxuries themselves. In my view the rulers of Teotihuacan would have used force, provided some benefits, created a myth that made sense of the world and of everyone's role in it, and created a convincing show of living up to their values. The notion that all past cultures relied primarily on brute force as social control is based on the Enlightenment concepts of human rights in which governments are believed to crush human liberty unless they are consensual and constitutional in the modern sense. We have thus inherited the idea that all ancient states were absolute and evil.

Concentrating the population in one large city may have been an easier way of enforcing control, but it was also dangerous in that uprisings or factional conflicts could occur on a much larger and potentially lethal scale. In fact, eventually, such an internal crisis may have resulted in the collapse of the city. As I see it, the ideology Teotihuacan propagated was twofold: partly it was defensive and relied on the power of the gods (and the priests who contacted them) to protect the city from environmental disaster, and partly it was positive and promised agricultural fertility, wealth, and social and cosmic order.

Unlike the arts of most of Mesoamerica that glorified violence and dissension, art at Teotihuacan emphasized harmonious coexistence. As striking as the lack of themes of conflict is the lack of dates. Teotihuacan presented itself as a timeless place, as if it had existed from time immemorial and would exist into eternity, outside of history and historical contingency.

Teotihuacan seems to have been the first culture in Mesoamerica to put the emphasis on the gods and the supernatural rather than on the human world in artistic commemoration. Most Mesoamerican monuments depict rulers, prisoners, ballplayers, and more rarely deities. Ancestor worship may have been the major cult of the elite, and many images (such as the well-known Monte Alban urns) appear to represent ancestors rather than gods. The deities in Classic Maya art are usually shown as small creatures under the control of the rulers or as a part of their costume. In the Postclassic period there are more deities, and the appearance is standardized in the divinatory codices.

Teotihuacan has few deities that are recognizable in the material remains. Two are based on ritual vessels—the Storm God and the Old God. Both of these antedate Teotihuacan and in various forms continued to be venerated until Aztec times. The Flayed God and the Fat God are known primarily in figurines and were thus important presumably in household ritual. These deities were known contemporaneously also in Oaxaca and Veracruz. The Flayed God was a major Aztec deity named Xipe Totec.

The most intriguing Teotihuacan deity is the Goddess, who seems especially strongly associated with masks. She is generically related to the various water, fertility, and death goddesses of Mesoamerica, but her specific form has no ancestry outside of Teotihuacan, and with the possible exception of some Xochicalco images, she has no visual descendants. Three colossal statues in Teotihuacan style depict this goddess as a neutral or benevolent power. The representational strategy of Teotihuacan was thus seduction rather than terror. A feminine major deity serves to emphasize cosmic rather than political issues, and a benevolent appearance emphasizes positive values.

One of the remarkable aspects of the Pyramid of the Sun is that it does not fit neatly into either the plan of the city or the surrounding landscape. From whatever direction one looks at it, it is a colossal individual monument, self-sufficient on its own, integrated with the other monumental architecture only artificially. It is an anomaly—sitting on one side of the Avenue without a symmetrical structure, without its own avenue leading up to it. (Modern site authorities created such a street with souvenir shops, as if unconsciously wanting such an axis.) Only further archaeology will reveal whether it was the first major monument at the site, but I argue that it might have been the first or among the first and that the original ritual purpose of attracting people to Teotihuacan was to build it, as in Millon's hypothesis. (Recently, Millon suggested that an even earlier structure might be inside the Pyramid of the Moon.)[17] The Pyramid of the Sun may have been located where it is because of (1) the location of a previous shrine that was enlarged; (2) a divination or mystic occurrence like the Aztec vision of an eagle on a cactus for the future city of Tenochtitlan; or (3) a desire to move away from Oztoyahualco and—without as yet a grand plan for the rest of the city—something of a random or geomantically divined choice of location to the south. Whatever the reasons and history, the Pyramid of the Sun always remained central but separate and unique visually. This visual uniqueness could reflect the distinctiveness of its cult and function.

The Pyramid of the Sun may have had a solar aspect, although I doubt that it was dedicated exclusively to a solar deity. It faces west toward the setting sun, and solar phenomena have been noted in relation to it.[18] Millon and, following him, Clemency Coggins have suggested that the Pyramid of the Sun is associated with a grand concept of time—the idea of the beginning of a cosmic era.[19] They relate this premise to the orientation of the Avenue, 15 degrees 25 minutes east of true north. However, this offset pertains to the site as a whole and not just to the Pyramid of the Sun.

The only deity image found in the Pyramid of the Sun was a tiny Storm God vessel dated to the Tzacualli phase (A.D. 1–150). Although rare in the Tzacualli phase, Storm God vessels are common in burials and offerings in the later phases. Nothing indicates that the pyramid as a whole was dedicated to the Storm God. A number of sculptures ornamented the later small *adosada* platform at the entrance; these sculptures included feline heads and paws.[20] Felines themselves were not deities at Teotihuacan, but they were associated with several deities and might provide a helpful clue in identification. But basically, nothing has been found archaeologically that would provide a definite deity identification for the Pyramid of the Sun.

Most of the pyramid was built during the Tzacualli phase. Various excavation galleries crisscross its interior, but the finds have been modest. The interior comprises Tzacualli-phase fill, including potsherds and figurines, which was useful in dating the structure. A youth was sacrificed in each of the four corners of the structure and buried, presumably at its foundation. Such foundation sacrifices are commonly associated with buildings throughout the world.

Doris Heyden suggested that the cave under the Pyramid of the Sun was like the Chicomoztoc, or Seven Caves of Origins, of the Aztecs.[21] According to Aztec migration legends, their barbarian ancestors emerged from caves. Karl Taube suggested a variant interpretation more in line with what scholars know of Teotihuacan: rather than a cave of origin and the beginning of a migration, he suggests that this was a cave of emergence more on the model of Hopi belief. (Although the Hopi actually believe that after emergence they did go on a migration.) He suggests that the people of Teotihuacan may have believed that they were autochthonous and that they came out of the earth at that spot.[22]

On admittedly slight evidence, I had developed the hypothesis that if the major deity of the Pyramid of the Sun was one of the ones we know, it was the Goddess. Although I am technically the "discoverer" of this goddess in the iconography of Teotihuacan,[23] others, such as Hasso von Winning and Clara Millon, saw her importance long before I did.[24] Hasso von Winning calls her the Great Goddess, but because of all the controversy that surrounds the concept of an ancient "Great Goddess," I call her "the Goddess." My original discovery of her was through simple Selerian identification. I noted that most Storm God images had very clear facial features and costumes: ringed eyes, a moustache-like upper lip, a water lily hanging from the mouth, and a five-knot headdress in the case of Tlaloc A and similar facial features, a long tongue, and a variety of headdresses in the case of Tlaloc B (Chapters 5 and 7). (As mentioned earlier, a larger sample studied by James Langley shows that this division is illusory because many intermediate forms exist.) I noted that several deities, such as the Jade Deity of Tetitla and the Deity of Tepantitla, which are usually called Tlalocs, lacked every one of these features. Instead, they shared a frame-headdress with a zigzag border and a bird in the center, a yellow face and hands, a mask, and a nose bar of some kind. At Tepantitla this figure was the major deity, and the Storm God was relegated to the borders. (Although these two deities usually have clear iconographic diagnostics, occasionally intermediate forms also exist.)

The femaleness of the Tepantitla and Tetitla deities was at first hard for me to accept completely, and I thought that they might be bisexual. The best evidence for femininity was the presence of a spider in both murals. Metaphorically, spiders represent weavers and are symbols of women and feminine activity from Mesoamerica as far as the American Southwest. (Taube goes so far as to call the Teotihuacan goddess "Spider Woman" as in Southwestern mythology.)[25] In addition, at Tepantitla the elite "priests" flanking the deity wear skirts and *huipils* rather than male garments. Whether they are male or female, they appear to be dressed as women; the priests of deities often dressed in male or female attire matching the gender of the deity in Mesoamerican rituals.

At Tepantitla the half-body of the Goddess rises from a *talud/tablero* platform ornamented with flowers and feathers. In the center of the platform, an upside-down U shape frames a space, in which seeds are represented, that I have interpreted as a symbolic cave. This central symbol emerges from a wavy body of water in which shellfish swim. Its top is an imaginary ground line on which plants such as maize and fruit trees grow. A branch or vine divided into a red half and a yellow half emerges from the back of the Goddess, full of spiders and butterflies. The tree is laden with flowers in bloom, seemingly weighted down by drops and streams of water, as after a rainstorm. Birds hover around it. Although the Goddess is masked, her hands with painted fingernails are very visible. She holds huge drops of water.[26] The Tetitla version of the Goddess lacks the elaborate setting, but the outstretched arms giving gifts are very similar. Instead of drops of water, she presents streams of liquid full of little green

Figure 6.2. Goddess mural. Overall view of copy of mural painting at Tepantitla, Teotihuacan. Metepec phase, A.D. 600–750. Painting by Agustín Villagra Caleti in the Museo
Nacional de Antropología, Mexico City. CNCA-INAH-MEX. INAH photo.

images—disks, animals, faces—which are most likely jade, the ultimate
treasure in Mesoamerican thought.

Both the Tepantitla and Tetitla Goddess images are from apartment
compounds and date probably to the late Metepec phase (A.D. 650–750).[27]
The Teotihuacan Goddess images are far less standardized in form than
are images like the Storm God that were established prior to the rise of
Teotihuacan. Because so much variety of representation exists, there is no
way to be certain whether all the figures I will mention represent one being or perhaps several. They share certain iconographic features, such as
yellow body color or a zigzag-bordered headdress, as well as thematic features such as cavelike interiors or hidden faces. I have argued in the past
that circumstantial evidence makes this protean figure one goddess, and I
still choose that interpretation to tell my story of Teotihuacan here. I am,
however, very aware that the Goddess is a construct and that other explanations may hold for the same images. I have no doubt, however, that
the three colossal stone images found at Teotihuacan—the so-called Wa-

Figure 6.3. Colossal stone Goddess. Basalt. Found near the Pyramid of the Moon, Teotihuacan. Height, 390 cm (154 in.); weight, about 22 tons. Museo Nacional de Antropología, Mexico City. CNCA-INAH-MEX. Pasztory photo.

ter Goddess, the so-called Tlaloc figure of Coatlinchan, and the fragment similar to the Water Goddess—all represent persons in female dress, thus making a female figure the most important visual image at the site.

The earliest representation of the Goddess is from the murals of the Temple of Agriculture, a structure on the left side of the Avenue near the plaza of the Pyramid of the Moon. Because these murals were found at the turn of the century and not properly protected, scholars know them only from copies.

In one mural the Goddess seems to be represented merely by a frame-headdress with the yellow and red zigzag borders, while the mural shows in abstract and decorative ways wavy lines for water, water lilies, shells, and sea creatures, and hidden among them, seeds: images of water, flowers, and agricultural fertility like the more anthropomorphic Tepantitla mural. The seeds are protected in cavelike enclosures. The presence of the goddess is merely implied by the headdress.

The other mural shows matching enigmatic forms at the two sides of the painting, blending the silhouettes of a mountain, a pyramid, and a woman wearing a skirt and a *huipil*. Each of these forms is personified by earplugs, nose bar, collar, and headdress, but is otherwise "faceless." The interior of each is cavelike, has a small structure, and contains scrolls that suggest smoke or sound. Small human figures present offerings to these two distant and seemingly indifferent beings. At the lower border, seeds are placed within wavy lines that signify water. In this mural the Goddess is present not as a person but as a personified mountain or temple, literally represented as a force of nature.

The two Temple of Agriculture murals may also represent the Goddess in a less human form than the later ones. She is represented either only by her headdress or by a very generalized and impersonal form. A vast gulf in size and scale separates her from humans. This difference in scale is not unlike what must have been the difference between the modest perishable homes of the Tzacualli phase and the Pyramid of the Sun.

Why should the Goddess be related to caves? Clearly she is an earth or nature goddess whose realm includes water, agricultural fertility, minerals, and wealth. She is shown as giving these as gifts. Sometimes she is shown only by hands pouring gifts. Three representations suggest caves: the mural of the Deity of Tepantitla and the two murals of the Temple of Agriculture. There was and is a great deal of cave lore in Mexico, and much of it concerns a powerful female enchantress who hoards seeds and treasure inside the cave. Bernardino de Sahagún documented some of this cave lore in the sixteenth century. Sahagún's informants explained that rivers, which are the property of Chalchiuhtlicue (the Aztec water goddess), flowed from Tlalocan, the earthly paradise of Tlaloc: "mountains were only magic places, with earth, with rock on the surface: . . . they were only like ollas or like houses; . . . they were filled with the water which was there." It was said, "This mountain of water, this water, springs from there, the womb of the mountain. For from there Chalchiuhtlicue sends it."[28] These traditions are remembered to the present day in many conservative areas. For example, some years ago a Tlaxcalancingo Indian reported a miraculous encounter with a woman who told him that she was the owner of a local source of water and who showed him her cave, which was full of water.[29] In present-day Tlaxcala tradition, the cave of Malintzi is full of jars—some of which contain water, and others, all sorts of seeds.[30] The story of an enchanted cave where men find riches is told in the villages in the Valley of Teotihuacan.[31] As a rule, in these stories, seductive women who live in caves approach men and offer marriage as well as riches. Often the men become rain priests, and after their death go to live permanently in the cave.[32]

Cave ritualism on an elite rather than a folk level near the Valley of Mexico is evident at least as early as 1000 B.C. at the site of Chalcatzingo, where a sacred rock with caves was venerated in both dynastic and nature ritual.[33] On one cliff a human figure sits inside a mouth representing a cave entrance. Cave-tunnels were built in a Puebla pyramid at Totimehuacan antedating the Pyramid of the Sun and its cave by hundreds of years. Frogs ornamenting the sides of a stone basin inside the chamber at the end of the tunnel refer generally to water imagery.[34] A Teotihuacan-style painting in one of the Chalcatzingo caves indicates a possible Teotihuacan familiarity with this site. Chalcatzingo was subsequently venerated as a shrine by the Aztecs. Caves continued to be important in Aztec times, and one cave that was important before the Spanish conquest has become a Christian place of pilgrimage and is the church of the Christ of Chalma.

Although the Storm God may also be associated with caves, because of the importance of the Goddess in Teotihuacan representation I have suggested that the deity primarily associated with caves, and by extension with the Pyramid of the Sun and its cave, was the Goddess. I have two reasons for this association of the Goddess and the Pyramid of the Sun: (1) the superior role of the Goddess in relation to the Storm God and the possibility that she was the major deity of Teotihuacan, and (2) the cave as ultimately a womblike feminine symbol. The realm of the Goddess was watery but, I suggest, mainly consisted of terrestrial waters—lakes, streams, seas.

At Teotihuacan, these types of waters have an underground association like that of caves. As René Millon has shown, the San Juan River could not have irrigated the lands needed for a city of this size, but the area is rich in underground springs, many located in the present village of San Juan Teotihuacan.[35] In addition, the water table at Teotihuacan is very high, and canals could have easily been cut to acquire further supplies of water. Both the water table and springs are underground features like the caves and are specific geographically to this area. The realm of the Goddess was therefore largely underground.

Janet Berlo suggested that the Goddess was associated with the Pyramid of the Moon because the mountain behind the Pyramid of the Moon was called Tenan, "Mother of Stone," in Aztec times.[36] Because of the cave in the Pyramid of the Sun, I think the argument for the Goddess's association with that structure is just as likely, and I have chosen to reconstruct Teotihuacan that way.

Though I imagine that the leaders, those who thought up the combined ritual and political attraction of what was to be Teotihuacan, were definitely powerful humans, I see them as having integrated their ideas not by setting up one of themselves as a divine king but by elevating the Goddess to colossal proportions. If the three-temple complexes were dedicated to a deity triad, the Goddess was perhaps one of the three deities. In the case of the Pyramid of the Sun, with the cave literally incorporated into the pyramid, a dedication to the Goddess seems like a reasonable conclusion. The lack of representations in the early periods has always been a mystery, but perhaps the Goddess was *literally* the cave and temple, rather than an image. Perhaps she, like the other gods, was represented by masked impersonations and not by permanent images. Her facelessness in early representations seems to suggest a reticence in giving her a fully human form.

Unlike Huitzilopochtli of the Aztecs, the Teotihuacan Goddess was not brought from anywhere else but seems to have been local. Like Huitzilopochtli, however, she may have had a civic and political dimension. Recent excavations in the Street of the Dead Complex, the administrative center of the city, unearthed a large sculpture of her made of blocks of stone. Hasso von Winning has suggested that the colossal so-called Tlaloc of Coatlinchan, now at the entrance to the Museum of Anthropology in Mexico City, is an unfinished version of her. Were Teotihuacan artisans working on it at the time of the collapse of the city in A.D. 750? When the number of murals and incense burners that represent her is compared to that of the deities, she emerges as the supreme deity of the city, at least from A.D. 200 to A.D. 750. If Teotihuacan had a patron deity, she may have been it. Curiously, however, she does not appear outside the city of Teotihuacan in important political contexts. (The Storm God, with or without the tasseled headdress, seems to have that role.)

Within the city the Goddess is preeminent. On many of the incense burners, the masks seem to represent a face like hers, the mouth covered by a nose bar. I have already argued that these composite incense burners reflect or idealize in their structure the apartment-compound make-up of the city, expressing the values of hierarchic order within which room for family or individual variation exists. The bodiless face, only a mask, set deep within this structure—as in a metaphoric cave—could be the Goddess herself.[37] Even more enigmatic and evocative are naked figures (not always clearly female) with hollow interiors with small, fully dressed Teotihuacan personages that are glued to the inside of the figures' chest, arms, and legs.[38] These figures evoke the image of a large, benign, vague being whose body is literally a dwelling place. Using that as a metaphor we could say that the people of Teotihuacan resided within the sacred body (i.e., earth) of the Goddess. Her powers were, however, local and specific to the Valley of Mexico.

Why should this civic deity have been female? Her status may have been entirely fortuitous, if the ancient cave deity was female in myths handed down by previous generations. Societies emphasize whatever deities they choose, and therefore, even if inherited, the deities are intentionally kept and reaffirmed. The female supreme deity may have evolved in contrast to the generally male semidivine dynastic rulers of Mesoamerica. Male gods, male rulers, and male culture heroes could blend easily, as the story of Quetzalcoatl indicates. Because women are rarely rulers (though some exceptions existed in the Maya area), their identification with nondynastic matters is more likely. A primary identification of the Goddess was with the earth, and I suggest the specific geographic landscape in the Basin of Mexico.

Female patron goddesses exist outside Teotihuacan. One notable example is Athena of Athens, who, like the Teotihuacan Goddess, is somewhat ambiguous sexually because her sexual or maternal qualities are not important. Like Athena, who is a goddess of war, the Teotihuacan Goddess has a claw-handed destructive side. Athena is almost like a man, but by being a woman she is credited with a higher degree of morality and deeper devotion. In most cultures, female symbols have often been associated with great positive ideals that symbolize the group as a whole and social integration. Sherry Ortner has noted that though women in general are associated with "nature" and accorded a lower esteem than are men, who are associated with "culture," paradoxically, supercultural values are often embodied in feminine figures.[39] As another example, though of course the United States has no civic deities, the Statue of Liberty functions as a civic symbol. A colossal woman holding a torch, she was given to the United States only in the nineteenth century, well after the development of this utopian country based on antimonarchic principles. "Lady Liberty" is not a dead idea but is frequently evoked and illustrated in a wide variety of contexts, from cartoons and magazine covers to wall murals. Articles about the statue or the people who take care of it are common on the Fourth of July. People customarily refer to the statue as though she were a real person. Although she is usually associated with the concept of liberty, the placement of the statue near Ellis Island indicates that she is also a symbol of the utopian future that immigrants will find, and of their integration into the community as a whole. In a general sense, both to citizens and to foreigners her image represents the United States. The United States also has a male symbol, Uncle Sam, who seems to function in a more military and political context; but as a symbol of integration, Lady Liberty is far more important. Like Athena and the Statue of Liberty, the Goddess of Teotihuacan expresses civic values beyond politics, symbolized by her femininity.

Linda Manzanilla's explorations of the caves of Teotihuacan have resulted in a major change in interpretation. Whereas at first the caves were all thought to be natural, they are now seen as artificial. Their purpose is alleged to be the removal of material for building, but Manzanilla suggests that subsequently they were used for ritual purposes. The issue is not certain at present, and whether they are natural or artificial is not totally clear. If they are artificial they create as many new puzzles as they solve. It does not seem particularly easy to excavate building material by making caves and tunnels—why not simply remove material from the surface of the ground? It is particularly difficult to see the cave under the Pyramid of the Sun, a narrow tunnel, as a great source of material. Moreover, its alignment, from the entrance to the center, suggests an architectural and ritual use. If the people of Teotihuacan were making artificial caves, that enterprise is perhaps even more remarkable than if the caves were natural. In either case, caves seem to be an important aspect both of the environment and of the ritual preoccupations of Teotihuacan. If the caves are artificial, then the emphasis may have been less on the initially sacred geography of the Teotihuacan Valley and more on the way in which it was "made sacred." Returning to the original scenario of the creation of Teotihuacan ideology in which the destruction of Cuicuilco may have played a role, one's attention is drawn to "dangerous mountains" with cavelike interiors, which erupt violently and unexpectedly. In the Postclassic period many volcanoes had deity names, such as Tlaloc, Popocatepetl, and Ixtacihuatl, and could be conceptualized as either male or female. If Xitle and the other monogenetic volcanoes emerged from the earth suddenly and unexpectedly, an earth goddess may have been the right being to propitiate them. An interest in volcanoes, caves, and destruction could relate to rituals in caves. All those artificial caves near three-temple complexes and within the Pyramid of the Sun may have been a part of such a ritual. Since Xitle never erupted again and the Cuicuilco disaster lost its powerful immediacy in time, some of the aspects that made Teotihuacan unique appear to have been lost in memory. If the Goddess was in some ways particularly related to these unique and local aspects that would explain her disappearance as well.

VII

The Pyramid of the Moon and the Storm God

IN CONTRAST TO THE ANOMALOUS POSITION OF THE PYRAMID OF THE SUN, in the grid plan, the Pyramid of the Moon is strongly integrated both in the city plan and in the surrounding landscape. It was evidently planned to be the focal point of the north-south Avenue, and a large symmetrical plaza in front of it enhances its importance. One of the most subtle features of the design of the Pyramid of the Moon is that it is located at the end of the Avenue that rises steadily upward—as a result, from almost anywhere in the city the pyramid looks elevated and its entire form is visible. Though not as big as the Pyramid of the Sun it is much more focal.

Teotihuacan is not impressive just because of its huge pyramids, but also because of the way the Pyramid of the Moon is set into a larger architectural plan. The Pyramid of the Moon, the temples surrounding it, the plaza, and the Avenue are the most dramatic visual demonstrations of hierarchy and order, suggesting something of the political structure that gave rise to the city. Whereas the Pyramid of the Sun with its chthonic cave seems to be associated with unpredictable forces, the Pyramid of the Moon as a part of the plan and of the orientation suggests complete intellectual control of the universe. I suggest that for Teotihuacan these rational forces were imagined as masculine and embodied in the Storm God. The Storm God should not be imagined as a simple and benign fertility deity, nor even necessarily as one deity. As the wielder of lightning, this god was power incarnate. He, or related aspects of him, were associated with warfare, sac-

rifice, and politics at every level of Teotihuacan society. In my view, the
Storm God may also have had patron deity aspects like Huitzilopochtli
of the Aztecs. The role of the various activities associated with the Storm
God, as of the orientation and the architectural layout, was to demonstrate
control. It is thus that the elite presumably convinced the population that
the world they were creating was good, harmonious, justified, and rational.
In the midst of unpredictable nature, Teotihuacan was built as a fortress
of order.

It is worth pondering the relationship of the Pyramid of the Moon to
the planning of the city. The city was oriented 15 degrees 25 minutes east
of north, a decision that has to have been made during the Tzacualli phase
(A.D. 1–150). This orientation is in striking contrast to Olmec orientations,
which were 8 degrees west of true north. Such a drastic change in orientation suggests a completely different cosmic justification for the city, as
though Teotihuacan were proclaiming a new era, a new creation, a new
contract with the gods and cosmic forces. (Changes in orientation were in-
frequent in Mesoamerican history. The Aztecs, for example, oriented their
structures 17 degrees east of true north, which is believed to be an imitation of Teotihuacan and other earlier orientations.) This new alignment of
Teotihuacan was in part astronomical and dealt with the position of the
setting sun and the Pleiades. René Millon suggested that on two days, Au-
gust 12 and April 29, the sun sets on the same spot on the western horizon
15 degrees 25 minutes north of west, across from the Pyramid of the Sun
and its cave. These dates can be linked up with the 260-day ritual calendar and the 365-day solar calendar. About A.D. 1 the Pleiades set close to
this same deviation off north.[1] All the astronomical data listed by Millon
are east-west oriented and associated with the Pyramid of the Sun, which
is why he feels that the Teotihuacan religious justification for the site was
that "time began at the Pyramid of the Sun." This supposition does not explain, however, why the great Avenue—the organizing axis of the city—is
aligned north-south. Why was the city not built along an east-west avenue? The north-south emphasis may have an astronomical explanation
that we do not yet understand.

Noteworthy in this context is the fact that all the major structures
of Teotihuacan are situated north or east of the Avenue and face a west
side that has only smaller structures. In many of the later apartment compounds the temple shrines are also on the east, facing west. This pattern
might suggest a privileged position of the west as the place to see from a
vantage point in the east. Privileged sacred orientation may have also de-

termined some of the ways in which the population was distributed in the city.

Pecked circles on Cerro Gordo behind the Pyramid of the Moon and on Cerro Patlachique to the west link up with a number of pecked circles near the Avenue. So far, archaeologists have found thirteen pecked circles at Teotihuacan. The crosses inscribed into the pecked circles point either to the north or to the Teotihuacan deviation from true north. Thus, they may have been used both in observations and in the layout of the city. Teotihuacan's interest in astronomical matters is also indicated by pecked crosses found near the Tropic of Cancer, near the site of Alta Vista. Here the sun reaches zenith on the summer solstice, and it is the northernmost point where the sun can reach zenith, a feature that probably interested the astronomers of Teotihuacan.[2] The people of Teotihuacan may have combined their astronomical interest with commerce, perhaps trading at Alta Vista for minerals such as cinnabar and possibly turquoise. Teotihuacan's astronomic orientation is also associated with commerce and travel

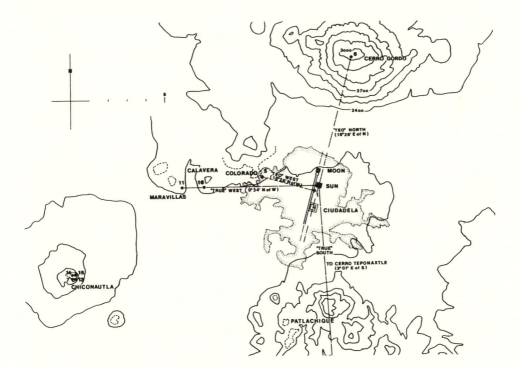

Figure 7.1. Orientation of Teotihuacan and location of pecked circles and crosses. From Aveni and Hartung 1982, fig. 2, p. 26.

at Uaxactun, in the Maya area, where another pecked circle was found in an astronomical structure.

Pecked circles often consist of 260 dots, which is the equivalent of the ritual calendar cycle, a combination of thirteen numbers and twenty day signs. This calendar was calibrated with a 365-day solar cycle. The aim of the 260-day cycle was largely divinatory—through its various combinations the gods made their will known. Both the calendar and the astronomic observations leading to the orientation of the site at 15 degrees 25 minutes east of north are complex systemic forms of knowledge. They are, like the grid plan of Teotihuacan, not just systemic, but complete artificial worlds in themselves.

A strong visual and planning relationship between the Avenue and the Pyramid of the Moon is evident. The Pyramid of the Moon gives purpose, completion, and an end to the Avenue—it is where it is *because* of the Avenue. It is thus central to the plan of the site. The Avenue is a colossal visual image of the Teotihuacan line of orientation. Though it could have been planned for splendid processions and rituals, it is in its everyday form a great arrow, with the Pyramid of the Moon at its apex, situating Teotihuacan in cosmic space. The point I wish to emphasize is that this cosmic space is largely related to the stars and to the sky, and to the mountains. In contrast, the Pyramid of the Sun and the Goddess refer more to the earth and the underworld.

Two very different sets of ideas might have been brought together simultaneously or sequentially at the founding of Teotihuacan. One set may have had to do with the Goddess and the Pyramid of the Sun, referring to the underworld, femininity, geomancy, and local power. The other seems to be related to the complex systems and sciences of astrology, mathematics, astronomy, and geometry and seems to have focused on the heavens, on external political and commercial contacts, on the world of men, on aristocratic power, and on the Storm God.

In Mesoamerican thought rain gods lived on mountaintops, because the dark gray clouds of thunderstorms seem to gather there prior to discharging their nourishing waters. One mountain in Mexico is still called Tlaloc, from prehispanic times, and many mountains had shrines to the rain gods.[3] The rain gods are sky beings. In text and images they create thunder and lightning by hitting a vessel with a weapon and pour water from a vessel. In Aztec lore their mountaintop homes were the paradise of those who had died from lightning or from a watery disease or drowning. Although some Aztec myths associate the rain gods with caves, the mountaintop location as the Tlalocan seems paramount.[4] The Teotihuacan Storm God may therefore have been primarily a creature of the sky and of the mountaintops.

Stephen Tobriner recognized the clearly designed relationship between the Pyramid of the Moon and Cerro Gordo looming behind it and linked the deliberate pattern to the then-known all-purpose Tlaloc deity. He noted that rainfall on Cerro Gordo is 50 percent higher than in the valley and that water from rainstorms flowing in its barrancas may have been used in irrigation.[5]

Again, as in the case of the Pyramid of the Sun, no archaeological evidence connects the Storm God to this temple-pyramid. Two sculptures of a colossal scale were found on or near the Pyramid of the Moon. One is very battered, but enough is recognizable to indicate that it was very similar to the other one.[6] The latter is magnificently preserved. It is a rectangular architectonic block representing a woman in an ornate skirt, *huipil*, and sandals. Her face is like a mask, and her earplugs, shoulder, and hip lines continue unbroken and disregarding the human body on its sides. She is popularly called a "water goddess" because the Aztec water goddess's name was Chalchiuhtlicue—"Skirt of Jades" or "Fancy Skirt"—and the statue has an elaborately ornamented skirt. She could very well have been a goddess, and possibly Hasso von Winning's Great Goddess,[7] the deity I am calling simply the Goddess. One might automatically assume that the Pyramid of the Moon was dedicated to her. However, I have argued previously that her domain was just as likely to have been the Pyramid of the Sun (Chapter 6). What then were these statues doing at the Pyramid of the Moon? Quite clearly they were architectural—indicated by their pairing and by their architectonic form. (Almost all Teotihuacan sculpture was architectonic.)[8] Their most likely function was that of a monumental gateway on some part of the pyramid, as secondary figures, perhaps an honor guard for the deity to whom the structure was dedicated rather than the deity itself. The deity may or may not have been represented—it could have been in the form of the lightning and storm or by some symbolic object unrecognizable by Western observers. (The dates of these sculptures are unknown.)

Unlike the Goddess, whose images are mainly at Teotihuacan, Storm God images abound outside of the city, and the Storm God is usually considered an element of Teotihuacan's external relations. The question of whether Teotihuacan had an empire is a much-debated and as yet unresolved issue. Teotihuacan definitely reached out beyond its boundaries in a variety of ways and on a variety of levels. It does not seem to have been a conquest empire like that of the Aztecs, organized systematically to collect tribute.[9] Some Teotihuacan activity, for example in relation to Alta Vista, was commercial but involved people with astronomical knowledge. Some contacts, as in Escuintla, Guatemala, and Matacapan, Veracruz, seemed to involve a considerable number of people from Teotihuacan moving and settling outside the city. They took their city cults with them and made images similar to the ones of Teotihuacan—figurines at Matacapan and composite censers at Escuintla. Some interactions, as in Kaminaljuyu in Guatemala, suggest that Teotihuacan conquered a local population. There the "conquerors" were buried in Maya-style splendor, but with some Teotihuacan-style artifacts.

Some relationships, as with the Maya city of Tikal, are quite mysteri-

Figure 7.2. Stela 31, Tikal. Drawing by William R. Coe. Courtesy of the University of Pennsylvania Museum, Philadelphia, Tikal Project 69-5-176A.

ous. The ruler Stormy Sky, the most powerful Early Classic ruler at the site, shows himself next to Teotihuacan-style figures carrying weapons and the image of a Storm God-related deity on Stela 31. These figures may have been Storm Sky's father, who, according to Clemency Coggins,[10] was a conqueror of Tikal originally from Teotihuacan (a notion which because of the distance is pretty mind-boggling) or who, according to Linda Schele,[11] was Maya but wore a Teotihuacan warrior outfit because a Teotihuacan type of warfare was accepted as superior by the Maya. Alternatively, as in the older theories, the figures may have been "Teotihuacan ambassadors" so important that their presence was thus invoked by Stormy Sky. Vessels in Teotihuacan style were also found in Stormy Sky's tomb. All these interpretations suggest detailed Maya familiarity with Teotihuacan and possibly interaction at the highest level.

The connections with the Zapotec city of Monte Alban, as represented on monuments, appear to be less personal and more diplomatic.[12] Teotihuacan and Monte Alban figures are shown as equal powers on the Bazan slab and on the Estela Lisa. Strangely, however, the sides of the reliefs that refer to Teotihuacan on the Estela Lisa were facing the pyramid and not visible to everyone, as if there was a need to hide this diplomatic relationship. Coggins suggested recently a more intense relationship with Monte Alban, including elite intermarriage.[13] Besides these major external contacts, enigmatic individual monuments exist, such as the Horcones Stela (representing the Storm God with the water lily emerging from its mouth), about which scholars do not even have a theory of explanation.[14] Evidently, the people of Teotihuacan did not stay at home—they were out in Mesoamerica, involved in everything from dynastic and diplomatic ties to commerce and new settlements. Although the "powerful state" hypothesis has suggested an astute state management behind all this foreign involvement, the varied material remains suggest something less coordinated and more entrepreneurial.

Teotihuacan apparently also welcomed foreigners to the city. In a barrio excavated in the 1960s in the western part of Teotihuacan, people were buried in Oaxaca-type tombs. Coggins's suggestion that this barrio was populated by a group of political exiles from Monte Alban is intriguing, though not quite provable.[15] Evelyn Rattray recently excavated a sector in the eastern part of Teotihuacan where Veracruz merchants seemed to have lived in a dozen large Veracruz-style round houses.[16] Some of their stockpiles of wares and burial offerings included Maya pottery. The major question, as William Sanders notes, is how were these foreigners integrated

Figure 7.3. Detail of Stela 31, Tikal. Height, 2.3 m (7.5 ft.). From M. Coe 1966, fig. 42, p. 70. Courtesy of the University of Pennsylvania Museum, Philadelphia.

Figure 7.4. Drawing of bazan slab. Alabaster. Found in Mound X, Monte Alban. 49 by 49 by 12 cm (19 1/4 by 19 1/4 by 4 3/4 in.). From *Indian Art of Mexico and Central America*, by Miguel Covarrubias. Copyright © 1957 by Alfred A. Knopf, Inc. Reprinted by permission of the publisher.

into the economy and ritual life of Teotihuacan? Both Teotihuacan and Tenochtitlan were cosmopolitan places in which ethnic difference may have been as common as craft specialization. Both initiated contacts with other Mesoamerican politics.

The Teotihuacan deity who seems to have had a major role in foreign relations is the Storm God, not the Goddess. As early as 1974 I was confused by the Storm God's various types of representations. One I called Tlaloc A had goggles, a moustache, fangs, a water lily in his mouth, and a five-knot headdress. It seemed to me then that he had a crocodilian origin.[17] I am no longer sure of that assumption, because earlier storm gods have since been found at Tlalancaleca with a form already conventionalized and showing no identifiable animal features.[18] Now I feel that the animal origins of the Storm God, if any, are unknown, and that his conventionalization is ancient—probably predating Teotihuacan. Another representation of the Storm God that I once called Tlaloc B has a serpent's bifurcated tongue, or even jaguar features. The headdress of this Storm God image is more variable, with a frame rather than the knots. I would suggest at this point that there were a variety of ways of rendering the Storm God, depending on the context or purpose of an image and a variety of animal aspects to which he related, as James Langley suggested.[19]

Finally, a number of deities (as well as human images) wearing rings, like eyeglasses, over human-appearing eyes seem to be related to the Storm God. Many of these deities carry weapons and are in contexts of war. For example, the Horcones Stela is a perfect Tlaloc A, whereas the shield carried by the figure on Stela 31 from Tikal has human-looking eyes within Storm God rings. I would now conclude that the Storm God could have also had a more warlike aspect.

This latter interpretation seems to be borne out by the curious fact that even after Teotihuacan had collapsed, emblems of the Teotihuacan Storm God combined with either blood or owl glyphs—all from the representations of war and sacrifice symbolism at Teotihuacan—were major images incorporated into the insignia of Maya rulers as warriors. Examples are present at Piedras Negras, Copan, Dos Pilas, La Amelia, and Aguateca—to name only the best known. Linda Schele and David Freidel argue that the images all refer to a warrior cult of Teotihuacan origins.[20] However, as the Horcones Stela indicates, the Storm God was also associated with water and fertility on some foreign monuments. The Storm God was thus a widespread image with two of its original Teotihuacan connotations—rain and warfare—intact for a long period of time. Closer to the Valley of Mexico, one of the major victorious warriors at Cacaxtla wears Storm God emblems, while a water-related Storm God is also present.

From this distribution of images I conclude that, like the Classical Zeus or Jupiter, the Storm God was a quintessentially male deity concerned with rain, with foreign relations, with commerce, with war, and with the highest elite of Teotihuacan and their dynastic and diplomatic contacts.

At Teotihuacan, he was closely related to the calendar and to the planning of the city but was somewhat subservient in size and importance to the Goddess. The Storm God and the Goddess could have been the major deities of the three-temple complexes. I have no suggestion for the third, except possibly a deity of local significance to a lineage or social unit. This notion is not inconsistent with Linda Manzanilla's suggestion that the three-temple complexes are barrio temples.[21]

These two gods are rarely shown as interacting—except that the Goddess is placed in superior positions, or frontally, while the Storm God, like an elite worshipper, is shown in profile. The rarity of interactions does not mean, however, that no relationship existed between the two deities. Here, again, an Aztec example helps. In 1978 a large oval stone was found representing a dismembered goddess with bells on her cheeks. Sixteenth-century stories relate that Huitzilopochtli's mother, Coatlicue, became miraculously pregnant from a feather and that her daughter, Coyolxauhqui ("She of the Golden Bells"), and her four hundred sons felt dishonored and vowed to kill them both. But at the moment of birth Huitzilopochtli emerged fully armed, cut off the head of Coyolxauhqui and scattered the four hundred sons. Mesoamericanists generally believe this is an astral myth—Huitzilopochtli is the sun who obliterates the moon and stars as it rises in the morning.[22] The point is that without the legend modern observers would know very little about the relationship of Coatlicue, Huitzilopochtli, and Coyolxauhqui and could not interpret the sculpture. Interactions of a variety of sorts were common among Mesoamerican deities, such as Quetzalcoatl sleeping with Xochiquetzal and feuding with Tezcatlipoca, as mentioned above. Mesoamericans imagined the relationship of the Christian "gods" in similar active terms. In various native villages in the twentieth century the sculptures of Christ and Mary are locked up in separate boxes at certain times of the year so they cannot make love to each other. At San Juan Teotihuacan the statue of the Virgin of Purification "visits" the Christ of El Divino Redentor in the Church of San Juan (built right in front of one of the major springs of Teotihuacan) for a week or so once a year. The erotic nature of the visit is not actually stated but vaguely implied.

There is no reason to assume that the Storm God (or the various storm gods) and the Goddess (or the various goddesses) were imagined in total isolation from one another. Though they were all gods of nature, water, and abundance as well as war and sacrifice, they also had a set of mutually contradictory and complementary features:

Storm God	Goddess
male	female
rainwater	groundwater
astrology	geomancy
sky	earth
science	nature
commerce	agriculture
foreign relations	internal affairs
dynastic values	collective values

These two major gods (or groups of gods) may have competed or fought, which does not rule out sexual relations or some family relationship. Ah, for an eighth-century Bernardino de Sahagún to provide a text that sheds light on the mystery! I am aware that I have just indulged in a form of structural analysis that may be as foreign to this material as casting it in the form of Greco-Roman gods. Not certain that it is necessarily more correct than previous hypotheses, I believe nonetheless that it is useful in that one can think about Teotihuacan and its gods differently.

At the foundation of Teotihuacan, though there were quite a number of three-temple complexes, only two colossal pyramids were built. This distinction suggests a duality not unlike the twin-pyramids of the Aztecs. There may be a further parallel in the deity dedications. The larger Pyramid of the Sun, like the Aztec one dedicated to Tlaloc, may have been dedicated to nature and possibly an ancient Goddess—though larger, this pyramid was in some sense isolated. The smaller Pyramid of the Moon, like the Aztec one dedicated to Huitzilopochtli, may have been closer to war and political enterprise in significance and was built in a centrally visible location that negated its smaller size. The Pyramid of the Moon has a vast plaza surrounded by a dozen good-sized pyramid platforms, creating the most significant open space and the largest clustering of ceremonial buildings at Teotihuacan after the Ciudadela. Taken together the plaza and buildings more than equal the Pyramid of the Sun's great mass. Considering this space, the overall mass, and the placement at the head of the Avenue with the mountain behind it, the significance of the Pyramid of the Moon has been underestimated in the various reconstructions of Teotihuacan.

Teotihuacan is not impressive just because of its huge pyramids, but also because of the way the Pyramid of the Moon is set into a larger architectural plan. The Pyramid of the Moon, the temples surrounding it, the plaza, and the avenue are the most dramatic visual demonstrations of hierarchy and order, suggesting something of the political structure that gave

Figure 7.5. Zapotec-style urn. Ceramic, pigment. Found in Oaxaca Barrio, Teotihuacan. Xolalpan phase, A.D. 400–700. 34.2 by 21.1 by 22.5 cm (11 3/8 by 8 1/4 by 8 3/4 in.). MNA 9-4878; INAH 10-39504. Museo Nacional de Antropologia, Mexico City. CNCA-INAH-MEX. INAH photo.

rise to the city. While the Pyramid of the Sun with its chthonic cave seems to be associated with unpredictable forces, the Pyramid of the Moon, as a part of the plan and of the orientation, suggests complete intellectual control of the universe. I am suggesting that for Teotihuacan these rational forces were imagined as masculine and embodied in the Storm God. The Storm God should not be imagined as a simple and benign fertility deity, nor even necessarily as one deity. As the wielder of lightning, this god was power incarnate. He, or related aspects of him, were associated with warfare, sacrifice, and politics at every level of Teotihuacan society. In my view, the Storm God may also have had patron deity aspects like Huitzilopochtli of the Aztecs. While Tlaloc was the "old" deity for the Aztecs, for Teotihuacan the Goddess may have played that role. The role of the various activities associated with the Storm God, as of the orientation and the architectural layout, was to demonstrate control. It is thus that the elite presumably convinced the population that the world they were creating was good, harmonious, justified and rational. In the midst of unpredictable nature, Teotihuacan was built as a fortress of order.

VIII

The Ciudadela
and Rulership

AFTER HAVING BUILT THE PYRAMIDS OF THE SUN AND MOON, THE
north-south Avenue, and associated structures within a period of a century, the people of Teotihuacan began a building project of similarly large
proportions in the Miccaotli phase (A.D. 100–200). This building project
was neither a three-temple complex nor a huge pyramid. Instead it was a
gigantic enclosure. This enclosure, 400 meters square, was built south of
the city (below the River San Juan) on the right side of the Avenue, facing
a similarly large space of less clear function on the other side. An east-
west avenue was built at the center of the enclosures, thus making the
layout of the city not just processional and directional, but also radial and
cruciform. Thus Teotihuacan was given a new center: the Ciudadela.

The Ciudadela enclosure, more than seven meters high on four sides,
and the Central Temple of the Feathered Serpent have enough material to
make up about two-thirds of the Pyramid of the Sun. The plaza is so large
that George Cowgill estimated that at its height the entire adult population of Teotihuacan could have gathered there.[1] Most of the Aztec Templo
Mayor could fit inside of it. The Ciudadela was probably a palace, Teotihuacan's version of the Chinese emperor's Forbidden City within the capital.[2]
Access to it could have been gained only through a single stairway on the
west that would have been easy to guard. The high barrier mound on all
sides means that from the exterior, view into the palace area was severely
limited. Two large habitations were built on both sides of the Temple of

the Feathered Serpent, suggesting the combination of palace, administrative center, and temple for the complex as a whole. The Ciudadela stands in opposition to the pyramids: it is a great negative space and open area rather than a mass. It is also restricted and lacks the more open access of the pyramids.

Another surprise is the form of the Temple of the Feathered Serpent. Although small, the temple was lavishly ornamented by stone sculptures. The Pyramids of the Sun and the Moon had simple sloping surfaces—the Temple of the Feathered Serpent is the first example of the use of *talud* and *tablero* (sloping base and rectangular panel) in the treatment of the plat-

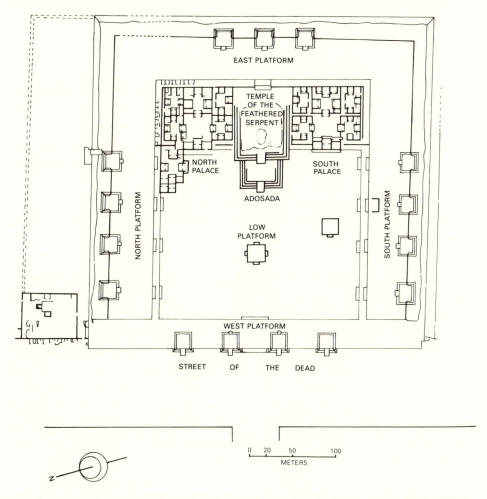

Figure 8.1. Plan of the Ciudadela, Teotihuacan. From Berrin 1988, copyright © 1988, by René Millon.

forms. The temple was thus both architecturally and sculpturally quite labor intensive—a jewel of fine craftsmanship on a monumental scale. The Temple was the first sculptured building at Teotihuacan, dated by archaeological context. Here too the temple on top and images are gone, so observers are left with the decoration of the body of the pyramid, which may be accessory to the main theme or image and is unlikely to be a major deity in itself.

Observers have spilt a great deal of ink on this imagery. On the *talud* feathered serpents are shown in an undulating position among seashells. These serpents face the stairway in the center. On the *tablero* is the low-relief body of a feathered serpent with a very clearly marked rattlesnake tail. Tenoned serpent heads project from the balustrade of the stairway. On the *tablero* the creature has two heads—the one on the left is always a serpent head, the long snout emerging from a collar of petal-like forms. It is the other head, near the tail, that causes all the questions and problems.

This head on the right is unique—no other head exactly like this exists in the art of Teotihuacan or anywhere else. It was first identified as a Tlaloc (as everything else was) because it has rings on its head, but the rings are *not* over the eyes but on the forehead above them. The eyes, inlaid with obsidian, are quite clear below the rings. The creature has only an upper jaw—its top teeth hang over the edge of the tablero. It has a face divided into rectangular segments that could be read as "scales," or "crocodilian" markings: with its long snout and teeth the creature has a saurian look. It has a looped knot at the top of its head, which led Alfonso Caso and Ignacio Bernal to relate it to a Monte Alban deity that also has a knot in its headdress.[3] Very likely the two heads represent some kind of an opposition: one is round, one is square; one has flower-petal forms, one has square scales; one is the head, the other is near the tail. Caso and Bernal saw this duality as the opposition of the seasons—rainy season and dry season—and compared the images to the feathered serpent symbol of fertility and the fire serpent symbol of drought of Aztec iconography. No one improved on Caso and Bernal's interpretation until recently. Focusing on the commercial power of Teotihuacan after the 1960s has led me to see the shells and feathers as connoting trade with faraway places and wealth, not just water and fertility.[4] Saburo Sugiyama has suggested that the saurian head is really a headdress and is thus an emblem of royal power.[5] Although I see what he means, I find the form to be too unlike the representations of headdresses in murals and figurines for that argument to be totally convincing. Mainly, I find that it works much less well than Caso and Bernal's dualistic theory, which, interpreted politically, suggests that through the power of the priest-ruler of the Ciudadela the cycles of dry and rainy seasons continue their appointed course. But Sugiyama is right in focusing on royal or dynastic power as an aspect of this symbolism, although I see that power working in a less direct fashion. In an ambitious essay, Alfredo López-Austin, Leonardo Lopez Luján, and Sugiyama interpret the feathered serpent as carrying the headdress of the day sign Cipactli (a saurian creature), the first day of the Aztec ritual calendar, and thus dedicated to the beginning of time.[6] Like René Millon's interpretation of the Pyramid of the Sun, this is yet another suggestion about a Teotihuacan structure being dedicated to the "beginning of time." These interpretations about time likely contain a kernel of truth, even if the specificity of association with a given structure is hard to prove or to disprove. Mesoamericans were obsessed with time and its various cycles; many buildings, artworks, and rituals present aspects of time, although little evidence for this focus on time is visible at Teotihuacan. Karl Taube sees the crocodilian head also as a fire serpent, which he associates with warfare.[7] Starting out as Tlaloc, the head has since become identified with wealth, with royal power, with the beginning of time, and with warfare—demonstrating, like inkblot tests, the possibilities of interpretations in multivalent systems. Every one of these interpretations may be a possible connotation, but none is a definitive meaning.

Let me leave the enigmatic head and focus on some other aspects of the building. First of all, the temple, with its large, three-dimensional heads, has surprising similarities to contemporaneous temple architecture in the Maya area: from Cerros to Tikal to Uaxactun to Mirador, early temples were ornamented with such paired and contrasting heads. At that time, Maya rulers were not yet commemorated in stelae and glyphic inscriptions. Linda Schele and David Freidel have suggested that as the cult of the divine ruler emerged between A.D. 200 and A.D. 300, the rulers put into their regal costume the imagery and insignia first found on architectural ornament.[8] The Maya architectural heads are modeled in stucco, whereas the Teotihuacan carvings are all in stone, making the Teotihuacan temple architecture all the more expensive in materials and labor. Still, I see a curious correlation between a building like the Ciudadela set up like a very exclusive royal palace, and an adjacent temple whose architectural ornament is similar to that of royal lords in the south of Mesoamerica. Did the person responsible for the concept of the Ciudadela have some contact with the Maya dynastic rulers?

What about the feathered serpent? We Westerners have an obsession with the feathered serpent, which we imagine was the major Pre-

Columbian deity (Chapter 2). It is no accident that D. H. Lawrence entitled his novel about Mexico *The Plumed Serpent*. Because of the apparent importance of the Aztec and colonial story of Quetzalcoatl, observers generally assume that the art of Mesoamerica will have lots of feathered serpents in it and that scholars clearly understand the meaning of the feathered serpent image. Yet the major early animal image of the supernatural was the jaguar in Preclassic Mesoamerica, and the jaguar continued as the primary symbol of both royalty and the supernatural in the Classic and Postclassic periods. Serpents appear on a few Preclassic images with a wing or a single feather, which might have been predecessors of the feathered serpent. The first truly feathered serpent is found on the Temple of the Feathered Serpent at Teotihuacan. No one can be certain whether the combination is a Teotihuacan idea, but unquestionably the mythical creature is here placed in a prominent position. The only other temple with a similar feathered serpent image is the one at Xochicalco, which flourished coeval with the end or right after the collapse of Teotihuacan. There the feathered serpent undulates over seated royal(?) figures and date glyphs. The Xochicalco feathered serpent is generally believed to be a conscious imitation of the feathered serpent image on the Temple of the Feathered Serpent at Teotihuacan. Perhaps the people of Xochicalco still knew what the Teotihuacan temple design signified or tried to link themselves visually with Teotihuacan, as they also used Maya and Zapotec motifs and stylistic details.

Was the feathered serpent a deity at Teotihuacan? This speculation is hard to answer. For instance, many more feline images than feathered serpent images exist in Teotihuacan. Except in this building, the feathered serpent is not the major image in art, especially in the murals of Teotihuacan. It is usually found as a border design, its long form appropriate as a framing device, although the Storm God and or Goddess do not have the feathered serpent border. On one shrine at Atetelco, which may "quote" the Ciudadela, Storm God faces and feathered serpents ornament the different levels of the structure.[9] The references are all to natural fertility and to wealth. However, processions of elite figures are frequently bordered by feathered serpents.

In a unique mural from the Tlamimilolpa phase (A.D. 200–400), various animals (including felines, birds, and feathered serpents) are shown moving in and out of stylized waves. It has been named the Mural of the Mythological Animals, since the creatures seem to be active and to enact some type of narrative. In this one context a feathered serpent on the far

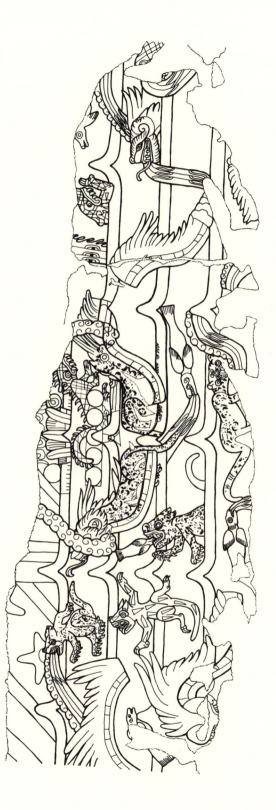

Figure 8.2. Mural of the mythological animals. Far right, feathered serpent; left, three felines. Drawing by J. Robertson.

right participates in a scene, but he merely spits out a stream of water. Far livelier are a group of felines, one of which catches a bird in its mouth.

Feathered serpent imagery does appear elsewhere in Mesoamerica in later contexts. For example, in Xochicalco, on the main pyramidal structure, human figures dressed like rulers or elite figures sit in the curves of the body of the serpent. At Cacaxtla and Chichen Itza, feathered serpents rear up above specific individuals; these feathered serpents have been interpreted as their names or emblems. Similarly, the Aztecs represented Quetzalcoatl as a man with a serpent rearing up behind him. These few illustrations indicate a strong association of the feathered serpent with men of great prominence in the Late Classic and Postclassic periods. The people of Xochicalco may have known what the Teotihuacan image signified, and it may have been both cosmic and political. They could have also used the image to refer directly to Teotihuacan's ruling power, the way the Aztecs imitated the sculptures of Tula to demonstrate their "Toltec" associations.

One more bit of evidence can be added to this question of how to interpret the feathered serpent at Teotihuacan. In 1942, Sigvald Linné found a pressed-ware orange bowl at the site of Las Colinas south of Teotihuacan.[10] This bowl has become one of the most famous objects in the analysis of Teotihuacan iconography. At its base is a Storm God with the water lily and five-knot headdress suggesting the forces of the cosmos. On the sides are four Teotihuacan elite figures with priestly bags. Three have animals in front of them: a feathered serpent, a bird, and a coyote. The fourth is rather special, having rings over his eyes and a segmented headdress and bearing as his emblem the tasseled headdress. Clara Millon suggested that these four figures may represent the four quarters of Teotihuacan and reflect in some way its social organization.[11] They could just as easily show the four highest titles in some significant order. At any rate, on the Las Colinas bowl the feathered serpent clearly identifies a person.

The feathered serpent may therefore have had associations with a title such as "ruler-priest", with a dynastic lineage, or generally with the elite. But the associations appear to be human and political, although in the case of the Ciudadela (and the Maya temples) I think the imagery was so worked out that the cosmic and the political coincided and rulership was associated with the alternation of the seasons, the beginning of time, sacred war, and so forth.

That the Ciudadela was most likely a palace has been suggested by both René Millon and George Cowgill on the basis of its plan.[12] The elaborately ornamented temple, with its feathered serpent imagery, does not contradict such an interpretation. What is striking about the Ciudadela is that it was not built earlier, along with the pyramids, but later; that it is huge in scale; and that in building it a new center was created for the city that made the pyramids peripheral. From many places inside the Ciudadela enclosure the pyramids are either not visible or only partly visible. The Ciudadela seems to be the architectural representation of a major change in the social and political structure of Teotihuacan.

I will resort to a hypothetical narrative to suggest what might have happened. As a result of the concentration of the valley's population in the city, a successful program of agriculture, and the beginnings of trade relations as far away as Belize,[13] the elite solidified their control over the commoners. If Teotihuacan was created partly by conquest and partly by the attraction of commoners to a heterogeneous, dynamic center, then the elite initially may have had some limitations on their power or may have felt that they could not freely use whatever power they had. Around A.D. 100 a powerful individual or family may have had enough wealth and political power to celebrate centralized power directly in something like the institution of royalty at Teotihuacan. A powerful leader may have literally redesigned the city, putting the palace—and thus rulership—at its center. He may have been in contact with other contemporary rulers in the Maya area and was perhaps inspired by their dynastic temples in building the Temple of the Feathered Serpent. I would guess either that he took the title of "Feathered Serpent" as supreme ruler or that "Feathered Serpent" was the name of his family or lineage. Either reason would explain the use of the feathered serpent image to identify important men at other Mesoamerican centers. (After all, Teotihuacan is likely to have had dynastic ties and alliances throughout the area.) Very likely the ruler also used the image of the feathered serpent to refer to the cosmos, implying that the proper workings of nature and its seasons were the result of his personal powers and ability to intervene with the gods.

Until a few years ago this "ruler" was a fantasy figure. However, excavations in the 1980s inside the Temple of the Feathered Serpent seem to suggest more of a reality. Cowgill, Sugiyama, and Rubén Cabrera Castro found a mass sacrifice of more than eighty young men, dressed as warriors, surrounding a series of burials.[14] The young men had their arms tied behind their back and were in a seated position. They wore many shell ornaments, but their most surprising adornment was a collar of human jawbone (maxillae) trophies. (Some of the maxillae were real and had probably come from captives; some were imitations.) Such a mass sacrifice of military individuals is very different from the limited sacrifices at the corners of the Pyramid of the Sun, which suggest the dedication of a building. Mass sacrifices of this sort are more usual in the graves of the rulers of great early empires from Peru to China. Sometimes the sacrificed individuals are servants, or wives, or, as in this case, warriors. No such buried mass sacrifice came to light in the Aztec Templo Mayor, though the Aztecs are known to have practiced sacrifice on a large scale. Sacrifice is likely to be a practice associated with burials, and early in the excavations of the Temple of the Feathered Serpent archaeologists hoped to find the ruler's tomb.

Not all the interior of the temple has been excavated. One major burial area was found, but it had been completely looted in prehispanic times. A number of other burials included women and children with rich jade ornaments. The looted tomb could have been that of this Teotihuacan supreme ruler, although another tomb, not yet found, could contain richer remains. The other personages buried in the temple may have been members of the ruler's family, suggesting a lineage burial temple rather than one devoted purely to an individual.

This attempt to celebrate dynastic rulership at Teotihuacan apparently did not succeed. In the Tlamimilolpa phase (A.D. 200–400) a large *adosada* temple was built in front of the Temple of the Feathered Serpent, rendering the Temple of the Feathered Serpent almost completely invisible from the front. *Adosada* temples are present in front of other pyramids, such as the Pyramids of the Sun and the Moon, but are nowhere near this large. Apparently the Temple of the Feathered Serpent was not dismantled or destroyed, but it was transformed and made visibly less accessible. William Sanders suggests that the complex became a school on the model of the Aztec *calmecac*.[15] The *talud/tablero* form of architectural articulation, without the complex sculptures, was adopted as a general Teotihuacan form and was applied later to nearly all civic and religious buildings. Apartment compounds were begun in their permanent form to house the general population of the city. They are remarkably like the Ciudadela in basic plan—a walled compound with central court and shrine and a temple on the east side. The composite incense burner was invented for apartment-compound ritual. The administrative center was probably shifted to the Street of the Dead Complex, straddling the Avenue and the center of the city and incorporating the old three-temple complexes. In the mural paintings of the apartment compounds and in the incised and frescoed pottery vessels, Storm God and Goddess imagery abounds, with the Goddess clearly ascendant.

One possible hypothesis for these remarkable changes is a shift in emphasis in the nature of rulership at Teotihuacan. The elite may have consolidated their power to such an extent that extreme display was no longer necessary. The Ciudadela may have remained a public space, but the political center may have shifted to the Street of the Dead Complex, a place of spacious administrative and habitation quarters and three-temple complexes but strikingly devoid of a large, theatrical open space for rituals witnessed by thousands. The elite were no longer interested in spectacular monument building and the theatrical ritualism that that implies, but were instead concerned with the city as a practical community. They initiated the building of relatively standardized apartment compounds fitting into the sacred Teotihuacan grid as suggested by René Millon.[16] While on the one hand this control over the development of Teotihuacan shows the power of the state over the life of every inhabitant, it is also an indication of the importance of the population in the eyes of those who would tax them or lead them into battle. The joint emphasis of the rulers and the population on integration and harmony focuses attention away from the rulers to the households. The material remains suggest but do not prove the existence of an internal organization as systematically and bureaucratically organized as the plans of the city and apartment compounds. This bureaucratic governmental system appears to have remained in place and functioned continuously from A.D. 200 to A.D. 750—more than five hundred years—until its collapse. Nothing like it ever existed in Mesoamerica before it or after it.

Symbolic of the new emphasis on officeholders rather than dynastic rulers is the emblem of rulership at Teotihuacan after the Tlamimilolpa phase: the tasseled headdress. This headdress usually consists of three layers—tassels on top, circles below, and triangular points below the circles. This is the headdress that the fourth figure has in front of him on the Las Colinas bowl. As mentioned before, this figure is also unusual because he wears rings over his eyes and a different helmet than the others. These four figures very likely represent four titled individuals. Because I feel that the tasseled headdress denotes a title—like a bishop's mitre—the bird, serpent, and coyote emblems are also likely to indicate titles rather than

Figure 8.3. Fragment of plano-relief vessel. Diego Rivera Museum, Mexico City. From Séjourné 1966a, fig. 87.

personal names. (They lack the idiosyncrasy of Aztec or Mixtec names in glyphs, for example.)[17]

The relationship of the tasseled headdress to the Storm God is particularly interesting. On the Las Colinas bowl, the human figure wears goggles. On Stela 31 at Tikal, the goggled deity on the shield carried by the figure in Teotihuacan dress wears a tasseled headdress. On Stela 1 at Yaxha, a man in military dress has both Teotihuacan-style goggles and a tasseled headdress. Many other examples show similar crossovers in Storm God and tasseled headdress imagery. The abundance of these examples suggests that

Storm God worship and patronage was closely linked to the institution of rulership at Teotihuacan—a hypothesis that has already been presented in Chapter 7. Clara Millon has devoted much scholarship to the subject of the tasseled headdress and was the first to deduce its essentially political significance.[18] Groping after similar ideas, I once suggested that the deity on Stela 31 with the goggles and tasseled headdress may have been the patron deity of Teotihuacan—like Huitzilopochtli of the Aztecs.[19] The tasseled headdress is sometimes associated with warlike attributes in representations, such as a design from a Teotihuacan plano-relief bowl on which a goggled figure with a tasseled headdress carries a shield and spears. It is *not* the figure on Stela 31 who wears the important tasseled headdress, but the deity on the shield; in many instances the tasseled headdress is associated with humans, as insignia, but is usually not worn by them.

The exceptions to this pattern can be found in a single set of murals and a group of throned figurines. In one set of murals from Techinantitla, dating from the last hundred years before the collapse of the city, humans with rings over their eyes wear tasseled headdresses. Moreover, emblems of various sorts, like names or titles, are placed in front of them. Storm God–related imagery and tasseled headdress parts are some of the elements of these emblems. Techinantitla was an unusually large apartment compound—perhaps even a palace—400 meters east of the Pyramid of the Moon.[20] Because of some of the garments worn, Clara Millon felt that these individuals were in military dress and named them "generals."[21] I suggest merely that they were high-ranking, perhaps among the highest-ranking of-

Figure 8.4. Techinantitla mural processional figures wearing tasseled headdresses. A.D. 600–750. Left, 79 by 121 cm (31 by 47 1/2 in.); right, 77.5 by 110 cm (30 1/2 by 43 1/4 in.). The Fine Arts Museums of San Francisco. Bequest of Harald J. Wagner, 1985.104.11 and 104.5. Tracings by Saburo Sugiyama from the original mural.

ficials at Teotihuacan, combining military and priestly functions. Despite the apparent high rank of these officials, they are not shown as individuals but as an anonymous group. We know too little about the paintings in the apartment compounds to infer whether these tasseled headdress–wearing elite individuals had lived in that compound or whether they were represented on its walls for other reasons. During the later phases these figures wearing or carrying the tasseled headdress insignia do appear to represent the ruling power at Teotihuacan.

The evidence of the figurines complicates this picture. During the same Metepec phase (A.D. 600–750) in which these murals were painted, mold-made clay figurines seated on thrones were common. Earlier handmade throned figurines differ from these later mold-made ones in having much less elaborate and specific dress and insignia. In their complex imagery the mold-made figurines are related to the murals. The throned figurines wear a variety of headdresses, including a butterfly and a feline; one of these is a goggled figure with a tasseled headdress. If only one type of throned figure (such as the one with the tasseled headdress) existed, it could more easily be interpreted as the image of ruling political figure. However, other types of throned figurines exist, and no hierarchic distinction is made visually between them. Perhaps in certain contexts (certainly external relations) the tasseled headdress symbol and its wearer were primary in importance, but in the city as a whole, it was just one of a series of important symbols and positions of rulership. Taking the images of the Las Colinas bowl, the Techinantitla murals, and the throned figurines together, scholars have no way to create a clear hierarchy of titles or even define the symbols of rulership in the later years of Teotihuacan.

We are thus left with a very limited story of rulership at Teotihuacan. Powerful leadership must have existed at the time of the building of the pyramids, but it did not commemorate itself as such figuratively in a permanent medium. Excellent evidence suggests that a powerful ruler or family of rulers built the Ciudadela before being buried in the Temple of the Feathered Serpent among lavish sacrifices of human victims. Perhaps the symbol of the feathered serpent legitimized their rulership. A reaction against such a flamboyant style of rulership in the subsequent periods seems likely, given changes in building patterns. An impersonal, collective ideology seems to have become codified. Rulership is later represented emblematically by the tasseled headdress, which is worn by both humans and deities to represent the highest titles at Teotihuacan—if not the patron deity and city as well. The tasseled headdress and its symbolism is related to the Storm God. Other representations—on the Las Colinas bowl and the throned figurines, for example—suggest an elaborate bureaucracy and system of titles on the basis of either headdress or symbolic attributes. As yet scholars cannot piece this structure together. It is noteworthy, however, that in the variations among headdresses and emblems, observers can discern the outlines of a ruling group but not the presence of any individuals.

The Great Avenue, looking toward the Pyramid of the Moon, Teotihuacan. Pasztory photo.

Cross of Tlaloc. Volcanic stone.
Tlamimilolpa-Metepec phases, A.D.
200–750. 129 by 104 by 12 cm (50 3/4
by 41 by 4 3/4 in.). CNCA-INAH-MEX.
INAH photo.

The Pyramid of the Sun, Teotihuacan. Pasztory photo.

Goddess. Mural painting at Tetitla, Teotihuacan. Metepec phase, A.D. 650–750.
© UNESCO 1958. Reproduced by permission of UNESCO.

Goddess. Detail of mural painting at apartment compound at Tepanti-tla, Teotihuacan. Metepec phase, A.D. 650–750. Copy by Agustín Villagra Caleti in the Museo Nacional de Antropología, Mexico City. CNCA-INAH-MEX. Pasztory photo.

Copy of mural painting at the Temple of Agriculture, Teotihuacan. Copy by Agustín Villagra Caleti in the Museo Nacional de Antropología, Mexico City. CNCA-INAH-MEX. Pasztory photo.

Serpent and saurian heads. Tablero ornamentation on the Temple of the Feathered Serpent, Teotihuacan. Pasztory photo.

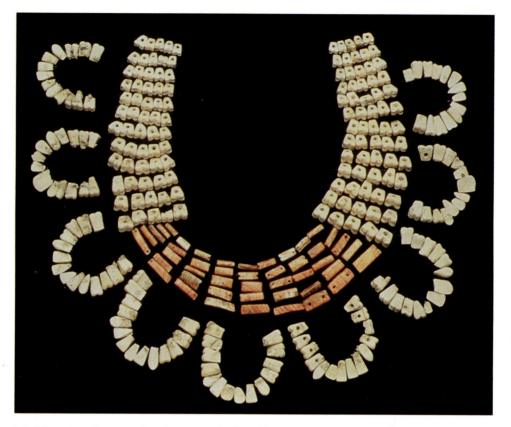

Necklace found on sacrificial victim. Shell and human teeth. Temple of the Feathered Serpent, Teotihuacan. Arranged on a board ca. 8 by 8 cm (20 by 20 in.). INAH 10-411076 and 10-411077. Centro de Investigaciones Arqueologías de Teotihuacan. CNCA-INAH-MEX. From Berrin and Pasztory 1993.

Alabaster mask with fresco detail on the cheeks. Atzcapotzalco, Teotihuacan. 17 by 17 cm (6 1/2 by 6 1/2 in.). Musée de l'Homme. Neg. no. C66.2110.493.

Mask. Green serpentine. Teotihuacan. 21.6 by 20.5 by 10.5 cm (8 3/8 by 8 by 4 in.). Courtesy of Dumbarton Oaks Research Library and Collections, Washington, D.C.

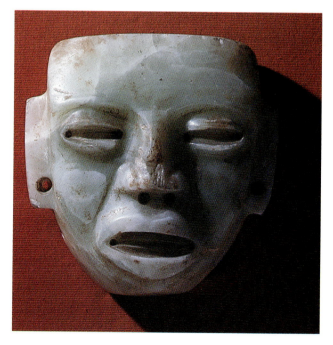

Mask. Alabaster. Musée de l'Homme.

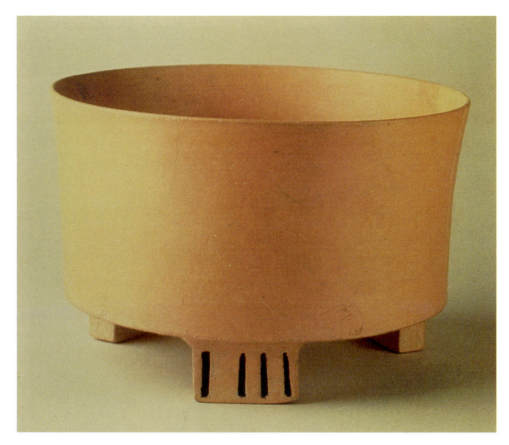

Cylindrical tripod vessel with slab supports. Thin Orange ceramic. Provenance unknown. Tlamimilolpa–Metepec phases, A.D. 200–750. 23 by 20 cm (10 by 8 in.). The Art Museum, Princeton University. From Berrin and Pasztory 1993, fig. 152, p. 260.

Standing male figure. Greenstone. Found at the House of the Priests near the Pyramid of the Sun in 1905. Miccaotli–Tlamimilolpa phases, A.D. 150–250. 71 by 23 cm (28 by 9 in.). MNA 9-3158; INAH 10-81806. Museo Nacional de Antropología, Mexico City. CNCA-INAH-MEX. From Berrin and Pasztory 1993, p. 177.

Censer. Ceramic, pigment, mica. Found in the early 1960s at La Ventilla. Xolalpan phase, A.D. 400–600. 72 by 39 cm (28 1/2 by 15 1/4 in.). CMCA-INAH-MEX. From Berrin and Pasztory 1993, fig. 70, p. 218.

Net-jaguar and temple. Fragment of a mural painting from Tetitla, Teotihuacan. Metepec phase, A.D. 600–750. Courtesy of Dumbarton Oaks Research Library and Collections, Washington, D.C.

Coyotes and deer. Fragment of a mural painting from Teotihuacan, probably Techinantitla. Probably Metepec phase, A.D. 650–750. 61 by 147.5 cm (24 by 59 in.). The Fine Arts Museums of San Francisco, Bequest of Harald J. Wagner, 1985.104.12.

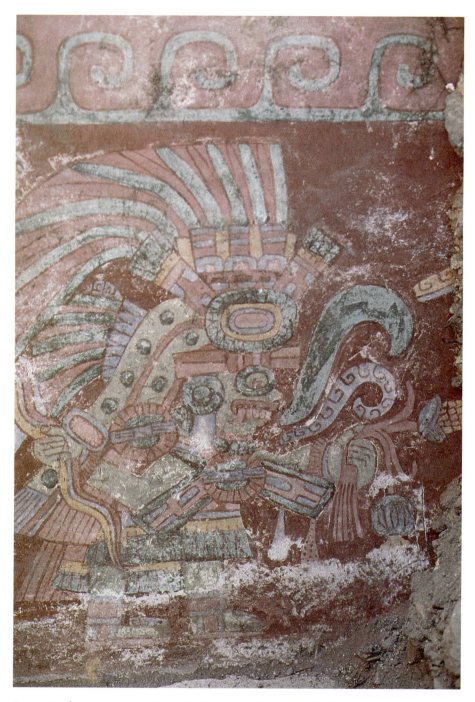

Storm God in procession. Detail of mural painting at Techinantitla, Teotihuacan, A.D. 600–750, found in 1984. In situ. Pasztory photo.

Little bird and spear. Mural painting fragment from Techinantitla, Teotihuacan, A.D. 600–750. 29.5 by 31.5 cm (11 1/2 by 12 1/4 in.). The Fine Arts Museums of San Francisco, Bequest of Harald J. Wagner, 1985.104.9.

Wide-band headdress figurine. Ceramic and pigment. Provenance unknown. Early
Tlamimilolpa phase, A.D. 200. 14.4 by 9.4 by 3.7 cm (5 3/4 by 3 3/4 by 1 3/4 in.).
The Saint Louis Art Museum, Gift of Morton D. May, 233:1978.

IX

Minimalist Aesthetics

Plain and Simple Things

THE GREATEST ART OF TEOTIHUACAN WAS UNQUESTIONABLY architecture. Most authors single out the awesome size of the Avenue and the pyramids and the regular, clearly planned layout of the street grid. They generally applaud the fact that such a colossal and well-ordered plan should have been created by people without metal tools, beasts of burden, or the wheel. But the real commendations of aesthetic appreciation go to other sites such as Monte Alban, Tajín, Palenque, Chichen Itza, Uxmal, and Mitla. These sites have certain features in common. In planning, all of them deviate from strict symmetry or a grid, while maintaining an overall balanced arrangement. Monte Alban is especially popular, with Mound J and Systems IV and M breaking up the symmetry of the plaza. Many of these sites, especially Tikal, have a rather ornate platform articulation; Mitla and Uxmal are loved because of the geometric stone mosaic ornament that appears crisp in the tropical sunlight.[1] Thus, after noting the hugeness and order of Teotihuacan, architectural critics generally dismiss the site as otherwise boring or monotonous.

None of the arts of Teotihuacan, including architecture, yield their pleasures and satisfactions at first glance. Indeed, the Teotihuacan *talud* and *tablero* form with which platforms are articulated is quite simple and repeated without change from one building to the next. It is unlike the varied use of niches and flaring cornices of Tajín, the overhanging corner moldings of Monte Alban, or the complicated apron moldings of Tikal. Teotihuacan architecture lacks the stucco sculpture common at Maya sites and the stone reliefs common elsewhere. Of all Mesoamerican articulations, the Teotihuacan one is the simplest—a rectangular form over a sloping base. This articulation results in long horizontal lines stacked up one above the other. Although in its time, heavily plastered and sometimes covered with murals, it would have been more elegant and decorated than it is now, simplicity of form would have been its overall effect because the ornament was mostly two-dimensional. Why not take that as a positive trait, or at least an intentional one? The architectural image Teotihuacan made for itself was the look of monumental simplicity. This simplicity contrasts with the remarkable social, political, and economic organization that had to have gone into the creation of the city and was probably far from simple. Appearances may be deceptive.

Looking at these "monotonous" *talud/tableros* in greater detail—adjusting my eyes to small-scale changes—I find a surprising amount of variation in size and proportion. On the platform on the edge of the Ciudadela, each set of *talud/tableros* decreases in size from the ground to the top of the stairway, exaggerating the diminution visually. Platforms along the Avenue may be divided in many *talud/tableros* or consist of one large

Figure 9.1. Architecture showing *talud/tablero* articulation. Pasztory photo.

tablero over a small *talud*. Such minimal variations are the rule rather than the exception. This pattern of variation within what appears to be standardization characterizes all the arts of Teotihuacan.

Walk along the Avenue, disregarding the vendors and the tourists, and watch what happens visually to the *talud* and *tablero* platforms: they are never simply linear and horizontal but are in shifting vertical and diagonal relationships to each other. Patterns are created, as in the minimalist music of Philip Glass—repetitions followed by small-scale changes. It is an aesthetic different from that of Franz Schubert. The simplicity and subtlety of the *talud/tablero* have the further result of not detracting from the colossal scale of the pyramids and enclosures, which emerge in stark geometric forms. Next to Teotihuacan, most Mesoamerican sites can appear unnecessarily ornamented. Could Veracruz-style niches be added to the stark Teotihuacan structures without marring the dignity of the Avenue?

Also unusual at Teotihuacan is what is absent. Where is the equivalent of the Sphinx, the statues of the pharaohs, the miles of wall reliefs of ancient Egypt or Mesopotamia—or indeed Monte Alban, Tajín, Chichen Itza, or even Tula in Mesoamerica? Each of those sites has major sculptural programs on the exteriors and interiors of a number of structures. Olmec and Maya rulers, Monte Alban captives, Chichen Itza ballplayers and warriors personify and enliven architecture. Three colossal sculptures did exist at Teotihuacan (Chapter 6): two large Goddess figures may have stood in architectural contexts near the Pyramid of the Moon, while a third, even larger figure (popularly called Tlaloc but wearing a skirt), was found unfinished in the Coatlinchan quarry. Like the pyramids, these sculptures are more remarkable for their colossal size and geometric simplicity than their subtlety of posture or detail. In contrast to the smooth curves of Olmec and Aztec sculptures, these Teotihuacan sculptures look as though they were designed by architects. Such an architectonic quality characterizes the enigmatic sculpture of a skull within a wheel.

Almost all the rest of Teotihuacan sculpture is also architectural. Feline and serpent heads and rattles occasionally ornament balustrades, designed in rectilinear forms that echo the lines of *talud/tablero* articulation. Wall reliefs exist in only two structures: the Temple of the Feathered Conch Shells, dated to the Tlamimilolpa phase (A.D. 200–400), and the Palace of the Quetzal Butterfly, dated to the Metepec phase (A.D. 650–750). Several hundred years separate these two structures located very close to each other near the plaza of the Pyramid of the Moon. None of the images on these structures is anthropomorphic. Shells, flowers, flames, eyes, frets,

Figure 9.2. Colossal figure of Goddess. Found in the quarry of Coatlinchan; now in front of the Museo Nacional de Antropología, Mexico City. Length, 7 m; width, 3.8 m; depth, 1.5 m; 167 tons. CNCA-INAH-MEX. INAH photo.

Figure 9.3. Piers with frontal and profile birds, Palace of the Quetzal Butterfly, Teotihuacan. Probably Metepec phase, A.D. 650–750. CNCA-INAH-MEX. INAH photo cxv-53.

and quetzal birds in frontal and profile views are arranged in strictly geometric registers or rows. The first sense of these images is of clarity and order. As Pat Sarro observed, an effect of layering and three-dimensionality is created through variation in the levels of the carving, not through creation of figures in the round.[2] These sculptures are very much like the mural paintings and when stuccoed and painted must have looked even more like them. At the same time, because of the greater difficulty of cutting stone, some of the lively effects of the mural paintings are missing. The sculptures thus seem like rigid stone versions of murals. Whether for reasons of expense or aesthetics, such reliefs were a rarity at Teotihuacan. Whereas other sites are "peopled" by stone figures whom we imagine as "inhabitants," Teotihuacan has no such stone population. Observers have a strange sense, therefore, of a site devoid of its people.

Most Teotihuacan art is small in scale and dates to the history of the

Figure 9.4. Skull in wheel. Museo Nacional de Antropología, Mexico City. CNCA-INAH-MEX. INAH photo 2446.

city after the building of the pyramids and the Ciudadela. One has to make a strange mental leap from the colossal pyramids to the small incense burners, figurines, and masks. One would never guess from the modest objects in the Teotihuacan hall in the Muséo Nacional de Antropología in Mexico City that these are the major artworks of the greatest city in Pre-Columbian America. It is not just a question of size, but of appearance. These works do not call attention to themselves the way Olmec, Maya, or Aztec art does.

Figure 9.5. Jaguar vessel. White aragonite. Said to have been found near the Pyramid of the Sun, Teotihuacan. Length, 33 cm (13 in.). Copyright © British Museum, London 1926–22. Museum photo neg. no. xlvi/40.

An art collector once said to me that Olmec and Maya objects he found aesthetically inspiring but that the art of Teotihuacan left him cold. It has left most other collectors and museum curators cold, too, since only two significant collections of Teotihuacan art exist outside of Mexico. One of these collections is that of the Museum für Völkerkunde of Vienna, which has splendid greenstone masks and figures collected by Cristos Dominik Bilimek in the nineteenth century. Bilimek was collecting specimens for the newly founded Vienna Museum on the order of the short-lived emperor of Mexico, Maximilian, who was the brother of Francis Joseph I of Austria. These objects all came with registration cards carefully penned in an old-fashioned script, which made me very excited when Christian Feest first showed them to me. My hope in finding useful information in these cards faded quickly—the geologic name of the stones was carefully identified, but nothing was said of the place of origin or context of the figures. Bilimek collected these objects as specimens of stone and minerals, not as works of art or archaeological artifacts.[3] The second major collection is in Stockholm, excavated in the 1930s and 1940s by Sigvald Linné, and it includes incense burners, masks, and vessels of great beauty as well as absolute authenticity.[4] For the past thirty years this collection has been in storage, with no great urgency to put it on display.

What curators and collectors seem to want most are the masks from Teotihuacan, of which probably a large number have been faked since the nineteenth century. The masks are the only Teotihuacan objects that we Westerners have been able to see aesthetically. They have become for us the "face" of Teotihuacan. In the 1950s, Paul Westheim praised them as follows: "The artist aspires to both plasticity and to the plane, and with unparalleled sensitivity . . . he achieves the exact point where the two tendencies seem reconciled in a happy balance."[5]

Evidently what Westheim liked was the seamless blend between the abstraction of the flat geometric face and the subtle rendering of facial features and modeling of the cheeks. This preference was very much in line with Modernist twentieth-century aesthetics. Moreover, the West associates masks with Pre-Columbian art; they are our idea of Mexican canonical forms. Everyone assumed that masks were attached to funerary bundles as false faces, and that too lent them their proper archaeological cachet of having been found in burials. In fact, no Teotihuacan masks have so far been found in burials. In the excavations directed by Ruben Cabrera Castro in the Ciudadela and the Street of the Dead Complex, excavators found three masks on floors and passageways, some near niches.[6] Linné excavated the fragment of a small mask from Xolalpan.[7] But the apartment compounds tend not to have large greenstone masks and figures. All the excavated masks come from the temples and administrative/palatial structures along the Avenue: near the Pyramid of the Sun, the Ciudadela, and the Street of the Dead Complex.[8] They were evidently objects of the highest status. Perhaps a systematic early looting of the structures along the Avenue for collectors such as Bilimek has resulted in the finding of many of the masks now in collections all over the world.

Nor were the murals of Teotihuacan particularly valued aesthetically. The Mexican collector Josué Saenz recalled that looters offered him and many others portions of murals in the 1960s but that most collectors did not want the murals.[9] The murals were on crumbly wall fragments, creating great problems of restoration and display—unlike the masks, which often came with neatly drilled holes, ready for mounting. Many murals ended up on the Lagunilla flea market, smaller every week as they slowly crumbled away. It is hard to imagine that similar pieces of Maya murals would not have found a home and conservation much more quickly.

What is it that fails to attract Western observers to Teotihuacan objects? After years of handling objects of all sorts, I think I have an answer to that question. It is easiest to illustrate the answer by noting what it is that we *like* in Olmec and Maya art.

First, we prefer *naturalism*. Our Greco-Roman heritage and the privileged role of the Renaissance in European art history predispose us to like naturalistic art. Despite the importance of abstraction in Modernist twentieth-century art, most people's aesthetic is still based on the canons of nineteenth-century naturalism. Muscles, portraiture, varied and asymmetrical poses are to our liking. A veritable cult of appreciation around the rather anomalous Olmec Corona Wrestler embodies all of these features.

Second, despite the technical crudeness of much of twentieth-century art, we like displays of *skill and virtuosity*—shining surfaces, openwork, intricate details—all elements of jewel-like precision. This paradox can be explained by our notions of cultural ranking. We know our culture is technologically advanced because we put satellites and airplanes into the sky. Our art does not have to show technical skill because it has already done that with the Greeks and in the Renaissance—its purpose now is to evoke ideas. By contrast, our evaluation of an ancient civilization depends on large measure on the technical skill of its arts—what would we think of ancient Peru without its elaborate textiles, China without its bronzes, and the Maya without their stelae?

Third, we are attracted to forms that show *idealization and elegance,* that exaggerate grace and beauty, even if defined in exotic and non-Western terms. The tapering lines of Maya scrolls and the languid lines of Maya profiles are perfect examples of our preference.

And finally, we look for a *cult of the "aesthetic"*—that is, a self-conscious appreciation of art as separate from its ritual or other functions. Known in the West as "art for art's sake," this ideology developed in philosophy once artworks were more closely tied to aristocratic patronage and the market than to ritual. Because a cult of the aesthetic is seen as belonging to more advanced cultures, we value it in a non-Western tradition. In Mesoamerica this ideology is most evident in Olmec and Maya art. Maya representations of delicately held brushes in the hands of artists and representation of artists and their supernatural patrons indicate that the Maya singled out aesthetic activity as a subject for representation. Naturalistic, skillfully made, elegant forms also enable us to individualize the Olmec and Maya artist the way we individualize Western artists from Phidias to Picasso. Mayanists search for the names of artists in the inscriptions; failing to find names they give artists names such as the Metropolitan Master.

If these artistic elements are what one looks for at Teotihuacan, indeed they are absent. The close-ups of mural paintings reveal paint self-confidently but casually applied, with mistakes that were evidently acceptable to the patrons. Designs are organized, regular, and well-spaced but show no obsession with precision. Most objects are matte and not shiny. The aesthetic is not naturalistic; often objects show no spectacular display of skill and virtuosity (as, for example, in openwork). Nor is the hand of the individual artist glorified by an exaggeration of manner—although individual hands and workshops can be found, especially in mural painting. In fact, objects are frequently mold-made, which is anathema to the notion that ancient art must be handmade to qualify as art. (Someone's comment at the Teotihuacan exhibition in San Francisco was, "You've done the impossible, you've turned all these mold-made things into art": an astonishing response, since modern artists may paint black canvases and heap piles of dirt on gallery floors and still have their works accepted as "art." Ancient cultures are measured by different criteria.) Teotihuacan did not have a cult of the aesthetic and did not glorify the artist as someone extraordinary in relation to other professions. Artistic activity at Teotihuacan appears to have been taken as normal and unremarkable, the way we accept automobile design. In Mesoamerica the cult of the aesthetic seems to have been associated with dynastic powers and "theatre states" where the self-consciousness of appearances was highly developed. Perhaps it is also a value associated with individualism, which for the Maya was important, at least among the elite. Although Teotihuacan probably held great theatrical rituals in its spectacular public spaces, the very size of public spaces suggests mass events rather than a focus on the individual or the dynasty. The emphasis was on the impersonal and the institutional rather than on the unique style of an individual.

The emphasis on mold making, for example, is just the opposite of the emphasis on the virtuosity of an individual artist. At Teotihuacan, standardized little heads or *adornos* resulted from it. Although from an aristocratic point of view these *adornos* lack "art," could they have had some qualities that the people of Teotihuacan valued? Mass production could have meant several things. Inexpensive mass-produced objects could

Figure 9.6. Molds and *adornos*. Ceramic. From a workshop at the northwest corner of the Ciudadela, Teotihuacan. Tlamimilolpa- Metepec phases, A.D. 250–750. CNCA-INAH-MEX. From Berrin and Pasztory 1993, p. 120.

have been available to many people; expensive unique objects to only a few elite persons. The uniformity characteristic of mold-made objects allows everyone to partake in or belong to a group or ritual activity in an identical manner. It presupposes that workshops produced objects for a large population. The values that emerge just out of this one example emphasize the entire community rather than a single individual: for the most part the emphasis is on many similar works rather than on one unique masterpiece. The objects do not lack aesthetic value—they have value of a different sort.

There was indeed a Teotihuacan aesthetic, a preference for certain types of forms and images, but as it is very understated and minimal, it is not as easy to see and value as the art of some other Pre-Columbian cultures. The perusal of many Teotihuacan objects (as often in storage as on display) has resulted in my acquiring a curious taste for these nonaristocratic objects.

Take the pottery vessels that range from utilitarian wares to funerary offerings. (Only those that eventually ended up as offerings or in a burial survived whole.) The vast majority of these vessels are plain and simple. Storage jars, bowls, vases, and cups take a variety of forms, but generally these forms are simple. Instead of the complex concave and convex silhouettes of late Preclassic and contemporary Maya vessels, such as the exquisite bowls with basal flanges, the Teotihuacan forms are remarkably restrained. Most vessels are beige or brown; some have some designs in red paint, which does not stand out much from the brown color. At first I paid little attention to this unexciting pottery and focused on the fancier works, such as the plano-relief carved wares, or the fresco-painted pottery.

My conversion came about through the aesthetic discovery of Thin Orange vessels. "Thin Orange" is the technical name of a pottery that is very frequent at Teotihuacan—nearly twenty percent of the sherds at the site are Thin Orange.[10] William Sanders notes that at the rural Maquixco site fifteen percent are Thin Orange.[11] Evidently this was a luxury ware to which there was broad access in Teotihuacan society. As the name implies, the walls of the vessels are thin, though not very much thinner than other fine pottery (only a few millimeters thick), while the color is a bright, light orange. Most Thin Orange vessels are undecorated—or decorated with a few delicate lines and dots. Most commonly the ware appears as bowls on ring bases, but vases and tripods are also common. More familiar to museum goers are effigy vessels of dogs, armadillos, human beings, and a variety of other subjects.

Figure 9.7. Vase with appliqué design. Thin Orange ceramic. Height, about 36 cm (14 in.).
Museen der Stadt Köln. Museum photo 49704.

Figure 9.8. Bowl. Thin Orange ceramic. Height, 6.4 cm (2 1/2 in.); diameter, 21.5 cm (8 3/8 in.). The Metropolitan Museum of Art, The Michael C. Rockefeller Memorial Collection, Gift of Rene d'Harnoncourt, 1960, 1978.412.45.

My appreciation of Thin Orange first developed in the dark lower level of Anahuacalli, the museum that houses Diego Rivera's Pre-Columbian collections, where more than half a dozen large and completely preserved vessels are placed in one case. The stark simplicity of these forms took my breath away. One simple bowl of exquisite thinness, like orange eggshell, was placed next to a vessel that in its curves imitates a squash. These curving forms were in contrast to two identical tripod vessels, remarkable for their straight vertical walls, angled covers, and total absence of decoration. This is a pottery that needs to be seen in quantity—I began to imagine a market display. (I had wanted to display Thin Orange in quantity in a heap at the Teotihuacan exhibition in San Francisco, but this could not be done: museum convention requires that each object be seen as an individual masterpiece and exist in its own separate space.) What the people of Teotihuacan seemed to have appreciated throughout most of their history was not a fancy carved or painted surface, not even a *shiny* surface,

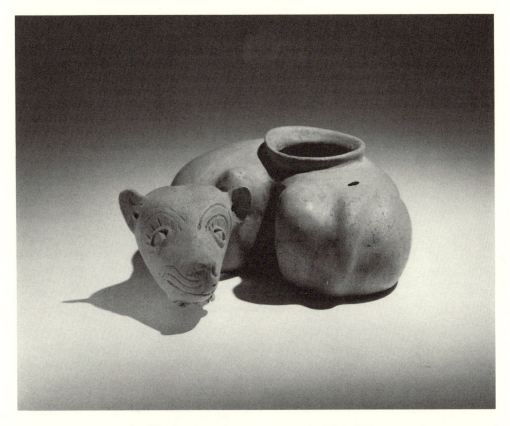

Figure 9.9. Dog vessel. Thin Orange ceramic. 16.6 cm (6 1/2 in.). Courtesy Department of Library Services, American Museum of Natural History, New York City, T293/2. Photo neg. no. 335319.

but thinness, lightness, simplicity of form, the bare surface of the orange clay—qualities of the material and virtuosity in handling such thinness. Understated values.

Archaeological excavations recently carried out by Evelyn Rattray demonstrated that Thin Orange was made not at Teotihuacan but in Puebla, one hundred kilometers away,[12] near the source of this special colored clay. But the manufacture and transportation of the ware was organized and controlled by the people of Teotihuacan—not just for their own use but as an export ware for other contemporary centers. After the collapse of Teotihuacan, it was not made again. It is thus a marker of the culture and aesthetic of Teotihuacan.

After Thin Orange, other categories of art emerged in the study of pottery. Characteristic of the more conventionally elegant pottery of the

Figure 9.10. Monkey whistle vessel. Thin Orange ceramic. Texmelucan, Puebla. Height, 13.5 cm (5 1/4 in.); diameter, 13.8 cm (5 1/3 in.); height of figure, 16.5 cm (6 1/2 in.). Musée de l'Homme. Museum photo N.H. 1. 1033.

Miccaotli and early Tlamimilolpa phases (A.D. 150–250) is a shiny black-ware most characteristic in a *florero*, a bowl-shaped vessel with a tall neck and a flat flaring rim. Although some blackwares are ornamented lightly through the contrast of matte and shiny areas on the flaring rim, essentially the focus is again on simple shape—long, elegant necks; dramatic proportions between rim and bowl; shiny black surface. Although these wares are quite refined by Teotihuacan standards, they are still basic in shape.

The black or orange color of these fancy wares stands in contrast to the

Figure 9.11. *Floreros* Black ceramic. Provenance unknown. Late Tlamimilolpa phase, A.D. 300–400. 9 by 6.8 cm (3 3/4 by 2 3/4 in.) and 9.2 by 7 cm (3 1/2 by 2 3/4 in.). The Saint Louis Art Museum, Gift of Morton D. May, 78.1980 1 and 2.

brown-to-black colors of the everyday ware. This pottery is much thicker and can hardly be described as "elegant" or "exquisite." Nevertheless, these flat-bottomed bowls and vases of many types have a family likeness. They have a sturdy simplicity, with attention paid to proportion, balance, pleasing curves, and only a minimum of ornament. Even some of the plainest vessels with a smudged brown surface as a result of uneven firing are aesthetically pleasing from the point of view of materials and form.

Some of these plain vessels of Teotihuacan are "ornamented" by being completely covered with a red paint called specular hematite, in which tiny bright specks of mica glitter through the deep red surface. This effect is much heightened by moving the vessel around. The same specular hematite is in the red background color of mural paintings and sparkles if the light is right. The effect is rich yet minimal.

The aesthetic of Thin Orange, blackware, and specular hematite is reminiscent of certain types of Asian aesthetics, evident in pottery such as Raku or in the use of cracking glazes, where material and form rather than decoration predominate in artistry. The rest of Teotihuacan pottery reminds me of twentieth-century industrial design—as, for example, in Pyrex dishes devised during the first half of the century—well-made but not individualized, ornamented, or in any way self-consciously artistic. These are household objects of a culture having a relatively high standard of living but no aristocratic pretensions.

Many Teotihuacan vessels were elevated. From the Miccaotli phase onward, many vessels have feet, ranging from little clay nubbins to big square openwork stands. Even many household items have such ways of elevating the vessel from the ground. Archaeologists have not determined whether elevating vessels has an ostensibly practical function, but aesthetically it results in the creation of a sense of importance for even simple forms. (Interestingly, its appearance coincides with the introduction of *talud/tablero* articulation in architecture, which similarly serves to divide platforms into a support, the *talud*, and a supported segment, the *tablero*. In both cases, the upper part seems to "float.")

Of all these vessels with feet, the cylindrical tripod vessel is the most important. Because so many cylindrical tripod vessels are present at Teotihuacan, scholars originally believed this vessel form had been invented there. Recent research suggests that it might derive from Veracruz.[13] Teotihuacan, however, made the vessel form its own; the cylindrical tripod vessel became the city's ceremonial pottery shape par excellence. Recent studies show that ashes are often found in its interior. It is the epitome of

Figure 9.12. Tripod bowl with alabaster inserts. Ceramic and alabaster. Tlamimilolpa–Metepec phases, A.D. 250–750. Museo Nacional de Antropología, Mexico City. CNCA-INAH-MEX. INAH photo.

Figure 9.13. Polished brown tripod bowl with lid. Brownware or Thin Orange ceramic. Provenance unknown. Early Xolalpan phase, A.D. 400–550. 21.8 by 19 cm (8 1/2 by 7 1/2 in.). Courtesy of the National Museum of the American Indian, Smithsonian Institution. From Berrin and Pasztory 1993, p. 245.

geometric simplicity with its straight or slightly concave cylindrical body and flat bottom supported on three legs. Only a small percentage seem to have had lids, which also are reduced to essentials—a slight angle, like a thatched roof, culminating in a sturdy knob. These vessels are more like treasure and jewelry boxes than like utilitarian pottery, but they are still sturdy rather than elegant. Recently, many tripod vessels have come to light in the Maya area with effigy-lid handles and elegant curves and designs, turning what is a simple form at Teotihuacan into artistic virtuosity for the Maya.

Lack of ostentation, simplicity, geometric form, and minimalism thus govern many Teotihuacan art forms from sculpture to pottery. They range from what we might call "industrial design" in their impersonal but well-made patterns to an understated elegance. They suggest a public more concerned with material and basic craftsmanship than with flamboyant form and imagery. Sanders suggested that such aesthetics are characteristic of state civilizations in which many objects are made for a well-to-do

Figure 9.14. Tripod vessel with pieces added to the interior, A.D. 200–750. 15 by 29 cm (6 by 11 1/2 in.). Museo Nacional de Antropología, Mexico City. CNCA-INAH-MEX. INAH photo.

urban middle class.[14] Marvin Cohodas goes so far as to suggest that this is a "consumer" aesthetic in which objects are made for a market and mold-made objects are "personalized" in the process of selection.[15] Both of these interpretations emphasize Teotihuacan's social and economic structure as a determinant of its aesthetic.

All art is to a large extent determined by its social and economic matrix; nevertheless, unpredictable characteristics and values, like the traits of an individual personality, also have great importance. Teotihuacan could have been all that it was as a state and had a different type of art: it could have had more decoration, it could have had less; it could have had supremely impersonal and distant images of its rulers; it could have covered everything with filigree ornament; it could have banned images altogether. The aesthetic of Teotihuacan has to be seen at least partly as a cultural choice expressing important cultural values. For Teotihuacan, simplicity and understatement expressed the power of the state and the quality of life of its inhabitants.

X

Assemblage

Organization Made Explicit

A STRIKING ASPECT OF THE HISTORY OF TEOTIHUACAN IS THAT FEW, AND few kinds of, permanent symbolic images were made at the time when the great pyramids and the Ciudadela were built during the Tzacualli and Miccaotli phases. Only a few whole vessels are known from the Tzacualli phase (A.D. 1–150) more from the Miccaotli phase (A.D. 150–200). These phases are known archaeologically largely from pots, potsherds, and fig- urine fragments. Perhaps much of the art was in perishable media. The layout of the site with its impressive Avenue, pyramids, and courts sug- gests its use for lavish ritual performance in which the entire city took part as performers or spectators. The advantages of having brought a large population into a city included not only the benefits of greater control and taxation but also the possibility of a rich civic life, including continuous and direct involvement in civic and religious ritual. Social integration may thus have been effected largely through active performance rather than permanent commemoration in images.

By contrast, during the Tlamimilolpa phase (A.D. 200–400) a veritable explosion of object and image making occurred, and it continued in the florescence of the murals of the Metepec phase (A.D. 600–750) phase. Some reasons for the paucity of early objects may have to do with the imperma- nent housing of early times and the far greater chance of their destruction. The extensive later rebuilding may also have disturbed remains. Despite such caveats, the contrast remains. With the building of the apartment compounds went a certain amount of wealth (previously unavailable to the general population), and some of this wealth was used to create new works of ritual art, of which a few pieces were preserved through burial under the floor. More than wealth, however, life in the later centuries of Teotihuacan seemed to require the making of objects charged with meaning in permanent media, as if just like the apartment compounds codified social and political relationships within the city, the artworks codified beings, rituals, signs, and symbols perhaps hitherto familiar only in the masks, costumes, and settings of performances.

I have already discussed the fact that much of Teotihuacan art existed in simple, minimal, well-made but nonostentatious forms. In this chapter I would like to single out the complex forms of Teotihuacan art and the way such complexity was created and what it might have meant. To begin with, I would like to mention two types of ritual works that antedate the Tlamimilolpa phase: Storm God vessels and Old God incense burners.

Because a little Storm God vessel was found in the Pyramid of the Sun in excavations directed by René Millon, we know that by the Tzacualli phase such objects existed.[1] This particular form is very simple, consisting of the facial features of the Storm God added in applique to a pot, and very likely the ritual it was used in involved some kind of pouring of water in imitation of the way the Storm God created rain.[2] This vessel certainly establishes the antiquity of Storm God ritual. Various Storm God vessels were made throughout the history of the city, and many were placed in burials in the apartment compounds. The form is usually a vase, later with nubbin feet, with the features of the face represented in coils of clay pressed onto the vessel. The vessel is not colored but is left brown or black or is covered in white. Large Storm God vessels may be fifty centimeters in height with openwork rims; miniatures may be the size of salt and pepper shakers. In general, however, the Storm God vessels are simple and conservative—facial features are added to a pot.

The second type of ritual object with ancient roots is the Old God incense burner. Found in clay in Cuicuilco and Tlalancaleca, the image of an old man holding a circular vessel on his head seems to have been widespread centuries prior to the growth of Teotihuacan.[3] However, every early known example is small and in clay. Small clay examples did exist at Teotihuacan; however, one of the innovations of the Tlamimilolpa phase seems to have been making these images in stone and making them much larger. The small stone ones are often about thirty centimeters tall, and fragments of one in the Teotihuacan storeroom of the site museum sug-

Figure 10.1. Old God brazier. Volcanic stone. Teotihuacan style. Probably Tlamimilolpa–Metepec phases, A.D. 200–750. 24.5 by 22 cm (9 5/8 by 9 in.). Museum für Völkerkunde, Vienna, 59.125.

Figure 10.2. Effigy jar of Tlaloc, the Storm God, A.D. 300–600. Ceramic. Teotihuacan style. Height, 4 3/4 in.; width, 3 3/4 in. The Brooklyn Museum 67.207.1. Gift of Mrs. Edward Holsten.

gest that it was larger than life-size. Such Old God incense burners were associated with the central shrines of apartment compounds, but several were also found during the excavations of the Ciudadela and the Street of the Dead Complex.[4]

Although these "Old Gods" are popularly thought of as deities, comparable to Huehueteotl, the Aztec god of the hearth, it is not clear what the images meant at Teotihuacan. The Aztecs made no images in stone of Huehueteotl for the burning of incense; Huehueteotl images are known only from the codices, and they share with the Teotihuacan image only their oldness. The Teotihuacan Old God figures have no special costume, insignia, or symbols. As supporting figures they may equally represent human beings. Scholars generally assume that a diamond eye design frequent on the vessels is a fire symbol because the vessels are associated with the burning of incense.[5] Could the old humans refer to ancestors and ancient rituals rather than to gods? Or could they be the kind of deities that include the notion of ancestor? This problem recurs in the interpretation of ceramic censers.

In contrast to the Storm God vessels, the Old God incense burners are quite imaginatively made. All the incense burners are made the same way, though surface details vary. One expects them to be quite solid, but actually they are openwork: the figures sit cross-legged, forming an open triangular base. The back of the figure then rises at the back of the triangle, the neck seems to be bent under the vessel, and the face hangs over the front, just above legs laid parallel one on top of the other. The entire center of the sculpture is empty space. The right hand is in a tight fist, while the left is extended. This ingenious open-centered, triangular-based design appears to have been invented, perhaps by a workshop, and repeated on all known sculptures. Some are crude and rough, some are delicate with the delineation of shoulders and spinal columns; some are small, and some are large—but they were ubiquitous.

Since at this point I do not know of earlier examples, I am assuming that the stone Old Gods are translations from Preclassic clay forms in the Tlamimilolpa phase, created to buttress or monumentalize the notion of continuity with a popular cult that preceded the founding of Teotihuacan. Unquestionably the continuity with the past and the sudden monumentalization of the form indicate a very strong emphasis on the veneration of past ritual. Like so many objects made for the apartment compounds, these vessels were mass-produced on a basic plan, but no two are exactly alike. Like the Storm God vessels, the form of these Old God incense burners is simple: a circular vessel on the head of a seated man.

The objects associated with antiquity at Teotihuacan are therefore ritual vessels—one for burning (probably incense) and the other for pouring water. As mentioned above, in much of early Teotihuacan life the emphasis was on the *performance* of rituals and not on their *representation*. One of the questions to be raised later is *why* there was a need for representation after A.D. 200.

In structures dated to the Tlamimilolpa phase, representations exist on murals, incised and painted vessels, composite clay censers, and host figures. Each of these forms is new. They fall into one of two categories: assemblage from many bits and pieces, as if complexity was created out of simplicity; and two-dimensional puzzles, as if the three-dimensional objects of assemblage were translated into two-dimensional forms for walls and vessels. The archaeological information is insufficient at this point to indicate whether three-dimensional assemblage preceded two-dimensional puzzles or whether they developed simultaneously. My sequential treatment here is purely for the sake of discussion and not to imply any difference in time.

Figure 10.3. Mask from a ceramic censer. Museo Nacional de Antropología, Mexico City. CNCA-INAH-MEX. Pasztory photo.

Mold making was introduced at Teotihuacan also in the Tlamimilolpa phase. (It was known in Veracruz and Oaxaca as well at the same time, and its point of origin in Mesoamerica is unknown.) At Teotihuacan, the first objects made in molds were probably the *adornos* of composite censers and later the heads and bodies of figurines.[6] Besides cheapness, mold making results in the replication of standardized images, which may well have been a value promulgated between A.D. 200 and A.D. 750.

Mold making was applied most spectacularly to the so-called composite ceramic incense burners with the covers in the form of a "doorway" through which a mask is looking out. Both the mask and the *adornos* attached to the flat framing panels were mold-made. The *adornos* consist of a wide variety of images and symbols: bird heads, butterflies, spears, flowers, bits of mica surrounded by feather shapes, trefoil designs, shells, knots (dozens of separate *adornos* have been identified). Many of these images are included in the 230 signs into which James Langley divided the Teotihuacan symbol system.[7] The meaning of many images is clear: flowers and shells connote nature and wealth. Others are less clear: butterflies are common, but their meaning is hard to deduce from Teotihuacan examples alone—they have been associated with fire, war, death, and water. The Aztecs saw butterflies and moths as the souls of dead warriors and sacrificial victims visiting the earth and sucking the nectar of flowers. This idea does not seem directly applicable. Like the serpent shedding its skin, the butterfly emerging from its cocoon may also be a symbol of new life, immortality, or transformation, a symbolism that might be relevant to a variety of contexts. Other elements, such as knots, appear in other places like glyphs. Whatever its exact individual meaning, each *adorno* is a sign and a symbol of a thing, an idea, a quality, or a deity. The point of the composite incense burners is that each one is a different combination of the various signs. Unique to the incense burners are rectangular plaques called *mantas*, all of which seem to combine with a trapeze and ray glyph with squares drawn as if in perspective. Although the *adornos* all seem alike superficially, Langley noted eighty-eight types.[8]

These *incensarios* are representational, in that their function—the burning of incense—is incidental to the image. The message of the image is in the masks and surrounding signs. This message is not narrative (it does not tell a story), nor is it an embodiment (it is not the image of a being). It is structural in that the message is coded in the selection and relationship of signs and masks. Modern observers will never know whether a diviner suggested a set of *adornos* for a particular event, whether the se-

Figure 10.4. Censer. Museo Nacional de Antropología, Mexico City. CNCA-INAH-MEX. INAH photo 2207.

lection of images was up to the individual, or whether families had their own patterns and traditions. What the incense burners tell us is something of the subconscious thinking of the people of Teotihuacan, the way they patterned their lives using ideas of which they may have been unaware. For example, consider the deep mistrust of anthropomorphic representation. This mistrust is evident not only in the lack of dynastic ruler images, but in the fact that on the incense burner the central face does not represent a person but a mask—a mask is essentially a device that hides one's identity by placing another identity over it.

Masking is most common in the sociopolitical context of village societies, in which power is in the hands of elders who are often the leaders of various ritual, clan, or men's societies. Because power is not vested in an individual chief or ruler, spirits are invoked that uphold the traditions of the group, including the punishment of deviants. These spirits are impersonated by the members of the society who wear masks and are ostensibly transformed into the spirits embodied in the masks. The spirits are usually nature spirits or ancestor spirits. The whole point of the masquerade is the fiction that the masks really represent these beings and are not someone's husband or brother-in-law wearing a mask. From the finding of clay masks in burials in Tlatilco dating to about 900 B.C. in the Valley of Mexico, and from the prevalence and importance of masks in later Mesoamerica, Mesoamericanists may reasonably suppose that the village cultures of Preclassic Mesoamerica had flourishing masking traditions, probably in perishable materials such as wood, barkcloth, or basketry, and that such masking may have existed prior to or in early Teotihuacan.

In ranked societies masks undergo changes in function and meaning. They no longer represent the egalitarian power of the elders but are instead in the hands of chiefs, and the masquerades legitimize and uphold social differentiation. Cecelia Klein argued that in ranked societies masks do not hide power but denote power.[9] In some situations masquerades are abandoned altogether, although the chief may wear symbolic masks as parts of his costume—as a pectoral or on his headgear—which suggest his personal control over or access to the same natural and ancestral forces. But this is a different form of spiritual access, not impersonation. In the case of the Olmec, surviving masks and jade mask pectorals suggest that both of these strategies in transforming the mask were used. Maya art is full of mask forms that have been transformed into other functions, including glyphs.

The mask, then, stands for an otherworldly being who descends to the human world and enters into a human surrogate. Its function is ostensibly religious but is always also political. Because the being comes to life literally, it is not usually represented in inanimate sculptures. Perhaps in state-level cultures, in which distinct deities are represented in sculptures and murals, they ultimately hark back to the spirit beings of earlier societies, through a series of transformations. In any case, the artists at Teotihuacan appear to have been reluctant to represent fully anthropomorphic deities in art; in the incense burner, the being remains a mask. This is a sort of intermediate situation in which the mask is no longer a mask that is worn and comes to life, but it is not yet an anthropomorphic being with a life of its own. Masks are paradoxical and contradictory images—they represent an important new reality, but they are false in that they are not the real being.

The Storm God and the Old God are represented as real beings—divine or human. By contrast, in many representations the Goddess is just a mask, or a nose ornament and earplugs, or a headdress. Her reality is hidden or mystified. On the incense burners the mask is emphasized as a mask. (The makers of the provincial incense burners from Escuintla, Guatemala, tended to create a real person with hands out of the Teotihuacan mask, thus suggesting a reinterpretation of the being or the significance of the ritual.) Clemency Coggins suggested that the incense burners represent ancestral spirits rather than gods, similar to the urns of Monte Alban.[10] Perhaps the masks are the transformations of ancestral spirits once propitiated in masked rituals. However, some gods may be further transformations of such spirits. It is hard to tell where the spirit ends and the god begins. At any rate, the deity closest in appearance to the masks in the incense burners is the Goddess. Rather than visiting the village for a certain period every year, these masks become permanent fixtures of everyday life. A different arrangement with the sacred is suggested. The beings hover somewhere between a mask and a personalized being—not quite one or the other. The mask's (and the Goddess's) identity is further hidden by a large nose bar that covers the mouth. The nose bar appears to be an item of jewelry that many gods and elite figures wear in Teotihuacan art, making a more precise interpretation impossible. This ornament is not as prevalent in other cultures in Mesoamerica. Hiding the mouths of images is a very effective suggestion of silence, noncommunication, or distance. They look literally "shut up."

By contrast to the distancing effect of the masks, the message of the *adornos* is friendly, since so many *adornos* represent rich and growing things. Their "text" is multilayered, as each sign relates in some symbolic way to every other sign, without a linear order to the reading. Though the specific resonance of these readings is lost, the people of Teotihuacan were clearly preoccupied by the organization and arrangement of a limited set of signs. This aesthetic organization is so reminiscent of the building of similarly planned apartment compounds that one may be tempted to think of the people of Teotihuacan as fascinated by human engineering and social organization as well. Because the composite incense burners were invented when apartment compounds were being built and Teotihuacan was codifying its social organization into new patterns, I think in an unconscious way the construction of the incense burner is a model of the civic organization that was being created. The ritual of burning here was secondary to the image that made manifest the structure of the relationship of the Teotihuacan gods and elite to the population. A major value in this structure is variety and individual or family choice within a collective system. The beauty of the Teotihuacan ideology is that it combined uniformity and standardization (mold making) with individual variety (selection of *adornos*). Uniformity and standardization were necessary values in a huge, heterogeneous city that had a large immigrant population and considerable foreign enclaves. The emphasis on uniformity seems to have been created to mold a Teotihuacan citizen out of this complex group. At the same time, the incredible scale of variety (more than eighty different mold-made *mantas*, for example) suggests a safeguarding of difference. It is hard not to see this as a winning combination. The two themes—uniformity and civic belonging on the one hand and variety and individual difference on the other—indicate a Teotihuacan preoccupation with the imagery of integration and separation, which artisans did literally in the process of creating objects of assemblage in which masks and symbols were arranged in various ways.

Perhaps the most enigmatic objects of assemblage are what Warren Barbour has called "host-figures."[11] These figures are structurally the reverse of the incense burners—the exteriors are plain, and the complex mold-made figures are all on the inside. Host-figures vary in size from those that are as little as ten centimeters tall to examples that are about fifty centimeters tall. The external being's legs are either crossed or to the side, which Barbour interprets as a sign of gender. Regardless of whether the figure is sometimes male and sometimes female, it is never sexualized or dressed in gendered or status-related garments. A sense of nakedness is very strong. The faces are all doll-like, and in one mysterious instance the face is a mask, which does not quite attach to the body—one wonders how

Figure 10.5. Host-figure in two pieces. Ceramic. Height, 20.5 cm (8 in.). Courtesy Department of Library Services, American Museum of Natural History, New York City. Museum photo neg. no. 332943.

it could have been used. (In the Teotihuacan exhibition in San Francisco a special stand had to be attached to the neck to hold it.) Another, almost surreal, image is a body without facial features, split along the sides to open up like a clam. Painted yellow, it almost looks like a dead body. Most commonly, the figures are in seated postures, either cross-legged or with their legs together, knees flexed and legs stretched out to one side. Also common is a panel or "door" in the chest, recalling a Christian reliquary figure. When the door is opened or removed, a mold-made figure is on the inner part of the door or on the interior of the chest of the figure. Smaller figures are at the shoulders, elbows, knees, and feet. Sometimes, besides figures attached to the host, small mold-made figures were found arranged around it when it was excavated. One such host-figure was found as an offering at the Maya site of Becan, placed in a Maya-style incised cylinder tripod.[12] The host figure is plain in features and costume, but the figurines inside are just the opposite: they are very complex, with rich clothing and fancy headdresses. Host-figures fall into different categories—some are larger and fancier than others, and even among the same types headdresses differentiate different types of persons. Are these gods or human beings?

Since deity attributes do occur, such as Storm God goggles, that is a possibility that needs mentioning. However, following Barbour, I am more of the opinion that the figurines are humans, while the naked external body is supernatural. Perhaps the facelessness of one exceptional figure and the mask on another unique figure make me deduce that these figures are divine, not human. Their scale as well leads to this conclusion—they seem to hold an entire human community divided into social classes inside themselves. As a hypothesis, perhaps in these host-figures the people of Teotihuacan represented quite literally their idea of the "body politic." What we may see in this naked form is the *real* face and body of the gods of Teotihuacan. Because of the womblike interior of the figure I am tempted to see this deity as another aspect of the Goddess or, if not, at least the concept of the maternal and pregnant. I think the generalized form and nakedness of the host-figures represent Teotihuacan—Teotihuacan as a sheltering, womblike, cavelike space. Just as the city held different social groups within its buildings, the host-figures hold figurines in different costumes within their bodies. The city of Teotihuacan was held within the Valley of Teotihuacan, which held the farms and fields that supported its population, so that the city was within the nature realm controlled by the Goddess. If the figure is a metaphor for the city or some of its parts, then the city chose to represent itself through an organic image.

I imagine that host-figures, like the incense burners, were made for specific persons and purposes and therefore their interiors are highly variable and may have been event specific. Archaeologists know them from offerings, not from burials, and have no evidence as to what, if anything, was done to or with them—they seem to be definitive statements. They do appear to demonstrate some point when the door is opened and the interior is available for inspection. Given the small size of some of the host-figures these moments of revelation could have involved only a few people.

Figure 10.6. Host-figure. Ceramic. Xolalpan–Metepec phases, A.D. 500–750. Height, about 12.5 cm (5 in.). Museo Diego Rivera de Anahuacalli, Mexico City. From Séjourné 1966b.

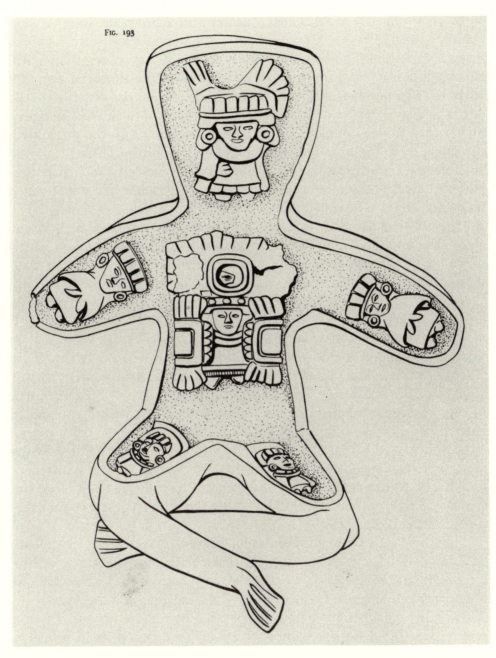

Figure 10.7. Drawing of back piece of host-figure in fig. 10.6. From Séjourné 1966b.

In great contrast to the host, the interior figures are smothered in clothes and headdresses. Clearly their social and political status is of primary importance. They vary greatly in size. The larger ones are in the chest, while the smaller internal figurines are in the limbs, or generally "inside." The number of figures ranges from one (on the chest) to over a dozen. Social hierarchy is thus related to the body of the host. The figures may belong to one compound, or to all of Teotihuacan—the principle is the same. As in the mural of the Temple of Agriculture, there is an overwhelming sense of the distance in size between the deity and the people. However richly people are attired, they are minuscule in comparison to the being within whose body they are found.

The host-figures also create an image of social order through assemblage. The relationship to the enclosing deity is very close, suffocatingly so, and people are attached to the larger body with only a door for an opening, as if they had been eaten, were unborn fetuses in a womb, or had been buried in a tomb. Whereas the incense burners are airy and open, the host-figures are womb- and tomblike, rigid in their hierarchy. These are probably the most surreal, the most evocative images in Teotihuacan art. Visitors to the Teotihuacan exhibit audibly gasped when they saw them. "If only Freud had seen these images, what might he have made of them?" asked a friend. To me they seem to express the negative side of the emphasis on religious/social organizations. In these figures structural integration had reached a point of immobility and lifelessness. The host deity appears more lifelike and full of life than the beings inside her. The host-figures raise the intriguing question whether toward the late Xolalpan and Metepec phases Teotihuacan society had become so structured and integrated that is was rigid and calcified, and whether this rigidity was a factor in the city's eventual collapse.

Only with the excavations of Rubén Cabrera Castro in the 1980s has it become possible to visualize what the major religious images of Teotihuacan might have been like in the temples, and they too may very well have been composite images. Excavations in the Ciudadela and the Avenue, especially, brought to light half a dozen large figures in various colors of semiprecious hard stones. Some of the figures are clearly male, others female.[13] They do not wear any deity insignia, and some are nude while some are simply dressed. They are quite reminiscent of the splendid greenstone figures found by Leopoldo Batres in a platform in front of the Pyramid of the Sun.[14] Similar figures are in museums in Vienna, Hamburg, and New York. They range in size from over thirty centimeters high to the half-life-size

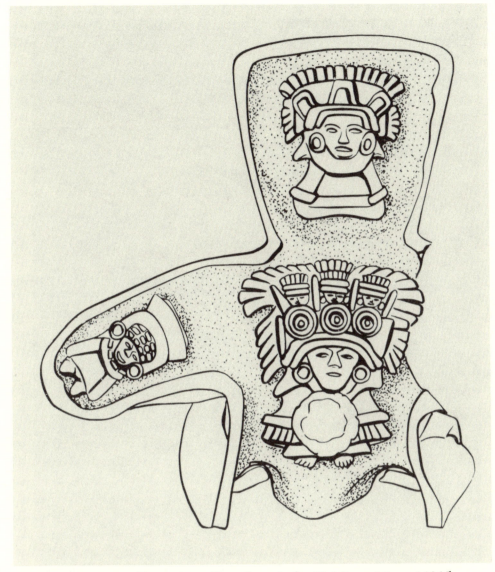

Figure 10.8. Drawing of front piece of host-figure in fig. 10.6. From Séjourné 1966b.

naked youth found by Batres.

No such large figure has ever been found in an apartment compound at Teotihuacan. In fact, neither have the famous stone masks. Like the figures, the masks seem to come from the temples and palaces on the Avenue. Although some figures have been ritually dismembered, scattered, and buried, most are found as though they had been in use in a room, in the general rubble.

Figure 10.9. Female figure with rosettes in headdress. Greenstone with traces of pyrite. Probably Tlamimilolpa–Metepec phases, A.D. 200–750. 40.5 by 20 cm (16 by 8 in.). Museum für Völkerkunde, Vienna, 6270.

What is striking about the figures is their variety of style. These figures vary from the delicately naturalistic to the square and clumsy. One figure has a strongly Olmec-style mouth and suggests an heirloom. Large blocks of uncut greenstone still lie in the corridors of the Street of the Dead Complex as well as other buildings along the Avenue, indicating the material from which some of these images were made.[15]

The masks appear to relate to the figures functionally. The masks were more abundant, and more standardized. The various holes in the back and sides suggest attachment to something. On the basis of the mural paintings, my hypothesis is that the greenstone figures were richly dressed in textile garments, jade jewelry, and feathered headdresses. The most sacred, or highest-status, figures appear to be the full-figure ones, whose whole body is precious greenstone. The masks were attached perhaps to wooden figures that were dressed in a manner similar to that of the full-figure statues and were still very high-status but less rich versions of the full-figure statues. A faceless ceramic bust with a mask attached to it found in an incense burner workshop zone north of the Ciudadela represents the sort of image to which I imagine the stone masks were attached.[16] This bust would have been easy to drape with garments. The headdresses and garments of deities in the murals are covered with signs and symbols, and this may have been the case with the deities in greenstone. The *adornos* of the ceramic censers may refer in a more abbreviated way to this symbolic insignia. The ceramic censer may be a miniature and more modest version of a greenstone masked deity as seen in its temple doorway, just as the apartment compound is a miniature version of the Ciudadela royal palace. I can imagine how each of the temples of the mound surrounding the courtyard of the Ciudadela could have housed a greenstone image dressed in elaborate attire.

Who were these gods? Nothing in Teotihuacan imagery suggests a pantheon as large as that of the Aztecs. Teotihuacan seems to have had a few major deities of whom images were made. Besides the Goddess and the Storm God are the so-called Fat God and the Flayed God, both known only from figurines, and the Old God that was restricted mainly to braziers. Why then the preoccupation with variation?

Previously I have suggested that the greenstone figures and masks could have represented "not deities but idealized ancestors of various social groups."[17] Coggins elaborated on the ancestor identification of the censers in a recent article.[18] My suggestion is based on the lack of deity identification and insignia; hers is based on the belief that the religion of Classic

Mesoamerica revolved around ancestor worship rather than deity veneration. She suggests that as the Monte Alban urns have been designated
as ancestors, so might the Teotihuacan incense burners. By this means
one could designate most Teotihuacan images as ancestors or deities. This
paradox suggests that the criterion of ancestor versus deity is the wrong
criterion. What exactly is the difference between a deified ancestor and
an anthropomorphic divinity? In many cultures spirits and ancestors are
the same being, as among the Hopi, whose kachina masks represent simultaneously rain spirits and ancestors. Though I have emphasized the
supernatural rather than the human aspect of these beings, I recognize that
both are present. In fact, my major point is that it is not *who* these figures
are but what they *do* that counts.

Because of the preoccupation with social and political integration since
the Tlamimilolpa phase I have been considering the idea that the various
groups—apartment compounds or barrios—were tied to the center through
temples and images and that everyone worshipped the Goddess, the Storm
God, the Old God. For some reason, the image of the Goddess may have
varied slightly from group to group, suggesting a specific relationship. Each
apartment compound may have been linked to a three-temple complex,
to a temple on the Avenue or to both. The role of images (greenstone figures and masks in the temples, incense burners in the homes) was to make
these connections clear.

That premise brings us back to the question of the explosion of image
making after the Tlamimilolpa phase (A.D. 200–400). The city is large, the
population over 100,000. The relationship of the elite and city dwellers is
being codified on a new basis. The elite are greatly preoccupied with a problem created by urbanism—the lack of a sense of belonging and integration.
This problem is solved practically by the building of apartment compounds
and the sociopolitical rights and powers those dwellings imply; it is solved
symbolically by the creation of images that in themselves express the
structural principles of the city—hierarchy and variation. Though the gods
and ancestors are nominally the subjects, the structures express human
relations. The most mysterious of these objects, the host-figures, are set
up almost like time capsules, expressing the human relationships within
a divine body. I have no doubt that further readings of these assemblages
will lead us closer to Teotihuacan sociopolitical thought.

Symbolic language, the language of art, is needed especially when the
practical is not quite adequate. It is a way of creating a mental reality. It
indicates a problem and a suggested solution. The solution hovers near re-

ality as perceived and near the ideal of what things ought to be. Because symbolic language does not clearly separate reality from the ideal, it helps to create the illusion that the ideal is real. It thus works by fostering the positive ideals encoded in it.

The move from the representation of a symbolic language in performance to permanent objects suggests a need for external sources of truth. Material works of art have an objective reality very much like trees or stones. At the same time, human beings project emotions, living qualities, and a psychological reality into images. (Which of us rational creatures are willing to put a pin through our own photograph without feeling strange?) Though they are made by human beings, once finished, works of art have a life of their own and can outlast their makers. This gives to them an authority the performing arts lack despite their immediacy. In comparison to the simple Storm God vessels and Old God incense burners with their direct ritual associations, the composite censers, host-figures, and greenstone mask figures are complex creations with multiple layers of meanings. They reflect a need to codify in permanent form the values that created the identity of Teotihuacan. It is particularly interesting that Teotihuacan artists chose to make images that seem to be in the process of construction and not fully envisioned as organic beings. This preoccupation with making order manifest as a process lasted throughout the life of the city.

Because images made largely to communicate ideas hover between the real and the ideal, their interpretation is difficult in relation to actual culture and history. Was Teotihuacan a supremely organized place, and the arts *reflect* this quality; or was it somewhat disorganized, and the arts in representing order were hoped to *create* it? The difficulty is that humans deal with a bit of both—creation and reflection. Modern observers read Teotihuacan through its art, knowing that its art was never neutral but fostered various values. This problem is especially great in the case of mural paintings.

XI

The Net-Jaguar and Other Two-Dimensional Puzzles

IN 1945, ROBERT AND MARIAN BLISS, PASSIONATE COLLECTORS OF EXQUISITE
Pre-Columbian objects, acquired a mural fragment from a newly discovered apartment compound—Tetitla. I do not know whether the Blisses
admired its rarity, its beautiful color and preservation, or whether its pe-
culiar design—a net-jaguar walking toward a temple—intrigued them. The
Blisses' taste was definitely Modernist-elegant. They loved abstraction and
distortion of form, but they liked rounded edges, smooth surfaces, subtle
sophistication. They have much Olmec, Maya, and Aztec jade and greenstone and a great deal of South American gold in their collection, which
now belongs to Harvard University's Dumbarton Oaks Museum in Washington, D.C. Their Teotihuacan collection was limited to a few objects:
masks, frescoed vessels, and especially the mural. Chance brought this particular mural to the Blisses, and by chance it is one of the most complex
and quintessentially "Teotihuacan" murals of the site.

In a previous book I edited, I once made the embarrassing mistake of
printing the mural upside down! Arthur Miller wrote the corresponding
text, in which he explained, very cogently, that one strange feature of Teotihuacan murals is that they are hard to see: the color values are close and the
spatial conceptions may be confusing.[1] Without the accompanying drawing (page 184, above), and especially in black and white, the Tetitla mural

(page 134) is almost meaningless. In life, the mural glows with the four primary colors of Teotihuacan mural painting: blue, turquoise green, yellow, and several shades of red. These are rich, "jewel" tones, but because of the usual absence of white and black, their tonal range is close, thus making the forms hard to decipher. The most pervasive color is red, used for backgrounds, and when mixed with specular hematite, it sparkles with bright light. The colors alone are lush and beautiful.

I doubt that many museum goers get much beyond admiring the colors and feeling befuddled by the rest. The yellow line with red footprints is very clear at the bottom and seems to signify universally and in any language a road or path with someone moving along it. The road turns ninety degrees up toward the left of the mural, where it meets a square design not unlike what children draw for houses with a big door. The house is embellished with jaguar-skin spots and feathers and seems to be wearing a feathered headdress. It stands on a little *talud/tablero* platform painted in red. Some scholars have designated it a "temple" because of its fancy and elaborate roof, *talud/tablero* platform, and single doorway.

So far one can imagine delight in the abstract, yet ornamental and neatly painted mural. Pre-Columbian art is supposed to be "religious"—how nice to have a scene of someone walking to a temple. But what exactly is a net-jaguar supposed to be?

That confused welter of lines on the right half of the mural can, with some imagination, turn into a feline/man combination kneeling on one knee, his tail raised high, holding two enigmatic feathered objects, a stream with objects coming from its open mouth. He is dressed like a man in a loincloth and headdress, but he has the clawed feet and fanged maw of a jaguar. Or does he? His body is not the solid flesh of either man or feline but is made of insubstantial ropelike net that twists in on itself. The net is green, while the body is mostly blue, and the closeness of green and blue is hard to decipher. Even harder to decipher is the face, which is the same red as the background, thus creating the illusion that the net-jaguar is a jaguar-shaped net in which empty space has been caught. In the mural at Atetelco and in Zone 5A other such strange empty-space creatures walk about. On the Tetitla mural, this confusing and insubstantial creature is very clearly outlined on his back, tail, arms, and legs with the saw-tooth insignia of the Goddess and feathered ruffs.

The net-jaguar seems to be a quintessentially Teotihuacan creation in that some portion of the being is left out and other things, such as costume and symbols, make up for it. The net, however, remains mysterious

Figure 11.1. Drawing of net-jaguar and temple. Copy of fragment of mural painting from Tetitla, Teotihuacan. Metepec phase, A.D. 600–750. From Séjourné 1966a, fig. 13.

Figure 11.2. Drawing of net-jaguar holding a maguey plant. Copy of mural painting at the Palace of the Sun (Zone 5A), Teotihuacan. Xolalpan-Metepec phases, A.D. 400–750. From A. Miller 1973, fig. 119, p. 81. Courtesy of Dumbarton Oaks Research Library and Collections, Washington, D.C.

for many reasons. The twisting of the "ropes" over and under seems to suggest a preoccupation with showing the figure in three dimensions (in an art that is primarily two-dimensional).[2] But what do the three dimensions reveal? The figure seems to be most of the time literally nothing, as if the essence of this creature were its invisibility.

Yet other animals are substantial, such as the coyote on the Atetelco mural that alternates with the net-jaguar, each hair carefully delineated, or the various birds: parrots, doves, owls, quetzals, and eagles. The only "transparent" creature is the net-jaguar. Yet in some contexts felines are portrayed naturalistically as jaguars with spots and mountain lions or pumas with tan fur. Curiously, on the Las Colinas bowl, where coyote and serpent and bird appear to designate people, there is no net-jaguar. Yet net-jaguars are often semihuman in form and posture or are shown wearing human dress. Are they some kind of mythical creature, or do they refer to a person or title?

In their mystery, they remind one of the Olmec infant and jaguar combinations, improbable for the mixture of vulnerability and ferocity. The net-jaguar is a similar paradox: something that clearly exists in three-dimensional space and yet is totally absent at the same time. It may have a relationship to the Goddess, in that in one mural yellow hands (similar to the ones with which she usually scatters water or jades), hold small net-jaguars, perhaps cubs. The net-jaguar in its emphasis on inside/outside is also reminiscent of the host-figures. However, the host-figures incorporate a complex internal structure hidden within an exterior that is striking in its simplicity. The net-jaguar has a complex and highly structured exterior and may wear elaborate costume, just as the figurines inside the host figures do. But in the net-jaguar, everything is on the outside, and there is no inside. The net-jaguar image never appears in art outside the city of Teotihuacan.

In Mesoamerica, the woven patterns of nets and mats are well-known symbols of royalty. I have wondered whether the net-jaguar could be a reference to some important Teotihuacan title or position in which the image represented only the external paraphernalia and not the various persons who held it. The net-jaguar seems to be as complex an image as the feathered serpent. However, the net-jaguar image was restricted to the city and disappeared from imagery after the fall of Teotihuacan. The net-jaguar ranges from an anthropomorphic form to a creature that in posture is entirely animal in form, apart from the fact that its body is formed by the net pattern. It is present in both fertility and military contexts. Like the elite priests, the figure performs rites and services presumably for the deities.

Curiously, both the Goddess and the net-jaguar are strongly invested in being partly invisible. This correlation has made me wonder, if Storm God
images, feathered serpents, and tasseled headdresses relate to families or
titles that deal with the outside world and therefore even have some dynastic associations, then do net-jaguars relate to internal persons or concepts
of power whose identity is played down?

The net-jaguar image in the Tetitla mural belies the apparent simplicity
of the path and temple. Western observers often believe that all painting styles that lack Renaissance-style one-point perspective and modeling
in light and shade are primitive and simple. This difference in technique
was first analyzed in detail in Egyptian art, which was compared—to its
detriment—with Greek art. In Egyptian art, the size of figures varies depending on their importance, not on their distance from the viewer. They
have a heavy outline, and the colors are filled in without regard for light
and shade. Their postures are impossible—often they stand with heads and
feet in profile with torsos in frontal view. This style is not unlike that of
Teotihuacan art (as well as the art from many other parts of the world,
from Celtic manuscripts to Persian miniatures).

A recent study on perspective by the geometer Margaret Hagen has
shown that there are only four possible types of projections in representation:[3] similarity, metric, affine, and projective. European Renaissance
perspective she calls similarity projection. It is based on one station point
from which the viewer "sees" a scene. A number of elements such as right
angles have to be distorted for such a projection to work. In metric or or-
thogonal projection, planes and projection lines are parallel but the viewer
is assumed to take multiple station points. Multiple station points are like
an imaginary conveyor belt that moves past the object seen. Egyptian and
Teotihuacan art use metric projection and multiple station points, rendering houses, roads, people in their broad, flat dimensions against a flat
background. The advantage of this perspective is that things such as the
walls of houses remain the same size and deciphering the image is thus
easier. Understanding that a small tree behind a large human is meant to
be far away is not the result of vision but the learning of a convention of
projection. In affine projection the planes are not parallel to the viewing
angle, but the projection lines are and station points are multiple. This
results in a kind of bird's-eye perspective common in Japanese paintings
and used in many details in Teotihuacan art to give the illusion of three-
dimensionality. Hagen's last category, projective projection, uses a central
station point but not parallel planes and is found mainly in Chinese and

European art. This seems to be the most "naturalistic" and "perceptual" type of projection, but in fact it distorts actual size and spatial relations the most. "Metric projection assumes a huge, stable world that requires multiple station points for the observer in order to be experienced. Similarity projection, by contrast, is man-centered: it shows the cone of vision from a single station point. The view may be 'deep' but it is also 'small and narrow.' In Hagen's view, neither metric nor similarity projection is any more realistic than the other, they simply measure reality differently."[4]

Scholars have often said that the Egyptians and other artists producing "primitive and simple" styles used metric perspective, flat color, and contorted postures for the sake of clarity, to make everything as simple and visible as possible. This premise clearly does not apply at Teotihuacan, however, where the images are often visual puzzles and far from being simple and easy to read. (Nor is the premise true of Celtic manuscripts or Persian miniatures.) The net-jaguar holding a maguey on a mural from the Palace of the Sun is a good example. One can eventually figure out what is the maguey and what is the net-jaguar in this representation, one can make out the streams of water that flow from the flower and enclose it in a medallionlike space of its own—but this deciphering is by no means instantaneous. It requires active looking and decoding. Most likely, the people of Teotihuacan were familiar with their image system and "read" it more quickly than we can. Imagine, however, their visitors from Veracruz or Oaxaca—to visitors, these images must have been much less accessible. This fact suggests that in their murals, as in their other arts, the people of Teotihuacan pursued their own ideas and were not interested in impressing or being comprehensible to outsiders. A careful study of murals suggests that the people of Teotihuacan enjoyed the complex and puzzlelike qualities of their images.

Playfulness, cleverness, even humor is suggested by some of the borders of Teotihuacan murals. As in the marginalia of European medieval illuminated manuscripts, there the artist had the chance to try out new and different ideas, while the main figures were more set in traditional forms. The early murals of Teotihuacan rarely had borders, but later murals in the apartment compounds almost always had rich borders with complex imagery. Borders seem to have been seen as liminal spaces, where the bodies, beings, and symbols of different parts of the mural were merged in dizzying combinations.[5] At Tepantitla, on the doorway border, a Storm God and Goddess face are merged—the two main deities of the main mural are combined in a single composite creature. At Atetelco, the *talud* border is

Figure 11.3. Net-jaguar holding a maguey plant. Copy of mural painting at the Palace of the Sun (Zone 5A), Teotihuacan. Xolalpan–Metepec phases, A.D. 400–750. Center detail of fig. 11.1. From A. Miller 1973, fig. 119, p. 81. Courtesy of Dumbarton Oaks Research Library and Collections, Washington, D.C.

also a composite creature, combining the coyote and the net-jaguar into a single being, which also has serpentlike qualities. At the Palace of the Sun, a border design joining the head of a bird with the body of a feathered serpent surrounds the main mural painting, which shows two priests in bird costumes. There is no reason to assume that the Storm God/Goddess, the coyote/net-jaguar, or the bird/feathered serpent were discrete supernaturals or mythical beings—the combined images are unique within their own murals. They are profound, clever, humorous ways of expressing the conception that the Teotihuacan artists and audience seem to have had regarding the borders of murals: that borders are important and necessary to separate images, but that they are also places where opposites come together and unlikely combinations are made.[6] In these borders, playing with multivalence is at its apogee.

I could extend the metaphor of borders to the city as a whole. The high walls of apartment compounds serve as borders, and perhaps the various wards or lineages emphasized their separation in rituals and customs. At

Figure 11.4. Coyote and net-jaguar. Mural painting at Atetelco, the east porch, Teotihuacan. Xolalpan–Metepec phases, A.D. 400–750. CNCA-INAH-MEX. INAH photo xlix-39.

the same time, Teotihuacan was obsessed by integration, which is shown in the borders by the many combinations, thus knitting the separate units together. This balance suggests some form of open, spontaneous coming and going between groups that mitigated the tendency toward separation. Although I cannot determine how closely this ideal expressed in art and architecture approximated Teotihuacan's social reality, I *can* suggest that it was a preoccupation.

When and where did mural paintings start at Teotihuacan? The best-preserved ones belong to the latest times in the city, the late Xolalpan and Metepec phases (A.D. 550–750), and are mostly in apartment compounds. The earliest mural paintings, few in number, are from the Tlamimilolpa phase, circa A.D. 250, and are in temples on the Avenue near the Pyramid of the Moon: the Temple of Agriculture murals, the Mural of the Mythological Animals, and the birds on the early Temple of the Feathered Conch Shells. One fragment came from an apartment compound at Tlamimilolpa. These early murals are characterized by black outlines around each of the figures and a lack of borders surrounding the murals. They consist of repeated motifs that extend across the entire field of the mural, like water lilies, birds, animals, or seeds, much like the individual *adornos* of the incense burners. The only motif that suggests a context is a wavy line, known in all the murals, which represents water. In one of the Temple of Agriculture murals, the headdress that looks like that of the Goddess suggests her existence and importance in ritual. In the other mural, two goddesses are vaguely rendered with human worshippers. This small sample suggests that human and deity figures were rarer in the early murals than were allegorical symbols such as water, plants, and animals. The lack of borders is also significant in that these murals are conceived of as existing and extending into space indefinitely—a total surround of a watery domain.

One puzzle for everyone working at Teotihuacan is that more murals have not been found in the temples and palaces along the Avenue. The Ciudadela palaces and the Street of the Dead Complex have yielded no major murals. On the Avenue, one large puma is the central figure of a mural on a *tablero* facing a stairway, and another probably faced it on the other side. Some murals have been destroyed in this much-looted, much-examined central area; however, the elegant apartments in the so-called Viking Group (a part of the Street of the Dead Complex) have well-preserved walls, but no frescoes. The only major palace with frescoes on the Avenue is the one in front of the Pyramid of the Sun, the Palace of the Sun (known more prosaically as Zone 5A). Otherwise murals are known only from apart-

Figure 11.5. Feline sitting on a metate. Mural painting at Tetitla, central patio, Teotihuacan. Tlamimilolpa phase, A.D. 250–400. In situ. Pasztory photo.

ment compounds. Of nearly a dozen compounds excavated, seven were either completely or extensively covered with mural paintings. Archaeologists still do not know whether such painted apartment compounds were the exception or the rule.

One thing, however, is clear—the quality of painting is as good at Atetelco, quite a distance from the Avenue, as in the Palace of the Sun. Mural painting may have begun in the temples, but it was not an exclusively sacred or aristocratic medium. It was evidently available to a wealthy segment of society. Its pervasiveness is evident from the way the Aztecs saw and imitated Teotihuacan structures at the Templo Mayor. Flanking the pyramids to Tlaloc and Huitzilopochtli are small buildings on either side in a style reminiscent of Teotihuacan. These are painted in red and blue with large and simple eyes, one of the most common motifs in Teotihuacan murals that they must have seen. Though observers do not know the extent of the decoration, Teotihuacan was a painted city.[7]

Art historian Meyer Schapiro once wrote an insightful article on the nature of painting, how the wall or paper form in itself determines issues such as the center, the edges, and various hierarchies that are built into the space to be used.[8] He noted, rather in passing, that painting does not come to be until such flat surfaces are available. This point deserves elaboration. Few flat walls are created in nature; they do not exist until humans build them. Much painting is on cave walls, on human bodies, on pottery vessels—but most of these forms are curved or irregular. There is flat bark-cloth or other cloth, there are flat shields, there are wooden houses, but somehow on them paintings are more like carvings or ceramics and the other arts than like murals or manuscripts. Mural art requires a lot of wall space. When Teotihuacan became a city, and especially with the building of the city in permanent stone, all of a sudden a huge amount of rectangular, flat wall space became available. Monte Alban, Oaxaca, Classic period Veracruz sites, and Maya buildings also have murals, but because of the two thousand apartment compounds, Teotihuacan had by far the largest wall space of any Mesoamerican culture. The Teotihuacan custom of covering the stone buildings with stucco resulted in smooth, creamy white surfaces. This surface was ideal for decoration. Colorful stucco had already been used for pottery in the late Preclassic period, so the idea may have a precedent in pottery. Teotihuacan artists also applied fresco to pottery vessels in the style of the murals, but because the vessels date generally from the same time as the mural paintings, precedence is hard to establish.

Undoubtedly, Teotihuacan also had painted books and manuscripts. Because of the climate, no manuscripts survive from the Classic period anywhere in Mesoamerica. (Excavations in Maya buildings have yielded a few calcified manuscripts, turned to a solid mass by water dripping through limestone structures.)[9] There are good reasons to believe that books existed in Oaxaca in the Classic period as well as among the Maya;[10] I would argue that they must have existed at Teotihuacan as well. Certain residents of a large and complex city that functioned in the Mesoamerican culture area (where books are sure to have existed, at least in some regions) must have made and used books as well. Books would have been very valuable for commercial and religious purposes. The Aztecs had a great variety of books, including histories, maps, tribute collections, and religious-divinatory books—to name only the types of which examples have survived. A more specific argument for the existence of books has to do with the question of writing at Teotihuacan.

Mesoamericanists have long noted that in comparison with inscriptions at Monte Alban and in the Maya area, Teotihuacan seems to have had no dates and texts. However, this observation needs to be stated more carefully, to more precisely reflect the nature of the evidence available to us: Teotihuacan had no major tradition of *public inscriptions*. Murals and frescoed vessels generally show figures with long sound-scrolls and not glyphs. The idea they all express is oral communication.[11] Sometimes the speech-scrolls contain images like the streams that pour from the hands of elites and gods. These too are beautiful or precious things—flowers and shells.[12] One gets the sense that another preoccupation at Teotihuacan was talking things out rather than writing them down, which may be related to the city's antidynastic bias. Much of the writing and use of calendars in Mesoamerica developed to demonstrate the antiquity and legitimacy of royal houses. Writing and public inscriptions were ways in which rulers advertised their power. This use for writing is especially true of the Maya, whose states were precarious and needed much ceremonial and artistic demonstration. At Teotihuacan, power was firmly based in the city (with its irrigation agriculture, craft specialization, and long-distance trade), and the elite seem to have found public inscriptions of the sources of their power unnecessary. The rulers of Teotihuacan might have intentionally avoided the personality cult of the dynastic art and writing to the south.

Yet, glyphs exist in the city. Isolated glyphs appear in the murals of Tepantitla, Techinantitla, and Tetitla. At Techinantitla especially, emblems in front of personages with goggles and tasseled headdresses may be their titles,[13] while at Tepantitla the glyphs are attached to the speech-

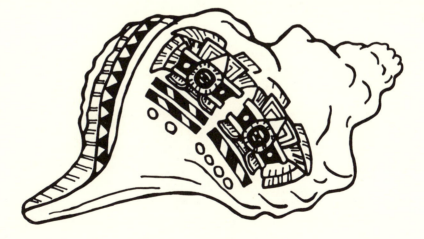

Figure 11.6. Conch shell with glyphs. Shell with stucco and paint. Provenance unknown. Xolalpan–Metepec phases, A.D. 400–750. 15 by 38 by 20 cm (6 by 15 by 8 in.). Museo Nacional de Antropología, Mexico City. CNCA-INAH-MEX. Drawing by J. Robertson.

scrolls of little figures.[14] Glyphs also appear on sculptures, pottery vessels, and a variety of miscellaneous objects.[15] Outstanding among these miscellaneous objects are two conch shells with dates in the Mesoamerican bar and dot system. But the most impressive are nine glyphs in the trunks of nine flowering trees in the murals of Techinantitla.[16] Each tree has a different type of flower, and the glyph may be the name of the tree. The glyphs are very much like Aztec place glyphs in composition, consisting of juxtaposed elements, some of which are recognizable as having been drawn from nature, others of which appear to be abstract, including a human hand, a flower, and a rectangle. These murals leave no doubt that writing had to have existed in some form, which was, most likely, that of the book. This is one of the many frustrating questions scholars will never be able to answer—what originated in books and what in mural paintings? Who painted and owned the books? Were they common or scarce?

Teotihuacan as a culture was in a position to develop painting on walls and in books, and evidently Teotihuacan artists did just that. At first, various symbols (like the *adornos* or the glyphs in books) appear to have been simply transferred to the walls in repeating or alternating series. Later murals exhibit the creation of more complex deity and human figures as major themes surrounded by elaborate borders. The paintings of the rooms were often interrelated. For example, the Dumbarton Oaks mural of the net-jaguar and the temple came from the apartment compound at Tetitla. It was found in rooms that flank—and are thus secondary to—a porch facing

Figure 11.7. Divine hands mural. Copied from the painted mural at Tetitla, Teotihuacan. Pasztory photo.

the central courtyard with a small shrine. The mural in the porch is that of the Goddess pouring jade treasures from her hands. In this case, the inner room beyond the porch is also painted with abstract emblems with yellow hands pouring seeds—a kind of close-up of the divine hands of the Goddess outside. Many apartment murals form such interrelated subjects in the paintings of the rooms. Each painting is only one piece of a larger puzzle.

In art history, as it is usually taught, art is believed to develop from a "nonrealistic" Egyptian or Medieval style to a "realistic" Greek or Renaissance style. This premise implies that the Egyptian and Medieval artist tried to be naturalistic too, but did not achieve that goal as well as the Greek or Renaissance artist. Leaving aside the more complex aspects of the change from an Egyptian to a Greek type of representation, I want to emphasize that in thinking of the difference in styles as a progression, observers see the non-naturalistic styles in negative terms. Art historians instead should find out what the Egyptian artist *could* do that was not possible for the Greek artist. In the case of Teotihuacan, I would say that the artist had a style with remarkable range and flexibility—precisely due to its composite puzzle quality. If he chose, as in the murals of Tepantitla, the artist could compose a naturalistic "scene" out of the signs—trees bordering a meandering stream of water, irrigated fields, squash plants, people sitting beneath the trees. A representational option existed, and was sometimes adopted by the artist, as in the three-dimensional interlacing of the body of the net-jaguar or, in another mural, the way a diver and shell collector moves in and out of the stylized "waves" of the wavy lines. A Goddess hand holding a plume or plant is also three-dimensional. When the artist felt like it, he played with three-dimensional "naturalistic" effects.

Artists, also were capable of going in the opposite direction and creating diagrams and surreal combinations. Instead of an anthropomorphic deity, two isolated hands may emerge from a medallion surrounded by S-shaped lines over diagonal bands of water in which shell creatures or water birds are rendered purely as symbolic forms.[17] Nothing in this composition can be considered naturalistic except for the individual little creatures. Such diagrams are reminiscent of the curious assemblage of *adornos* on incense burners that also obey non-naturalistic rules.

In the nineteenth century Désiré Charnay described walls at Teotihuacan "ornamented with figures, as [the] principal subject, with a border like an Aubusson carpet."[18] Modern visitors see them, especially the interlacing trellis designs, as resembling wallpaper. Comparisons to rugs and wallpaper indicate the decorative quality of the murals. This has also been seen as a negative quality, since our culture considers ornament an

Figure 11.8. Mural of hands and water creatures. Drawing from mural painting at the Palace of the Sun (Zone 5A), Teotihuacan. From A. Miller 1973, fig. 128, p. 84. Courtesy of Dumbarton Oaks Research Library and Collections, Washington, D.C.

Figure 11.9. Shell diver. Drawing from mural painting at Tetitla, Teotihuacan. From Séjourné 1966a, fig. 178.

Figure 11.10. Net-jaguar in yellow hands. Copy of mural painting at the Palace of the Jaguars, Teotihuacan. Copy by Agustín Villagra Caleti in the Museo Nacional de Antropología, Mexico City. CNCA- INAH-MEX. Pasztory photo.

"empty" form of art because it often lacks symbolic meaning. Many cultures in the past have developed elaborate systems of ornament as a way of celebrating both secular and sacred subjects. Ornament is always celebratory, and in pre-industrial cultures without mechanical reproduction, its labor-intensiveness is a part of its value. Ernst Gombrich has shown in a more subtle sense the ways in which ornament embodies the sense of order of a given society.[19] I have emphasized the idea that an ornamental matrix[20]—rather than a naturalistic view of a scene—is ideal for an art that oscillates between the abstraction of diagrams and the presentation of scenes. An ornamental matrix allows for a realm of fantasy, of the mind, in which any images can be juxtaposed without visual contradiction or the tyranny of perception. Moreover, because an ornamental matrix comprises multivalent signs, most images read as both ornament and symbol. The sign is never naked—as, say, in a painting by Paul Klee—but is set into a rich, honorific enclosure.

What Teotihuacan mural painting rarely does is tell a story. It is a non-narrative art. By contrast, in the Oval Relief from House E at Palenque, Pacal's mother presents the young ruler with a crown. The focus of this Maya artwork is individualistic, psychological, and narrative. Viewers feel that we are in on a dramatic scene where the action is occurring. Such an image is unthinkable at Teotihuacan, where the imagery is more fragmented and viewers have to put it together. For example, the relationship of the net-jaguar to the Goddess at Tetitla is implied and never clearly stated.

Did some of the people of Teotihuacan, like Medieval scholastic philosophers, discuss their murals, the complex interrelationship of their symbols, and did they relish this multifaceted art? Or were many happy with the lively colors and beautiful patterns? Whichever was the case, they knew that they were living in a very special place where their living quarters were transformed into other worlds. Their houses were also temples, with the gods and their symbols present. Since a large majority of paintings deal with nature and water symbolism, they were living within a verdant paradise. Whatever Teotihuacan was like—noisy with craft work, smelly with unsophisticated sanitation, dusty with the seasons of drought—the painted porches were a shady relief from sun or a protection from rain, and the paintings represented an endless sacred universe of natural bounty. Whether the promises of the founders of Teotihuacan came true, we do not know, but the people of Teotihuacan made them a reality in the paintings on the walls of their houses.

XII

The Human Body in Parts

Hearts and Footprints

IN THE SYSTEM OF FRAGMENTATION THAT RULES TEOTIHUACAN ART BOTH human and divine bodies appear to be chopped up into pieces as if for a cannibal's meal. As in picture writing, the part clearly stands for the whole. This is not writing; however, it is a metaphoric way of representing reality—not necessarily the observable reality, but the culturally felt reality. Nowhere in Teotihuacan art is the organic wholeness and coherence of figures emphasized, except perhaps in the small figurines. The fragmented style suggests that the whole figure did not matter, but the parts did. Also, the body parts chosen for representation differ between humans and deities. Human body parts are passive and consist of hearts and footprints (the first an item of sacrifice and the second a mere imprint), while deity body parts consist of effective and articulate parts of the body, such as eyes, mouths, hands, and claws.

Laurette Séjourné was right: the ovoid design with an ellipse at the top, with vertical divisions and sometimes a drop hanging from it, is undoubtedly a human heart.[1] The mural from Atetelco in which a goggled figure cuts through it with a sacrificial knife supports this premise. The representation of the heart is another detail where the artist shows an understanding and a way of representing three dimensions. The same theme is present on a mural from the Palace of the Sun and on frescoed vessels. The heart often exists by itself, as an independent sign or emblem. It is frequent in front of the maws of animals like serpents, raptorial birds, and

Figure 12.1. Heart on sacrificial knives, from mural at Zacuala Patios, Teotihuacan. Drawing by J. Robertson.

felines, both in this form and in a related trefoil form.

The art of Teotihuacan has more representations of hearts than that of any other Mesoamerican culture—even the Aztecs. Apart from images painted in manuscripts, hearts occur in Aztec public art mainly on sacrificial vessels and on a few major sculptures such as two colossal statues known as "Serpent Skirt" and "Heart Skirt." In monumental art it is not an ever-present motif. If it were not for the documents of the Spanish conquest with all their dramatic illustrations and textual descriptions, Westerners might not consider heart sacrifice so important among the Aztecs. More archaeological evidence indicates decapitation and the placing of skull trophies on a rack; Aztec art also shows many more representations of skulls than hearts. Indeed, a carved skull rack came to light in the Templo Mayor excavations.[2]

At Teotihuacan there are not only many representations of hearts, but a few rare scenes of heart sacrifice. Although this form of sacrifice was not invented at Teotihuacan, as I once speculated that it might have been, I feel that it was turned into a central ritual activity perhaps more here than anywhere else.[3] Clara Millon noted, quite rightly, that heart sacrifice may be represented in the Preclassic period (900 B.C.) on the San Jose Mogote Danzante-like image: the figure has a trilobed symbol on his chest.[4] In general, however, in the imagery of the Monte Alban Danzantes more seems to be made of genital mutilation than of heart sacrifice. Some Teotihuacan

Figure 12.2. Priest with heart on sacrificial knife. Drawing from a mural painting at Atetelco, Teotihuacan. Xolalpan–Metepec phases, A.D. 400–750. Figure is 0.5 by 0.75 m (20 by 29 in.). From Kubler 1967, fig. 14. Courtesy of Dumbarton Oaks Research Library and Collections, Washington, D.C.

figurines appear to wear the flayed skin of a victim, like the Aztec Xipe Totec, the Flayed God. Skulls are also occasionally shown, in a variety of media, as in one example of a priest carrying a skull on a stick toward a frontal-view feline from a plano-relief vessel. As in the rest of Mesoamerica, Teotihuacan evidently had a wide variety of ways to sacrifice victims, but judging from the representations, heart sacrifice had a special meaning or privileged position in its ideology.

Human sacrifice is one of the hardest subjects to discuss, and the theoretical understanding of it is remarkably limited. There are essentially two schools of thought in explaining it: the all-powerful state theory and the transgression theory. In the powerful state theory, the powers that rule do so by force and use bloody sacrifices to enforce compliance.[5] The massive sacrifices of the Aztecs are usually seen as a demonstration of the power of the state. These sacrifices seem to me an attempt to create control rather than a sign of control. In other words, the massive sacrifices of the Aztecs seem like the bullying tactics of a very insecure power.[6]

The related phenomenon of bloodletting by priests and rulers has been brought out in recent studies by Clara Millon, Cecelia Klein, and Linda Schele and Mary Miller.[7] The basic premise of their studies is that autosacrifice is justified by the elite ideologically as a way of contacting and nourishing the gods and politically as a way of indicating their good faith toward the population, some of whom will be expected to undergo the more drastic and fatal forms of total sacrifice. In this theory, sacrifice and bloodletting are forms of social control. People put up with it because they have no choice.

The traditional and overt explanation for sacrifice provided by sixteenth-century native informants and many modern authors is that sacrifice exists because it is dictated by religion—it is demanded by the gods in exchange for survival and fertility. If one considers that gods and religion are human creations, this explanation of the phenomenon is inadequate both psychologically and sociologically.[8]

The second theory, which I call the transgression theory, was proposed by the surrealist writer Georges Bataille and has been discussed by René Girard and others.[9] In the powerful state theory, the sacrificers are represented as guiltless sociopaths drenched in blood. (A modern comparison would be to hardened criminals who have no feeling toward their victims.) Bataille argued that the phenomenon of sacrifice makes sense psychologically only if guilt is involved; sacrifice is a transgression of the normal rules of life that include the high value placed on life itself—universally. He suggested that the very horrendousness of sacrifice is its purpose. According to him, participating in a shared act of guilty violence can bring victim, sacrificer, and witnesses together in a shared state of consciousness. (He would have said a higher and mystical state of the experience of the sacred.) If we remove his mystical language, what he suggests is that the participation in a sacrificial ritual forges both emotional bonds in a community and altered states of consciousness. This theory is intriguing because it suggests another possible functional reason for sacrifice besides naked threat.

In fact, both theories may throw light on different aspects of the problem. Sacrifice has both a sociological and a psychological dimension. Though Westerners no longer practice literal sacrifice, our language, behaviour, and concepts are full of the ideas of "sacrifice" and "self-sacrifice." We seem to understand its meaning all too well.

One of the problems in dealing with sacrifice is in understanding why it occurs in a given context. Man's inhumanity to man needs no demonstration in the century of Auschwitz and Hiroshima. There are those who have argued that *Homo sapiens* began their rule on earth by wiping out the Neanderthals. Almost all human groups, large and small, feud and war among themselves, and the taking of trophies, especially heads, is common worldwide. War and its atrocities seem universal, and modern society accepts war as a necessary evil, "diplomacy continued by other means" as Carl von Klausewitz put it.[10] No one is really horrified by Teotihuacan images of human and bird and animal warriors carrying spears and spear throwers: we expect a powerful culture to be military. We even accept the grim disemboweled victims in the Cacaxtla battle scene on this basis. Our notion of "human rights" does not extend to war.

Human sacrifice—that is, killing outside the context of immediate warfare for the ostensible purpose of deity veneration or to accompany the dead into the afterworld—is, however, anathema in modern thought, as the great religions (Judaism, Christianity, Islam, and Buddhism) forbade it centuries ago. (Horrendous punishments were and are still allowed, however.) The sacred texts of these religions denounce both sacrifices and idolatry, and we have inherited their attitude and language. Scholars write about war and its atrocities as something understandable, but writings on sacrifice are as weird as if the topic were extraterrestrials or extrasensory perception. One can disapprove or be titillated, but it is not a part of comprehensible life.

Human sacrifice occurs infrequently in most types of societies, except for chiefdoms and early states. Because most of these societies are now defunct or at any rate no longer practice human sacrifice, modern sources of information about them are often limited to archaeology, oral traditions, or texts by outside observers. Why is it that at a certain level of sociopolitical development human sacrifice emerges as a custom? And why does this change occur precisely when cultures arrive at what modern observers see as the threshold of "high civilization"?

As I see it, the essence of sacrifice is its theatrical nature. Unlike killing in the heat of battle or in the secrecy of ambush, this ritual is presented as a spectator event dramatized in dress and in plot. The victim and the slayer play clearly defined roles. The event is planned, directed, premeditated. Why? Why do the trophy heads brought back from battle or ambush not serve the same purpose? Why did the Aztecs waste time on the battlefield trying to take live victims for sacrifice rather than killing indiscriminately on the spot like the Spanish? Why did they try taking high-ranking enemy warriors, and why were victims often commemorated on monuments with the glyphs of their names or home towns added? Mesoamerica seems to have had as much of an obsession with the defeated as with the victors.

Both large chiefdoms and early states have certain organizational problems. They have large and diverse populations divided hierarchically into rank and class that must be integrated into a smoothly functioning whole. Kinship relations are no longer adequate. A major problem for these ruling groups is social control, which they try to create by some form of ideology of belonging to the body politic. Smaller village societies can create integration partly by kinship and partly by focusing their hostilities on their neighbors in feuding. Human sacrifice seems to have been invented in many different cultures as a way of creating political bonds in the context of the insecure power of chiefdoms and early states. In more complex, later, and bigger states, human sacrifice is less significant or abolished because social integration is created by other means. Public violence remains in punishments, holy wars, crusades.

One cannot simply dismiss a custom independently invented in many parts of the world and practiced as right and sacred. Human sacrifice seems to have worked as a bonding device for various reasons. Whether the victim was a prisoner of war or someone selected for a ritual, the entire population participated in a ritual that was likely to bring forth complex and intense emotions that could range from fright and quiet to exultation and disgust. The theatricality of the event probably resulted in a distancing of the horror. If the victim was an alien prisoner of war, the deed could be cheered on ethnic or polity grounds. If the victim was one of themselves in a ritual, the deed could be admired as the ultimate in altruism. Participants could have identified both with the killer and with the victim. This was the ambivalent Aztec attitude toward sacrifice—the captor addressed his victim as "my son" and saw him as a surrogate for himself but was also, quite understandably, anxious to avoid the same fate. No doubt such a theatrical ritual also expressed the power of the ruling elite, conveniently deflected onto the gods, and implied a threat to anyone thinking of acting against the elite. Sacrifice may have been invented both to express the power of the gods and rulers and to cement human relations in the context of early states with populations too large and too diverse to be held together by family or sodality ties. The victims belonged to everybody. The theatrical killing dramatized a blood pact of social unity.

What is curious about the representations in Teotihuacan art is that the hearts do not belong to anybody. The usual Mesoamerican drama in which the victim plays a crucial role is subverted. With one exception, in the murals of Tepantitla, the victim is not usually shown. The heart is isolated and could belong to anybody—alien or citizen. The Teotihuacan insistence on heart sacrifice seems to be an insistence on ritual killing and not something taken over from war, like trophy heads. (Not that trophy heads and heart sacrifice are mutually exclusive.) In the ritual of heart sacrifice a new symbolic center is defined for human beings: the heart rather than the head. The heart is an anonymous organ without the individual personality and the features of a face. It is an absolute way of deemphasizing the ethnic or family origin of the victim or even his or her individual existence.

Unlike the head, the heart is unlikely to be the center of reason or intelligence. It signifies raw physical life as well as the life of the emotions—as in the racing heart of fear or joy. In Western culture the heart is the seat of emotions. We cannot know if this was the case at Teotihuacan, but it was true for the Aztecs. "Heart" and "face" were placed as parallel and opposite concepts in Aztec thought as the following lines indicate:

In reverence do I hold your faces, your hearts.
[Y]ou surrender your heart to each thing: aimlessly do you lead it.
Perchance, are we to live a second time?
Your heart knows it:
Only once have we come to live.
It was said that he had God in his heart, that he was wise in the things of God.[11]

Miguel León Portilla concludes that for the Aztecs the heart signified dynamism and that the word for "heart" was related to the word for "movement."[12]

Whatever the heart signified for Teotihuacan, the choice of the heart as a symbol of sacrifice has very different connotations from the choice of the head. Focusing on heart sacrifice in ritual and image may have been Teotihuacan's way of making clear that these were *sacrifices* to the gods and not trophies of warfare. Teotihuacan has not a single representation of a warrior holding the victim by the hair such as occurs in Maya, Mixtec, and Aztec art. The emphasis of heart sacrifice is on biological life—the province of the cosmic gods—and not on individual and ethnic life. Other Mesoamerican polities that were organized around semidivine kingship (the Maya and Zapotec, for example), tended to represent their victims not by hearts alone, but as full figures kneeling with arms tied, or less frequently already sacrificed, and usually identified by name glyphs of their person and place of origin. Society was unified around external conflict that

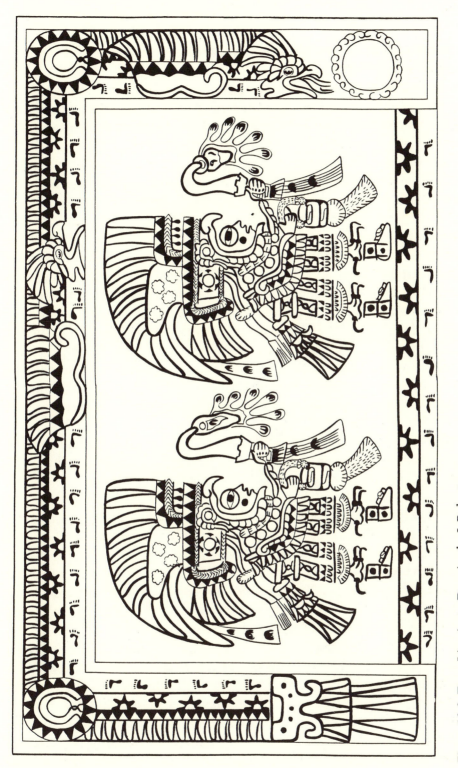

Figure 12.3. Zone 5A priests. Drawing by J. Robertson.

was commemorated on monuments in which the identity of the foreign victim was important.

Who do the Teotihuacan hearts represent—residents of the city or conquered outsiders? There is of course no way to determine the answer to this question from the images alone. However, the representations at Tepantitla show insiders. In addition, no one knows with whom Teotihuacan might have been carrying on battles to bring captives into the city. René Millon suggested Tlaxcala, the traditional enemy of the Aztecs.[13] The nature of the representation leads me to interpret the image not as a symbol of ethnic conquest (although I do not deny that conquest and prisoner sacrifice took place) but as a symbol of the cosmic requirement of sacrifice, which fell on the people of Teotihuacan potentially equally and anonymously.

Probably most of the gods of Teotihuacan required sacrifices. Sacrifice was general in Mesoamerican religious practice and was performed both for gods of fertility and creation and for gods of war and destruction. Indeed, the Teotihuacan Goddess is shown in the Tetitla mural with two hearts in her headdress. As has been suggested, sacrifice (especially human sacrifice) is common in the chiefdom and state context worldwide. What is necessary to ascertain at Teotihuacan is in what way sacrifice was interpreted and presented in this society. I think Teotihuacan strove as much as possible to separate sacrifice from the taking of captives and intergroup warfare, and to present it as a cosmic and "natural" event. The mural in which two coyotes are shown ripping out the heart of a deer may be the representation of such a cosmic justification of sacrifice. Although the allegory the animal figures may represent is hard to interpret specifically, it certainly implies that sacrifice is the order of things in the natural world. The issue of sacrifice is therefore exclusively between man and the gods, rather than between men and men. The gods signify the personified powers of nature that are a source of both bounty and disaster, and man is seen generically as a human being, without ethnicity and rank being of significance in the act of sacrifice. The apt symbol for this is the human heart, which therefore signifies potentially everyone's heart. Teotihuacan's innovation in sacrifice may have been the emphasis on the victim's anonymity in ritual sacrifice. The choreography of theatrical rituals climaxing in sacrifices not related to war but to the cults of the dieties on a lavish scale may have been an innovation at Teotihuacan aimed at the internal ceremonial and emotional life of the inhabitants. Self-sacrifice was highly valued by the Aztecs, and its ideals were inculcated in children. I think Teotihuacan might also have emphasized the values of self-sacrifice and altruism rather than focusing on the humiliation of enemies. Not only inequality, but self-sacrifice were to be made attractive enough to be embraced voluntarily.

A unique little figure at Tepantitla is an example of how Teotihuacan artists represented sacrifice. A stream of red (blood) bordered by blue (water) flows from his chest. Tears fall from his eyes—unquestionably "suffering" is the intended message in part. Otherwise, he is still standing and waving about a branch that is used elsewhere in the mural in a dance and is therefore likely to be ritual. From his mouth emerges one of the longest speech scrolls, consisting of five loops, and it is adjacent to a butterfly and to a water glyph. In the context of this mural the suggested purpose of

Figure 12.4. Sacrificial victim. Detail of a mural painting at Tepantitla, Teotihuacan. Xolalpan–Metepec phases, A.D. 400–750. In situ. CNCA-INAH-MEX. INAH photo clxii-46.

the sacrificial ritual is natural plenty. The lack of an executioner and the fact that though crying the figure stands and waves his branch suggests voluntary participation in the ritual. The victim is seen as both dead and alive—he utters a great and powerful cry and his blood flows directly into the stream beneath his feet.

The notion of man at Teotihuacan as an anonymous and to some extent collective everyman is supported by the recent finds of sacrifices in the Temple of the Feathered Serpent in which groups of identically dressed soldiers were buried. Because so much Teotihuacan imagery outside of Teotihuacan seems to be in military contexts, Mesoamericanists have speculated about the military power or advantage Teotihuacan might have had in Mesoamerica. In a very interesting paper, George Cowgill suggested that Teotihuacan's military fame may have rested on a style of collective warfare.[14] While other centers practiced a strategy emphasizing the exploits of the individual as much for the sake of personal glory and prestige as for success, Teotihuacan may have gone to battle with well-drilled units of soldiers who were less interested in individual prowess and more in the success of the enterprise as a whole—that is, willing to die anonymously. (This attitude is especially likely if they were not or did not see themselves as nobility.) Though archaeological evidence does not indicate that Teotihuacan was a great empire, Cowgill suggests that that lack of evidence does not rule out the possibility of some spectacular, if ultimately temporary, conquests. Enemy hearts may have been treated as anonymously as hearts from within the city.

The other human body part frequently represented in Teotihuacan art is a footprint. In contrast to the manifold connotations and evocations of heart images in Teotihuacan art, footprints appear to be much more conventional and much less interesting. They are found in other Mesoamerican arts in similar ways and, though common, do not play as spectacular a role in Teotihuacan art as hearts. What is striking about the footprints is that they represent the only other body part in Teotihuacan art that has a human significance. Footprints in art generally belong to humans or to hybrid creatures such as the net-jaguar. They occur in scenes as well as in emblems and diagrams. The general significance of footprints is to show the act of walking as well as the direction of walking. In a few instances footprints are randomly dispersed, which can be interpreted as dancing or jumping around. Since many deities are shown without feet, just as busts (as if somehow transcending lower bodies), footprints belong specifically to the human world and to its lowest part, closest to the earth.

In fact, technically, footprints are not really a part of the human body at all but an imprint on the earth or path. Footprints therefore are a sign that symbolizes human presence and absence simultaneously. The prevalence of footprints in Teotihuacan art suggests an image of man that is evanescent and insubstantial.

XIII

Divine Intervention

WHEN THE AZTECS PUT UP TWO BUILDINGS EVOKING TEOTIHUACAN STYLE at the Templo Mayor, they painted their walls with large disembodied eyes in Teotihuacan style. Clearly they must have seen such murals at Teotihuacan, since no other Mesoamerican art has such images. No one knows exactly what symbolic meaning the Aztecs assigned to these eyes, but I will argue that disembodied eyes, mouths, hands, and claws represent body parts of spirits in Teotihuacan art. In contrast to the sacrificial heart and the barely present footprint in the representation of humans, these body parts are articulate and active and refer to seeing, talking, devouring, giving, and grasping. I suggest that they all refer to deities or to supernatural concepts.

I have noted previously that Teotihuacan has few organically coherent images and that even the gods come in parts or can be lacking facial features altogether. The two deities most often in pieces are the Storm God and the Goddess.

The Storm God may be represented either by goggles over eyes or by a mouth with fangs and sometimes a bifurcated tongue. Although it is not clear whether all goggles denote Storm God symbols, as I once argued,[1] the goggles clearly are his major attribute and hence might show a potential relationship among other goggled figures. Most interpretations of Tlaloc's goggles suggest that they signify some form of visual enhancement—like modern "eyeglasses" or in Mesoamerican terms through some other device such as mirrors.[2] Since Teotihuacan inherited the form of the Storm God from earlier cultures, the aspect that is new is the separation of the goggles from the deity and their placement on other figures. They are thus found on animal images, such as the saurian creature on the Temple of the Feathered Serpent, as well as on elite figures, as on the Atetelco sacrificer. They are present on foreheads as well as over eyes.

Karl Taube has catalogued all the homologous circular forms that could stand for one another in Teotihuacan art, indicating a wide variety of possible visual metaphors and substitutions.[3] I am not suggesting that all these forms relate to the Storm God specifically. They do relate, however, to the idea of the supernatural, as represented by enhanced vision, which is borrowed like a mask by a variety of figures.

Why the Storm God should be associated with vision is not clear from a given ritual or myth in later times. If he were to create lightning from his eyes, it might make sense, but all textual and ethnographic information indicates that lightning is created by an axe or weapon struck against a pot or box, and the Storm God is so represented at Teotihuacan. One can hypothesize that he needs special vision in the thick, dark storm clouds or that the original meaning had been lost in the mists of antiquity and was merely a convention by Teotihuacan times. It is worth noting, however, that goggles are frequent on sacrificing figures and on warriors as if activities related to the shedding of blood needed visual enhancement or were in some way related to the Storm God.

The mustache-like upper lip usually placed over a set of fangs and sometimes a long tongue of the Storm God also appears by itself occasionally as an abbreviated symbol of the deity. More interesting are examples where the disembodied mouth is used as a symbol in another context. Mouths are, in general, symbols of openings such as doorways in temples or caves in the earth. This idea is pan-Mesoamerican, and representations can be found from Olmec to Aztec art. The well-known Aztec earth monster carved on the base of many sculptures metaphorically swallows the dead and sacrificial offerings through its huge open mouth.[4] The Aztecs conflated Tlaloc and the earth monster, and sometimes Tlaloc is found on bases.[5] Such an association with the earth and the bottom of objects is visible in the Las Colinas bowl, where a Storm God is shown at the base. The isolated Storm God maws at Teotihuacan also seem to suggest openings in temples and caves, but they are usually in a benign context, containing either various glyphic symbols or seeds within the opening. Frequently the fangs are missing, thus removing the animalistic power symbols entirely.

Storm God body parts function as enclosures and literally "encircle" features such as eyes or seeds. They appear as medallions, as little "islands"

Figure 13.1. Zacuala patios mural of mouth and eyes. Drawing from mural painting at Zacuala, Teotihuacan. From Séjourné 1959.

in the space of Teotihuacan designs. By contrast, disembodied eyes appear scattered throughout the Teotihuacan visual field, especially in the contexts of water. Within nearly all representations of water are disembodied eyes in rows, regardless of whether figures dive in the water or, whether it is part of a stream in a landscape or a stream emerging from a serpent's maw. George Kubler saw this motif as an adjective, suggesting that it signified "brilliance," perhaps referring to light effects on bubbles of water.[6] In his view, eyes are a metaphor for water because eyes are moist and produce the wetness of tears. The Aztecs sacrificed children to Tlaloc in preparation for the rainy season because children cried more and through sympathetic magic would create more rain.[7] Many other water symbols, such as shells, waterlilies, and starfish, are ubiquitous in Teotihuacan imagery. However, unlike the eyes (which are merely body parts, curious and unsettling when removed from a figure), the latter symbols are complete objects. The disembodied eyes leave the impression that a consciousness—either human or divine—is pervading all of nature and "watching" through it. The juxtaposition of fish and eyes as if they were equivalent types of things has a surreal quality. The overall effect is as though through its murals Teotihuacan were pervaded by some kind of an all-seeing spirit, whose eyes were in water, and because water was represented almost everywhere, this spirit too was everywhere. In the later Mixtec and Aztec cultures, eyes represented the stars, which also were shown as "seeing" what goes on on earth, but in a more distant fashion, limited to upper borders representing the sky.

The isolated eyes of the murals remind me of the fact that the masks, which might have represented deities, usually had inlaid eyes: black obsidian pupils and white shell eyes stared out of the semiprecious stone faces. The best-preserved example is the Teotihuacan mask found in the Templo Mayor. Because of this association I would like to suggest that the significance of eyes in water is not just "brilliance" but "divinity." Eyes signify that the water is "divine." All water may have been, by definition, "divine water" at Teotihuacan, whether it came from streams, springs, or rain. Divinity may have been imagined as being literally the water, in the same way that for Mesoamericans the corn god literally was the corn that they were eating. These eyes may thus belong to the cosmos in general or to a specific deity. Though no concrete evidence supports my hypothesis, I suggest that the deity might have been the Goddess (partly because the Storm God eyes are already represented by the symbolism of the goggles). Because she usually wears a mask or is faceless, she has no characteristic eye form. The large statue of the so-called Water Goddess has human eyes like the eye motif in the murals, but that face is also like a mask.

In the mural of Tepantitla the Goddess wears an eye mask that has on it the rhomboid eye form of the Old God of the stone censers. The rhomboid eye is so consistently associated with the Old God incense braziers that it has even been seen as a fire symbol. The relevant point here is that the Old God is yet another Teotihuacan divinity identified by a specific eye form that in fact always occurs disembodied (the Old Fire God never has such eyes; the eye form is merely a design on the vessel type associated with him). The rhomboid eye always appears to be a mask worn over the face and instead of the face, as on a series of compound emblems, or that is used as a border, in a four-part compound sign that is generally felt to represent water and fire elements tied together. Like the visage of the Storm God, the rhomboid eye, related to the Old God, may also be an old motif in Teotihuacan

Figure 13.2. Rhomboid eye. Four-part motifs. From Kubler 1967. Courtesy of Dumbarton Oaks Research Library and Collections, Washington, D.C.

art. Like the Storm God body parts, the rhomboid eye is also usually found in specific contexts and less pervasively spread out than the natural eye.

The natural eyes that pervade Teotihuacan imagery thus seem likely to be those of the Goddess, who is otherwise masked or faceless but who "sees" literally through all watery places. I imagine her eyes as having been displaced from her body to the entire cosmos. If the natural eyes in fact are not hers, my alternative interpretation might be that they belong to nature or the cosmos in general and not to a particular deity. Actually, in some ways these two interpretations overlap. A good indication of the way Teotihuacan uses the imagery of body parts is in the mural of Tepantitla where the Goddess figure emerges from a platform with a Storm God mouth opening of a "cave-womb" and wears an Old God–style rhomboid eye-shaped mask, and the tree that grows from her back is dripping with water with attached disembodied eyes.

Since the natural eye is so often a symbol in water, it is often presumed, on the basis of associative reasoning, to be a positive fertility symbol. In

Figure 13.3. Goddess with clawed hands. Mural painting. Probably from Techinantitla, Teotihuacan. Probably Metepec phase, A.D. 650–750. 66 by 107 cm (26 by 42 1/8 in.). Staatliche Museen zu Berlin, Preussischer Kulturbesitz, Museum für Völkerkunde, IV Ca 46106.

terms of the frequent Teotihuacan practice of masking and covering the face, the eye motif acquires other potential meanings. Why does the Goddess hide her face? After all, she gives water, jades, seeds. Why the need for invisibility or for a mask? On a recent visit to Teotihuacan with non-specialist museum trustees, on seeing the many eyes as border designs at the Palace of the Quetzal Butterfly, several of these visitors exclaimed in mock horror: "Beware, big brother is watching you." Teotihuacan produces a sense of being watched by all these eyes, which emerge and are a part of nature as it is depicted, and the feeling can be unsettling. In view of the fact that the Goddess can trade in her hands for claws, can take off her nose bar to reveal teeth, and clearly has a destructive aspect, her eyes under the mask may also be powerful and dangerous.

Whereas the disembodied eyes are difficult to relate to a specific deity, isolated mouths and hands and claws belong mostly to the Goddess. Although the Goddess wears a nose bar that hides her mouth in contexts where she is giving, on a number of murals the nose bar is missing. In the latter cases, her lips are parted to reveal her teeth, creating a menacing impression. In one mural from Techinantitla she consists of only a mouth full of teeth from which water and water lilies emerge. Her hands are raptorial claws. This mural seems to show the Goddess in her destructive rather than creative form. Mouths full of teeth surrounded by flames, presumably also associated with the theme of destruction, are visible in a border fragment from Tetitla. There the mouth is a pun for the door of a temple, and no anthropomorphic personage is indicated. The deity association is not clear in this mural, because the central subject has not been preserved. In a striking mural from Zacuala Patios, eyes in horizontal bands flank a central mouth design surrounded by rays that even without a specific military or sacrificial context seems menacing. Mouths can be metaphors for temple doorways, for shields and even glyphs can function in such a fashion. The RE glyph (named "reptile eye" because the oval with an S-shaped curve above it reminded early scholars of the representation of a reptile's eye) is most likely a glyph, perhaps even a day sign. It is associated with dots numbering one to nine, and therefore James Langley feels it is part of Teotihuacan's writing and numbering system.[8] Nevertheless, rather than being shown itself as a glyph, this symbol is often placed under some eye design, such as the rhomboid Old God eye panel, to form a mouth and thus, together with a headdress, to create a "face" or a "mask."

Some observers have suggested that Mesoamerica was an "oral" civilization, particularly obsessed by themes of eating and devouring. I have mentioned the Aztec earth monster that devours everything, and one could refer to sacrifice as a way of "feeding the gods." Since Mesoamericans also saw the eating of staples like maize as the eating of the body of the maize deity, gods and men alike clearly indulged in mutual eating. Or, to express that idea another way, eating was a basic metaphor in divine-human interaction. Note that in the Techinantitla mural with the Goddess shown as claws and teeth, divine water emerges from the mouth, just as in the Tepantitla mural, suggesting that the mouth is the origin of both benefits and disasters. (In this context one might refer back to the sacrificed soldiers in the Temple of the Feathered Serpents who wore necklaces of human teeth set in maxillae as trophy-ornaments, indicating the preoccupation with mouths and teeth.) In this obsession with mouths, one should remember the common use of the nose bar, which hides the mouth as if that were a dangerous or unseemly part of the body. A visible mouth is therefore something of a striking, "naked" body part that always calls attention to itself whether surrounded by flames or not.

Isolated hands, like mouths, seem to belong usually to the Goddess. Hands are just the opposite of the mouth in meaning—the yellow hands always represent giving and gifts, the benevolent aspect of the Goddess. They are among the most elegant and gracious representations in Teotihuacan art. The hands, sometimes with painted fingernails, have a surprising life and individuality in contrast to the remote, masked, or even absent face of the deity, as if all the positive energy was concentrated in the hands and not in any other part of the Goddess.

Claws signify the destructive aspect of creatures and of the Goddess, and like hands, they too appear by themselves. In a striking mural from the Palace of the Sun, jade treasures flow from claws that emerge from stylized S shapes made up of a net that suggest but do not represent arms. Instead of a face, the figure has a round net emblem and an isolated claw, topping a Storm God lip, is in the headdress. The border of this mural shows a band with alternating hearts, footprints, and shell creatures. The imagery combines ferociousness with giving, water and nature with wealth, fertility with sacrifice. Hands and claws are thus both opposites and synonyms.

It is worth pondering this mural as an artifact of Teotihuacan thought. Painted in shades of red, this mural is relatively difficult to read, like the jaguar-and-temple mural. Though the first impression is that of a frontal figure bust with a feathered headdress, one is immediately aware of the lack of a face. Further scanning reveals the hands, but even they turn out

Figure 13.4. Net-laced figure with claws. Drawing from mural painting at the Palace of the Sun (Zone 5A), Teotihuacan. Detail from A. Miller 1973, fig. 124, p. 83. Courtesy of Dumbarton Oaks Research Library and Collections, Washington, D.C.

to be claws. One's reading proceeds along similar contradictory observations. Though one first reads the image as a being, one quickly notes that its arms and face are made up of interlace over the flat background—that is, nothing. Though it appears to be a rich but two-dimensional ornament, both the interlace and the hearts in the border are rendered to create the illusion of three-dimensionality. There are endless repeating forms, such as the feathers, the drops, and the dots, but unexpectedly there is specificity in the little face, the nose bar, the shells, the flower, and the hand that flow from the claws. A similar surprise awaits in the border where an undulating band of flat footprints is punctuated by three-dimensional hearts, while, painted in yet another scale, different shell creatures "swim" in the resulting spaces.

This image provides two resolutely contradictory attitudes in relation to forms at Teotihuacan. First, there is a strong tendency to cut up bodies (human and divine); to define forms by turning them into discrete signs, glyphs, and ornamental units; and to reduce even shell creatures and flowers to types—as if everything in the Teotihuacan universe could be reduced to a kind of "Platonic" ideal form. Second, there is a drive to turn this compendium of image, sign, and ornament back into anthropomorphic form. The mural, after all, is constructed so that it reads like a frontal human. Or, as in the rhomboid eye and RE glyph panels, the glyphs together read as a face. Curiously, at least in the arts that survive, this potentially linguistic vocabulary of signs is not put in the service of writing; it is rechanneled into the construction of new images.

I am reminded of the often-quoted story of Siberian shamans, who, while in a trance, feel that their fragile biological bones have been transformed into iron. Thus strengthened, they awake from their trance. The nature of the art of Teotihuacan seems to suggest transformations of a similar magnitude—the world of nature and man has first been fragmented into artificial signs, but like the iron skeleton in the story, it is put back into natural-looking images. However, the Teotihuacan images are always clearly constructs, whether they are composite censers or mural paintings. One is never under the illusion that real beings, human or divine, adorn walls or vessels. The approach is insistently nonillusionistic. Unlike the Olmec colossal heads, which suggest the presence of an actual being, art at Teotihuacan never tries to fool one's intelligence—it always proclaims its own artificiality and the viewer's active role in making and unmaking it. But because body parts play such a crucial role in this image system, they stop the abstraction of the artificiality from being excessively distancing. (This is not unlike cubist painting in which details such mandolin strings and newspapers refer to the things of real life.) Viewers have (probably biologically inherited) visceral reactions to eyes, mouths, and hands, and the structurally complex images of Teotihuacan hold us through the emotional power of the dismembered human form.

In this sense Teotihuacan mural painting seems alive—it throbs with a heart, stares with eyes, and dances with its feet. As in the host-figure, where the deity has all of society inside it, visible through a door that opens to its "heart," all of nature at Teotihuacan is animated by the body parts of humans and gods. This fact suggests a social ideal in which everyone participates and is "lost" as an individual within a cosmic whole. The gods themselves are not individual but incorporate elements of each other in their being and insignia. In fact, their exchange of elements is as protean and on such a colossal scale that the only metaphors that seem appropriate to them come from modern natural sciences—the way we explain how the rains that flow into rivers finally make their way to the ocean and evaporate back into clouds, making more rain; or how the erosion of mountains into sediment that accumulates in ocean bottoms makes new layers of stone that are once more uplifted into mountains to be eroded again. These are vast cosmic cycles in which eventually everything is interrelated. In a geological sense of the cosmos what is earth is also sky, what is under water is above water, what is whole can also be in fragments. In its way, Teotihuacan represented a cosmos of similarly vast interrelating forces.

XIV

The Human Element

AFTER I ACCOUNTED FOR THE REMARKABLY FRAGMENTED AND reassembled nature of Teotihuacan images, a series of forms began to insist on their wholeness in my mind. Surprisingly, these were mainly human figures.

The lively little figures of the Tepantitla mural came to mind (which Wicke long ago compared in form to the figurines),[1] as well as the entire large corpus of the figurines, a subject to which I will return. It seemed as if figures could be whole, so long as they were small, or could perhaps be colossal, but not life size. Size seemed to be a part of the answer, but not the complete answer. Figures are more whole when they are humans than when they are deities even in the mural paintings. For example, the elite figures—priests or warriors or whoever they are—exist in an intermediate position between deities and commoners. Their size is that of deities, but they are in profile rather than being in the more dramatic and important frontal position. Their bodies are clearly human: their faces, arms, and legs are in the right biological positions. They are shown wearing existing types of dress, from sandals, loincloths, and mantles to headdresses and jewelry. They carry human artifacts such as bags, spears, spear throwers, shields, rattles. They speak, judging by the ornate scrolls in front of their mouths. (But then, in Teotihuacan art almost everything seems to utter sounds.) Like the deities, they wear huge headdresses, almost half of their size, and pour streams that can be interpreted as containing valuables—seeds, water, flowers. Although a hierarchy is clear in certain room complexes such as Tetitla or Tepantitla, with the frontal deities in central locations and the profile elite figures in flanking positions or even in flanking rooms, elites and deities are close in size and context. Moreover, in the known murals from Teotihuacan (disregarding isolated borders), there are probably more representations of such profile elite figures than of any other subject.

Because these figures are rendered in profile, they seem emotionally remote. Surprisingly little has been written about them as a class of representation at Teotihuacan. Everyone focuses on the signs and deities. Moreover, the figures seem to leave modern observers cold intellectually as well as emotionally. What can one do with these elaborately dressed short figures with all their monotony, despite their fantastic headgear and eager expression? Perhaps the most important fact to note is that evidently they were not boring to the people of Teotihuacan.

The main question asked has always been "Who are they?"[2] Do they represent the elite living where the murals are found, and hence, were they once thought of as specific persons? Do they represent groups from

Figure 14.1. Elite figure with maguey leaves. Fragment of mural painting, Tlacuilapaxco. Xolalpan–Metepec phases, A.D. 400–750. Length, 36.6 cm (14 1/4 in.). The Art Institute of Chicago. Photo © 1994, The Art Institute of Chicago. All Rights Reserved.

the ruling temples and palaces, honorifically represented in the apartment compounds? Or do they represent some generic idea of priest or sacrificer? After all, wall space must be filled and if doing so requires ten figures, the ten figures may have to be identical. Some murals may represent each of these alternatives at different times and places.

But if the city was not interested in glorifying dynastic rulers and their conquests, why are the human elites such an important subject in representation and so clearly whole? This is a late phenomenon; such elite figures were painted mainly from the Xolalpan phase onward. Early murals show flora, fauna, deity imagery. But from about A.D. 400, the powerful servants of the state are commemorated on many walls, as if in the last few hundred years Teotihuacan wished to show a human presence in a limited but pervasive manner. These figures are among the most easily recognizable and understandable images in Teotihuacan art. Visually, they project paradoxical qualities that remind me of the representation of seventeenth-century Dutch burghers by Rembrandt and Franz Hals—the burghers are sober and understated in their black dress and white lace collars, but their expressions are as self-confident and proud as if they were royalty. The Teotihuacan elite figures are similarly understated in being in profile and in groups, but they are glorified in being splendidly dressed and organically coherent. Such images of collective human power may have been as awesome in their way as the stelae of individual Maya rulers. While these rows of elites suggest power, they also suggest organization. Like a well-trained army stepping out on parade, they evoke a well-ordered elite world of civil and religious bureaucrats.

Perhaps they have interested modern observers so little because they appear constrained by the conventions of representation, and our favorite paradigms are symbols of individual freedom rather than regimentation—even if that freedom should belong only to rulers or gods. Paradoxically, however, though the elite figures show a limited range of pose and action, nevertheless, their size and costume are related to those of the gods. They are thus intermediate beings.

In fact, a whole group of representations cannot easily be assigned either to gods or to humans: profile figures with the upper bodies clearly belonging to deities and the lower bodies to humans. Many of these are Storm God images, which is interesting in that he is the deity most clearly linked to elite concerns such as war, trade, and dynastic and political matters. What is curious in these representations is that the lower body is indistinguishable from the body of elites, including loincloth or sandals. Either the gods were sometimes imagined in more anthropomorphic form or, alternatively, these are the elite figures wearing the masks of gods. In a marvelous study of the interrelationship of the concept of deity and impersonator—which included the deity's statue, priest, and sacrificial victim—among the Aztecs, Arild Hvidtfeldt has shown their inseparability.[3] For Teotihuacan I like the second alternative, which is that these are the gods as represented by the masked elite, but no absolute visual evidence compels the selection of the second rather than the first suggestion, which is that they are the gods imagined in anthropomorphic form. In either case, the system of representation makes a close visual connection between the gods and the elite—bordering on exchangeable identity.

As there is a curiously close relationship between gods and elites, there is a similarly close relationship between men and animals. Animals in Teotihuacan art seem to do what men do—they walk upright, they kneel, they dance, they carry weapons, they blow conch shells, they wear human dress, and speech-scrolls issue from their mouths. They range from figures that are completely in animal form to those that are so anthropomorphic as to look like humans in animal costume. For example, at least one anthropomorphic Storm God or Storm God impersonator very likely alter-

Figure 14.2. Jaguar and conch shell mural. Palace of the Jaguars, Teotihuacan. In situ. Pasztory photo.

nated with or was related to a feline scattering flames. The representation of anthropomorphic animals crosses over into definite representations of humans wearing animal costumes. Among the earliest representations is the enigmatic Mural of the Mythological Animals in which birds, felines, and a feathered serpent emerge from stylized wavy lines indicating water. Although the interactions are not clear, one feline seems to be catching a bird in its maw. The representation of the animals is varied and lively and almost suggests a narrative. A stream of water with eyes pours from the head of the feathered serpent, resembling another early mural from the Temple of the Feathered Conch Shells in which similar streams flow from the beaks of birds. These activities make the animals as much godlike as human.

What does the animal metaphor signify at Teotihuacan? The animals seem to be allegorical representations, but who do they represent: gods or humans or both? Like humans, they are usually in profile, usually whole (except for the net-jaguar), and usually related to the human realm in costume, activity, posture, or insignia. It would be tempting to conclude that these powerful creatures (largely birds of prey, coyotes, and felines), stand for the powerful elite, that through them the strength, protection, and danger of the ruling class were given visual expression. Laurette Séjourné and I began by comparing these animal images to the Aztec orders of knights, usually referred to as the "Eagle and Jaguar Knights."[4] Seeing these animal figures at Teotihuacan, almost everyone writing prior to the 1960s saw them as the Teotihuacan versions of the Aztec knights and assumed that such an institution of warrior orders existed at Teotihuacan. Instead the animals might represent certain qualities of the elite—eagle, quetzal, jaguar, and coyote could have been honorific terms that were, in the fanciful manner of Teotihuacan mural painting, given visual form.

The trouble is, some animal representations could also be deities. Many animals have human hearts in front of their maw, or blood drips from their beak. These images can be read at least two ways. First, if the animals are surrogates of the gods, they could be "feeding" on the hearts like gods. In that case their power relates to the deity and not to the human world. Second, as in the heart of a deer being ripped out by coyotes, the hearts could signify that the animals are sacrificers, like the human priests. It is impossible to decide categorically whether the animals signify one or the other. Perhaps the meaning depended on the context. Perhaps any distinction is meaningless—the point may be that the elite are for some purposes different from the gods, but for others like the gods. Similarly, animals are important symbolic substitutions for both humans and deities, thus making the situation even more complex.

What the animal imagery does is to insist that the world of the gods and the elite is not a human construct but the normal realm of nature. It suggests that the social order is a mirror of the natural order.[5] This strategy is not unique to Teotihuacan—all cultures imply, one way or another, that their ordering of the world reflects nature most closely. Even modern society's cult of "natural foods" (which seem to consist mostly of chips and cookies) is based on a concept of living closer to nature than is allowed by modern commercial culture. Peter Berger and Thomas Luckmann have shown the naturalizing tendency of all social systems.[6] What is specific to Teotihuacan is how this clearly complex and artificial urban entity chose to present itself as the "natural" result of a cosmic alignment and represented its social, political, and religious powers and organization through images of flora and fauna. The references to nature counter the other very clear references to artificiality and the manmade.

When one first encounters Teotihuacan imagery, human figures, animals, gods, and signs seem to be clear entities. Eventually, the imagery turns out to be one big ambiguous field of interrelationships. The elite, divine, and natural worlds could be one construct. Teotihuacan is sometimes easily dismissed as a theocracy, a word to which we have a hard time attaching specific meanings and that I am not going to try to define politically here. The art, however, suggests a possible world view that was widely, if not completely, shared: the ideal of collective power, intertwined with the concept of cosmic and natural order.

Ordinary people, commoners, citizens (or however one wishes to characterize them), are represented on only three known sets of murals—the Temple of Agriculture offering scene, the murals of Tepantitla, and the Pinturas Realistas fragments from Tetitla. Evidently such figures were relatively rare as a subject in mural paintings. These three examples are, also, very diverse. In each case miniature figures are distributed against a red background and the emphasis is on their activities, which are represented with ethnographic clarity. At Tepantitla, there are scenes of ritual, of various games (including a stickball game with a marker and an umpire), of curing, amidst a wide variety of plants. At Tetitla more richly dressed figures with Maya-style eyes seem to be grabbing at each other, but the fragments are too small for the narrative to be understandable. In the offering scene the figures stand or sit with what look like feathers, incense, birds, and foodstuffs that they are presenting to the deities.

These figures are whole but extremely abbreviated—the nearly naked Tepantitla figures look like stick figures. Their insignificance in relation to the elite figures is indicated by their smaller size, less clothing, and lively and sometimes undignified manner. Modern writers have tended to like them better, precisely because they lack hieratic gravity. They provide us with a glimpse of what we imagine as everyday life, that is, joy, playfulness, sadness, doing things—the stuff of the bourgeois imagination as exemplified by the favorite nineteenth-century literary form, the novel. Though apparently "informal" in organization by the usual Teotihuacan standards, these paintings also deal with the sacred realm. No one is shown tilling the fields, raising children, building houses, bartering at a market, or even hunting. These panoramas still reveal a sacred, ritual world, in which sacrificed humans stand up and people come in several colors including blue. But they show a lighter side of the sacred and indicate that playfulness and a certain informality were as much a part of the sacred ritual world as the formality of the neat line of the marching elites.

In fact, regimentation is given to the elite, while "the people" are allowed a freer and more casual appearance. More speech-scrolls with glyphic signs are associated with the little figures at Tepantitla than with any elite figure. Whenever observers are tempted to see excessive "order" in this Teotihuacan "theocracy," we come upon representations suggesting individual choice, personalization, or liveliness that contradict it. We cannot know if people were lively or not, but we can know that they sometimes liked looking at lively people in their murals.

While planning the exhibition of Teotihuacan art, my co-curator, Kathleen Berrin, noted the curious extent to which Teotihuacan art consisted of "little things," or small-scale objects: *adornos*, figurines, miniatures. This emphasis seemed in great contrast to the colossal size of the city and its architectural monuments. Unlike most other Mesoamerican cities, Teotihuacan is almost entirely without large-scale sculptures in stone, terracotta, or stucco. In the 150 years of excavation at Teotihuacan, only three colossal stone statues have been discovered. Teotihuacan's contemporaries and trading partners in Veracruz and Monte Alban made large terracotta sculptures, but these too are absent at Teotihuacan. Instead, Teotihuacan has yielded millions of figurines, small by comparison to Maya or Veracruz examples. Like the pottery, they tend to be minimal, especially figurines dated to the Miccaotli and Tlamimilolpa phases (A.D. 150–400) that are dressed in flat clay garments and are wearing flat, rectangular headdresses. There are mothers and children, leaders on thrones, simple

Figure 14.3. Wide-band headdress figurines. Ceramic and pigment. Provenance unknown. Early Tlamimilolpa phase, A.D. 200. Height, 10.5 cm (4 in.) and 14.5 cm (5 2/3 in.). The Saint Louis Art Museum, Gift of Morton D. May, 233:1978.

standing figures. Many retain their original bright colors, like the *adornos* of the braziers. These figurines have been made even less substantial by their flat garments.

Mold making was introduced into figurine manufacture in the early Xolalpan phase (beginning A.D. 400), and some types of figurines combine handmade and moldmade forms.[7] The so-called portrait figurines have mold-made heads, identical idealized forms like masks, and lively handmade bodies. They are like the painted figures of Tepantitla. Their hands seem clearly to have been made to grasp objects, with an opening left between curved fingers and thumb. The rigid masklike heads contrast strangely with the the lively bodies—like the contrast between standardization and individualism in the city as a whole.

Anthropologists do not know what people did with the figurines. They were household ritual objects, and some went into the trash and some into

Figure 14.4. Portrait figurine. Ceramic and pigment. Provenance unknown. Xolalpan phase, A.D. 400–650. CNCA-INAH-MEX. INAH photo.

Figure 14.5. Ball-game scene. Copy of painted mural at Tepantitla, Teotihuacan. Xolalpan–Metepec phases, A.D. 400–750. Pasztory photo.

Figure 14.6. Puppet figurines. Ceramic and pigment. Provenance unknown. Xolalpan phase, A.D. 400–650. Height, 17 cm and 16 cm (approximately 6 1/2 in.). The Saint Louis Art Museum, Gift of Morton D. May, 308:1978 and 231:1978.

burials. Did families have altars? Modern Mexicans often have household altars on which they place images of the saints, incense burners, and other ritual objects.[8] In fact, the modern guards have created such an altar in one of the rooms of Tetitla with an image of the Virgin of Guadalupe. Did specialists like curers use them? Modern curers also sometimes use small figurines in rituals; the figurines may represent either the helping spirits of the curer or the patient. Warren Barbour suggested that curers used puppet figurines, especially in rituals associated with pregnancy.[9] Most of the puppet figurines are female, and because their arms and legs are attached to the torso with strings, they could have been manipulated to inspire a similar result in the human patient. Puppet figures are not restricted to Teotihuacan but have a wide distribution in Mesoamerica both in time and in space.

Who did the figurines represent? Although some Storm God, Fat God, and Flayed God figures exist, most figurines seem to represent human beings. In the later phases of Teotihuacan, when the whole figure was mold-made, the costume was included. There are figures of rulers or leaders on thrones wearing a butterfly, a feline, or a tasseled headdress. Whereas in the murals the elite are represented as ritual performers, in the figurines they are enthroned and frontal. The individual and powerful social world seems to exist in the miniature world of figurines, with its images of men, women, children, rulers. This common clay is the least prestigious of materials; the everyday material, small size, great quantity, and use in ordinary household contexts all suggest the figurines lacked prestige. Though they may have been low down in the hierarchy of values, they were ubiquitous and owned by everybody. And on this low but pervasive level, the image of man and woman is whole—not broken up into body parts and signs. As in the case of the pottery, most often the figurines have not been turned into aesthetic objects. They are simple, straightforward, minimal creations.

Other items of everyday cult use that are almost as ubiquitous as the figurines are mysterious clay objects called *candeleros*. These objects, which all have two small holes, range from minimal blobby forms to textured or simply incised designs; some have faces or, rarely, are in animal effigy form. No other Mesoamerican culture has these objects. Archaeologists have considered them to be miniature incense burners or possibly containers to collect blood drawn in penitential rites. At any rate, like the figurines, they are ritual objects for the population as a whole, perhaps even on the individual level. Whether they were for bloodletting or for incense, they suggest the importance of the ritual activity of the individual and of the entire population. Their haphazard ornamentation suggests more individual variation than rigidly prescribed cult symbolism or ritual requirements.

There is thus a curious hierarchy in Teotihuacan art and architecture. The colossal is, with a few exceptions, reserved for architecture, which vies in scale with the natural landscape. Although a few colossal sculptures exist, most Teotihuacan art was not in large-scale stone. Most sculpture was architectural, attached to balustrades, walls, *tableros*, or roofs. At the other extreme are the millions of clay figurines of people rendered with lively charm and the mysterious ritual objects for the populace. It is hard to imagine these extremes in the same sociopolitical context. The

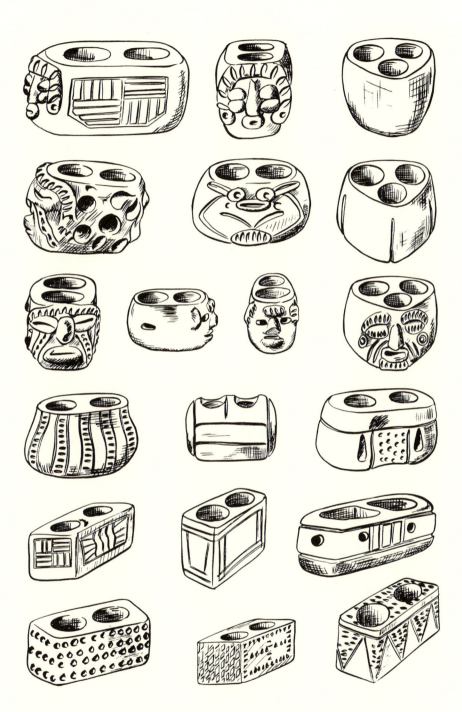

Figure 14.7. *Candeleros*. Clay. Provenance unknown. Tlamimilolpa–Metepec phases, A.D. 250–750. From Séjourné 1966b, fig. 19.

intermediate-size images—the incense burners, the host-figures, the murals, the tripod and sculptural vessels, and the smaller-scale sculptures (like the mouth and fang of the Storm God), are all in pieces—signs, symbols, and body parts are combined to form complex images of man, the gods, and the cosmos. These images create a web (or perhaps in Teotihuacan terms more properly a net?) in which the small people exist. Looking at the visual system another way, one could say that the colossal works of sculpture and architecture and the small figurines suggest the distance between the gods and their surrogate rulers and the people. The murals and other intermediate-scale arts express, in a series of diagrams, the infrastructure that connected people to each other and to the cosmos; the warp and weft of the fabric of Teotihuacan social life. These puzzlelike images of a natural paradise were presented as existing at the price of human sacrifice and were studded with the actively interfering body parts of supernaturals.

XV

An Experiment in Living

TEOTIHUACAN WAS A STATE-LEVEL SOCIETY AND AS SUCH CAN BE EXPECTED to have certain material features such as monumental architecture, an art evoking rulers or deities and showing power relations, craft specialization, and systems of writing and numbering. However, even if a state were to be "typical" (a condition that does not exist), these are very vague parameters for state art. The types of sociopolitical integration that have been called the band, the village, the chiefdom, and the state are generalities that have been derived from individual cultures whose peculiarities and unique features are as dramatic as their shared aspects.

Marcia Ascher and Robert Ascher quote a passage by Gertrude Stein in which she coined the term *insistence* to describe a person or a civilization: "When you first realize the history of various civilizations, that too makes one realize repetition, at the same time the difference of insistence. Every civilization insisted in its own way before it went away."[1] If one considers that the insistence of Egypt, for example, was on the afterworld and preservation, that the insistence of the Maya was on the ritual of dynastic rulers, then the basic insistence of Teotihuacan I would define as the appearance of impersonal order and organization. The mechanics of order and organization are so clear in the city plan, in the murals, in the censers and host-figures as to suggest an obsession. Impersonality is remarkable in the central role of clay and stone masks and the deemphasis of human figures, including the dramatic lack of large-scale sculpture in quantity. A second level of insistence is on nature and the divine, which are conflated as one. Insistent images of a paradisaical, verdant nature—flora and fauna, deities and elites in the act of giving—create a benevolent semblance of flourishing life. Human beings are very small or are merely represented by hearts and footprints in the context of this vital cosmos.

Can these elements be related to state-level organization? A comparison with the contemporary Maya is helpful to elucidate this point. Scholars have attributed the dramatic and personal monuments of the Maya to small, insecure states that created power literally through the process of dynastic theater. In other words, the impressive power shown on the monuments is a wish rather than a reality. The monuments worked, just as "whistling in the dark" works in keeping fear away. The lack of such boastful stone images at Teotihuacan may be indirect proof of the security of a solidly based power that did not have to rely on such propaganda to stay in power. The emphasis on impersonality and order may thus be attributed partly to the level of organization. State-level societies frequently resort to the abstractions of laws, separate from divine or human will as agents of more legitimate power. The appearance of impersonality helps to visualize this. However, other powerful ancient states, in Egypt and Mesopotamia, also erected impressive dynastic monuments, so this organizational aspect of Teotihuacan needs further explanation.

Another aspect of Teotihuacan that may be related to its being an urban state, with craft specialization and markets, is the use of mold making and the creation of an almost "consumer" culture in which standardized images are individually customized, as in the composite censers. This customization results from the presence of a large, reasonably wealthy population at Teotihuacan for whom many of the murals and ritual objects were intended. These features, however, are related not only to levels of integration, but also to Teotihuacan's concept of its identity and its way of visualizing itself.

The Teotihuacan state existed in a historic Mesoamerican context, and the lack of dynastic imagery may have very specific Mesoamerican references. Dynastic art is found in Maya, Olmec, Zapotec, Mixtec, Aztec, and possibly Veracruz cultures. Rulers are a major focus of art in Olmec, Maya, and Mixtec art. At Monte Alban, rather than representing the rulers, artworks show the victims of war with glyphs indicating their name or place of origin. In Aztec art there are clear representations of the rulers Tizoc, Ahuitzotl, and Motecuhzoma II, all identified with their glyphs in scenes of the capture of prisoners, of bloodletting at the dedication of temples or aqueducts, and in life-size portraits in Chapultepec Park carved into the cliffs. Many monuments—including the famous Calendar Stone—have name, place, and date glyphs. The only major Mesoamerican site that has no named rulers or prisoners is Tula, but Tula has several stelae atypical of central Mexico that seem to be provincial imitations of Maya dynastic carvings. Teotihuacan's avoidance of dynastic image making as well as glyphic inscriptions is highly unusual in this Mesoamerican context and suggests that Teotihuacan was avoiding this type of commemoration intentionally as inconsistent with its chosen identity as a "collective" rather than a personified power.

Just as unusual as the rejection of dynastic imagery is the rejection of the ball-game cult. The ball-game cult may have originated early in the Preclassic period in Mesoamerica. In the Classic period all areas of Mesoamerica had ball courts, many with reliefs of ballplayers on the walls. The Maya added the courts, the game, and the ritual to their dynastic cult—the ballplayers represented were the rulers. Teotihuacan is unique in having no ball court, although some scholars have suggested that sections of the Avenue could have functioned as ball courts. Nevertheless, the lack of an actual court suggests that this very distinctive aspect of the cult was not considered important enough to distinguish architecturally. Ballplayer imagery is particularly common at sites with limited or no dynastic art, such as Bilbao, Chichen Itza, and Tajín. We know little of the sociopolitical functions of the game, since most research has focused on its religious symbolism. Games could have been played among rival groups within centers as well as between centers. The division into teams emphasizes dualistic conflict and perhaps ethnic or polity hostilities. In the Postclassic period the ballgame could be the equivalent of war, or perhaps a form of symbolic warfare. Like conquest and sacrifice, the ball game is the ritualization of a conflict situation. Ballgame art usually depicts the players, the sacrifices, and the deities who are invoked. The images do not clearly indicate whether the ball players are specific human players, generic players, characters out of mythology, or a conflation of all three. Whoever they are, they are visualized as human and are represented on a heroic scale acting in a cosmic drama. They are neither clearly gods nor rulers but heroic humans. These images of ritualized conflict in a sacred setting ultimately glorify human activity. Such glorification and aggrandizement of the human is not characteristic of Teotihuacan art.

The people of Teotihuacan evidently played ball games, as the discovery of a marker from La Ventilla and a scene from the murals of Tepantitla indicate, just as they were familiar with glyphs. But they did not use the ball game and its imagery as a part of the state or household cult. In fact, the widespread popularity of the cult in Mesoamerica suggests that its absence at Teotihuacan in an official way was intentional. Something in the ball-game cult did not fit in with the ethos of Teotihuacan, which, as will be discussed below, chose not to glorify conflict.

Many aspects of the uniqueness of Teotihuacan lie in the negation of widespread contemporary or general Mesoamerican practices. Teotihuacan chose to put its emphasis on the world of the sacred in its imagery, which can be compared with the strategy of the Toltecs and the Aztecs.

Dynastic images are present in Toltec and Aztec are, but the more obvious strategy of the elite in those cultures was to create cosmic monuments consisting of deities, humans in ritual postures, and symbolic animals. Although this approach is similar to the Teotihuacan approach in general, it is very different in context and meaning. Most Toltec and Aztec art is monumental sculpture intended for an architectural context, thus rivaling and relating to the traditions of monumental sculpture that had existed since Olmec times. This characteristic was also true of ball-game art, which was either monumental sculpture in architectural contexts or small-scale sculptures worked in semiprecious stones. None of these arts are found in habitations. Moreover, the image of the Toltec and Aztec deities and the cosmos is warlike, conflict ridden, frightening, and malevolent, in great contrast to the harmonious and benevolent aspects stressed in Teotihuacan imagery.

Teotihuacan's strategy in art in Mesoamerica was unique. The Aztecs, Maya, and Olmec share more with one another than any does with Teotihuacan.

What can one make of this insistence? In some of my interpretations throughout this book, I have taken the view that some of these features "mirror" the structure of Teotihuacan. This premise includes first the idea that Teotihuacan presented the appearance of a more collective type of political structure than the more dynastic rulership usually characteristic of Mesoamerica and second, that it was preoccupied by social order and the organization of the first huge city in Mesoamerica rather than by ethnic conflict with its neighbors. I have argued that the myth that was the social glue was the promise of a safe "haven" away from natural cataclysms, such as volcanic eruptions, and the creation of a paradise on earth, which would be provided by the gods if the people of Teotihuacan followed certain rules, rituals, and practices. I have also implied that, because Teotihuacan lasted so long and because its population lived in such well-made habitations, to a certain extent this promise may have been fulfilled.

One can also turn all this information around and interpret it not as a reflection but as a false façade, thus viewing Teotihuacan as an evil empire rather than a utopia. One can look at the verdant universe of the artworks and see it as propaganda (the equivalent of happy people on tractors in the official art of the communists, or the constantly smiling faces in commercial advertising)—not the happy reality, but the façade a segment of society insists on presenting of itself to prove that it is indeed benevolent. One can argue that Teotihuacan was ruled by an absolutely powerful officialdom in an inhuman, totally controlling, and impersonal way.

I propose escaping this either/or scheme not by just suggesting a muddled "middle" course (saying something like "Well, it was a little bit of both") but by looking at some of the paradoxes presented by the city and its art. The paradoxes help avoid too-simple solutions, because they define Teotihuacan insistence on a deeper level.

Collective ideology versus hierarchy

Whatever art forms modern observers look at, we come up against the fact that at Teotihuacan there seems to be equal emphasis on hierarchy and separate but roughly equal units. Thus the Teotihuacan type of order and organization is one in which a great many elements sorted into relatively equal categories seem to be arranged in a hierarchic order.

Standardization versus individualization

Though the overall appearance of arts, including architecture, looks standardized, and standardization appears to have been valued, all arts were also individualized or varied. Like the concept of "fit" that Ascher and Ascher use for the Inca,[2] individualization and variation suggest the importance of the adaptation of buildings and images to local, seasonal, or personal needs.

Boundaries versus liminal spaces

Both in the architecture and in the arts of the city boundaries are set up and divisions are clearly made, and yet boundaries are represented as permeable and as complex spaces of interaction. Because modern observers are obsessed by the buildings, we have yet to consider the life of the streets of Teotihuacan! One can consider the great avenues themselves as both boundaries and places of commingling as important in the life of the city as the pyramids, if not more important.

Fragmentation versus assemblage

The insistence on fragmentation is the most puzzling aspect of Teotihuacan art. I have interpreted it as a way of expressing that the individual is but a small part of a total human or cosmic community and not a totality in him- or herself. Assemblage is a necessary complement of fragmentation, in that the pieces are put together in a new, culturally sanctioned way. As an example of the relationship between assemblage and fragmentation, censers were assembled from pieces and when buried were often disassembled.

Conflict versus harmony

Conflict is the warp and weft of Mesoamerican cosmic and political metaphor. Capture, sacrifice, monstrous blood-demanding deities or spirits are the rule. At Teotihuacan all such conflict is hinted at but not represented directly. The emphasis is usually not on the moment of conflict but on its peaceful aftermath. The weapons, the sacrificial knives, the hearts, the blood, the maguey spines are there, but the stress is on order and harmony. Violence is both present and insistently denied.

Visible contradictions

What is especially striking at Teotihuacan is that the paradoxes listed above exist clearly and have not been smoothed away. For example, in the case of fragmentation versus assemblage, even in the "culturally sanctioned images" the various units are visible. For example, faces are made out of glyphs that continue to look like glyphs. This characteristic suggests a preoccupation with process, with creating an image out of signs and glyphs rather than with the finished creation of an image. If observers could but read the images, Teotihuacan is presenting the naked interior skeleton of its thinking structure in its various open paradoxes.

Artificiality versus nature

This is one of the most interesting of the paradoxes, with the widest ramifications. Teotihuacan is literally a dissertation on the nature/culture problem. The city and the pyramids are presented as both nature and as the work of humans that is superior to nature in a bit of sophistic reasoning worthy of a Medieval Scholastic philosopher. Though the Aztecs thought that the pyramids were built by the gods, the people of Teotihuacan knew that they, or their ancestors, built them. This self-awareness applies to the entire city, its cosmic layout, its apartment compounds, its complex city life so different from the surrounding hills and valleys. Teotihuacan was the largest and densest artificial construct in Mesoamerica in its time. Yet it represented itself and probably "sold" itself as a place of nature. The pyramids were probably "mountains," the caves were real caves, the alignment was related to the stars and planets. The gods were nature gods and brought wealth and fertility. The city covered its walls with images of nature.

The truth of Teotihuacan is, however, not as simple as it seems at first. Clearly the "nature" referred to in the city is not the real nature of the Basin of Mexico. The city is clearly set up as superior to its surrounding natural environment. Its superiority is cultural, residing in its artificiality, its knowledge, its work, its power. This artificiality is not denied—in fact, it is celebrated in all those images that represent the relationship of things in process, in diagrams, in fragments newly put together. The leap of faith occurs in the implication that is then made: that this artificial nature, put together out of bits and pieces by the people of Teotihuacan, is greater than real nature or is the true nature behind the appearance of just plain real nature. Teotihuacan insists that it is nature, but nature reconstituted and improved, as it were, on a secret design of the gods—secret because the rest of nature and other cultures do not share it. That is how the city feels to someone at the site, as if nature itself must have heaved up these walls and pyramids, while at the same time one knows full well that it is a human creation.

Given the time of the creation of Teotihuacan, in the late Preclassic period, in a context with no other great centers yet built in the Valley of Mexico, this dialogue with nature makes sense. Teotihuacan was defining itself against nature and yet claiming to be nature. The Aztecs, who came six hundred years later, defined themselves against the great earlier civilizations, such as Teotihuacan, which they feared they could never rival. Teotihuacan had no such colossal cultures to pit itself against—it literally pitted itself against the stars and the mountains. If there was a cosmic Teotihuacan saga, I imagine it to have been about the necessity of building Teotihuacan on the order of the gods and along the plan presented by the gods, perhaps even to have been the abode of the gods. Do the artworks, the very walls of the city, not protest too much that Teotihuacan is "nature"? Ultimately, this was an economic, social, and political experiment on a colossal scale that was entirely "unnatural" and had to have been created by force and seduction.

Societies may be past or future oriented, traditional or utopian in focus. The Egyptians and the Maya, two of the better-known archaeological cultures, venerated the past, the past history of their ruling houses, and their royal ancestors in heroic portraits and long inscriptions. Teotihuacan was clearly not like them. It may be said to have been utopian in that it seems to have followed an innovative blueprint of a more future-oriented society.[3] Teotihuacan presented itself as a cosmic place, without history or with only a mythological history but without dynastic or political personalities. This may have been an attempt to emphasize its impersonal and natural aspects.

Although unique in many features, Teotihuacan exhibits partial similarities in its ideology, art, and architecture to other early states. These parallels help to check and to expand the interpretations that I have just made. Ancient Egypt and Mesopotamia are our ideas of "typical" early states, with their stone monuments representing rulers, gods, conquests, laws as human events. However, other early states did without stone monuments.

For example, the ancient Chinese art of the Hsia, Shang, and Chou dynasties consists largely of bronze ritual vessels in which often dismembered animal images predominate. There are no images of rulers, conquests, enthronements, or anything humanly heroic. These vessels were made for ancestral veneration and suggest a more collective ritual ethic. Yet inscriptions exist on both vessels and oracle bones, and their presence demonstrates that the ancient Chinese were dynastic and the rulers and their palaces were important. The bronzes were on royal and aristocratic altars. The Chinese royal palace was in the center of a walled town. The towns were laid out on new lands with the streets on a grid plan surrounding the palace. This plan seems to combine dynastic and utopian features. Thus, scholars cannot assume that just because a society does not represent kings, it has no kings. However, the existence of inscriptions in ancient dynastic China does suggest that writing and dynastic rulership are connected, as also noted for Egypt and the Maya. Thus the absence of *both* dynastic imagery and inscriptions at Teotihuacan may indeed suggest an anomaly. The Chinese bronzes are in some ways understated images of power—unlike Maya stelae or Egyptian sculpture—and values other than the overt glorification of rulers seem to have operated in their creation. One is reminded of the writings of Confucius and his frequent injunction that the task of the rulers is the proper performance of ritual. This emphasis on the understatement of service is the opposite of an individual personality cult. Moreover, the animals depicted on the vessels are interpreted as cosmic creatures, many of whom refer to transformation—a topic that was presumably relevant to the rituals in which the rulers used them. Thus ancient China was a cross between a culture with a dynastic focus and one with a cosmic focus.[4]

The only ancient culture that was even more impersonal in its art than Teotihuacan was the Harappan civilization of the Indus Valley. This civilization is particularly mysterious because it has neither writing *nor* figural representation. It is the most "minimal" of ancient civilizations. Mohenjo-Daro and other centers were built on a grid plan aligned to the cardinal points. The buildings had a uniform brick size, and the plans suggest much concern with privacy. All the artifacts are remarkably standardized and plain. There is no architectural ornamentation, no individualization of things, except for the use of seals. There is little clear evidence for a class structure. At the center of the city was a ceremonial complex including a great bath and possibly a granary, but no obvious temples.

Anthropologists have argued that Harappan civilization may have had a more "dispersed" power structure and that its leaders were distinguished by austerity rather than by conspicuous consumption. Daniel Miller suggests a moral ideology not unlike Buddhism and refers to blocks of cells that could have been reserved for the ruling monks.[5] He compares Harappan civilization to Puritanism and to the European Protestant work ethic that limited consumption while encouraging enterprise—since the Harappan civilization was successful economically. Noting that the concept would not have meant the same thing as in modern times, Miller refers to the ideology of Harappan civilization as "egalitarian" on the basis of the nature of its material remains.

Teotihuacan seems to fit somewhere between the austere Harappan model and the dynastic Chinese one: without clear evidence of a dynasty, except for early in its history, but with clear class divisions and a highly developed art. Its daily utensils are simple as the Harappan ones and show a similar minimalist love of basic forms; but its murals and other objects are structurally similar to the complex bronzes of China. One can imagine the Chinese bronze decor as the equivalent of Teotihuacan murals and find in its decorative, symbolic, and structural qualities many parallels to Teotihuacan art. Even the concepts of play and ingenuity within strictly set limits are similar.

A third parallel to Teotihuacan is the domestic sphere of the Roman empire, with its homes covered in murals as at Pompeii, suggesting a well-to-do social sector with access to art and a rich ritual life. However, nothing at Teotihuacan resembles the Roman portraits and deities carved in stone.

One of the major preoccupations of many early states is the integration of a large population into a coherent whole. I have suggested that at Teotihuacan internal integration may have been complex and multifaceted, if the arts are an indication of ideology and practice. More specifically, however, Mesoamerican parallels are not of much help, since no other Mesoamerican city or culture was quite like Teotihuacan. The emphasis on structure and relationships in Teotihuacan art reminded me strongly of the societies of the Andes, such as the Inca. Although scholars know that the Inca were ruled by powerful kings, no art represented and venerated kings—after death their actual mummies were kept and brought out for rituals. Figurative arts were very few and were found mainly in gold, which the Spanish conquerors melted down. Abstract rock shrines were carved in sacred places in which the forms of nature were evoked. As such, the model of a cosmic art form and a dynastic context among the Inca is not unlike that of ancient China. The Inca model is interesting because rich sixteenth-century sources permit detailed reconstruction of its social integration.

The city of Cuzco was divided into *ayllus*, or clans, each of which had its residential area. Each clan had a shrine for which it cared one day out of the year. The shrines, both in and around Cuzco, numbered close to 360 and were arranged on forty lines, or *ceque*, which began at the Temple of the Sun in Cuzco. The shrines clearly were also related to the solar calendar. Within this system social structure and families, shrines, and the calendar were related.[6]

Although I do not suggest a *ceque* system existed in Teotihuacan, the multiplicity of three-temple complexes, Avenue temples, apartment compounds, and the interest in structure lead me to wonder whether some formalized system linking society, religion, and calendar (different from that of the rest of Mesoamerica) did not also exist. I am assuming that something existed because the usual integrating mechanisms of Mesoamerica—intergroup feuding and ritualized hostilities such as the ball game—seem to have been missing or down-played. Because Teotihuacan emphasized structure, order, and harmony, I am postulating some integrative mechanism in which ritual, calendar, society, and politics were brought together like the *ceque* system of Peru.

I have long noted that Teotihuacan art and culture were in many ways an anomaly in Mesoamerica and that Teotihuacan's insistence on structure and harmony was more characteristic of the Pre-Columbian arts of Peru. The art of the Central Andes lacks both writing and the flamboyantly dramatic representation of human and deity figures, especially in stone sculpture. The Inca road system, the Nazca "lines in the desert," the complex textile techniques, and the knotted string recording device (*quipu*) are all structurally complex but visually quite minimal. Peruvian styles in all media are consistently abstract in form and play mental games with the viewer rather than being naturalistic narrative, and illusionistic.

One major exception to this pattern exists in Peru, and that is the art of the Moche (200 B.C.–600 A.D.), which is quite "Mesoamerican" in feeling. Moche art is naturalistic, dramatic, and narrative and insists on conflict or interaction, whether violent or erotic. In many ways Moche art is reminiscent of Maya art, and it is no coincidence that one of the major scholars of Moche art, Elizabeth Benson, is also a Mayanist. Moche art has as little echo in the later art of Peru as Teotihuacan does in Mesoamerica—it's as if Moche art never happened.

The Central Andean and Mesoamerican examples illustrate that entire cultural areas have a dominant form of insistence that characterizes them for most of their history and channels individual cultures within them into certain directions. We often attribute these insistences to ecological and geographic conditions, social conditions, the early development of certain arts, or even "chance," as in the great significance of initial conditions as defined in chaos theory. (The importance of initial conditions can be seen in the so-called butterfly effect: a butterfly flapping its wing in Singapore, creating a hurricane in Hawaii.) In fact, however, we have very little idea of how large-scale insistencies originate and are sustained over time. We do not know why anthropomorphic representation in clay figurines, introduced into both Peru and Mesoamerica from Central America and the Northern Andes, took hold and became important in Mesoamerican but not in Peru.

The examples of the Moche and of Teotihuacan arts and cultures show, however, that despite the prevailing insistence of a culture area, a given society can—under special circumstances and for reasons of its own—

develop in quite a different and perhaps even an opposite direction. (I am in no position to speculate whether Moche art was in contact with Mesoamerica, perhaps by way of Ecuador, and if the similarities are due to diffusion, but I am convinced that even if diffusion is a factor, it is the local conditions of the Moche that account for the special features of the Moche arts.) I am quite certain that the similarities I sense between Teotihuacan and Peruvian art are not the result of diffusion. No possibility of significant cultural contact between Teotihuacan and the Central Andes exists. Even if diffusion were to be the case in the Moche example, I very much doubt that an entire culture would be created on the model of a very different foreign one, unless conquered and colonized or in some other way "converted."

What the Andean and Mesoamerican cultural histories demonstrate is that civilizations develop in quite different styles, which mirror and promote different sociopolitical structures and views of the universe, and that escaping these mental templates is not an easy matter. But it is not impossible, and cultures do (rarely, to be sure) develop against the prevailing norms, trying new forms of sociopolitical integration as well as arts. I therefore see Teotihuacan as a rebellion against the norms of Mesoamerican life and art, an experiment in living differently, and the creation of an "Andean" style culture out of Mesoamerican building blocks. I imagine that the people of Teotihuacan would have been fascinated by objects such as the Tello Obelisk with its design of a male and female cayman giving plants, the Gateway God at Tiahuanaco with its anonymous attendants, the endlessly varied and complicated Paracas embroidered beings, and the fragmented and distorted Huari textiles. They would have been fascinated by a world of nuanced image systems without writing.

In contrast to the arts of Teotihuacan, which go against many Mesoamerican traditions, the Classic Maya arts are an exceptional intensification of the dynastic, asethetic, glyphic tendencies of Mesoamerican art since the time of the Olmecs. Teotihuacan and the Maya culture are interesting not only as extremes of contrast, but also because they were largely contemporary. Scholarly interpretation of the Maya culture usually takes into consideration the arts and symbolisms of other Mesoamerican cultures to which it is closely related, whereas access to Teotihuacan art and culture is more difficult to achieve through comparison with other Mesoamerican cultures.

I have suggested that the unusual aspect of Teotihuacan might be the result of historic events surrounding its founding (an initial "butterfly effect.") The trauma of the eruption of Xitle and its relationship to Cuicuilco perhaps led some minds to question the very nature of traditional society and religion and led certain individuals to devise a utopian new culture that would avoid cosmic disaster. These features included a focus on the cosmic and natural worlds rather than on the human and dynastic worlds, resulting in a political organization that was in some ways highly central- ized and heirarchic but that also structured very clearly the relationships, rights, and responsibilities of the population. Traditionally, Mesoameri- can societies were more open and less systemic. A greater emphasis on structured system seems to have been a Teotihuacan defensive measure.

I am not the first to think of an Andean parallel. Linda Manzanilla has looked for (but has not conclusively found) storage facilities at Teotihua- can similar to storage systems characteristic of Andean empires and less so of Mesoamerican ones.[7]

Judging by the plan of the city, life at Teotihuacan appears to have been much more structured and organized than in the rest of Mesoamerica. The psychological factors that may have led to this structuring were fear of cos- mic upheaval and a sense of common defense. The Aztecs, too, used fear of the end of the world as a religious rallying cry, but they employed it to create massive sacrificial violence as a form of social control. Although we do not know the extent of sacrifice at Teotihuacan, I imagine it to have been more carefully choreographed and exquisitely set up rather than em- phasizing blood. (Note in this context the beautiful dress of the military sacrifical victims in the Ciudadela.) In Teotihuacan, the specific fear of lo- cal volcanism may have been used to create a well-organized, disciplined society that put collective values first, presumably ready to deal with emer- gencies if they arose. Harmony and cooperation were more crucial to this view of the world than were violent confrontations.

The great pyramids literally put the gods on notice that here was a culture ready to deal with them on their own terms and nothing was go- ing to stop it from succeeding. Behind all the terrifying Aztec images, one can sense a great, bullying insecurity. By contrast, Teotihuacan gives the impression of a secure bastion of ordered civilization. This is largely a result of its architecture, which is breathtakingly spacious. There are an- cient sites in other parts of the world more dramatically situated, there are buildings more rich in carving or articulation, but no other ancient ceremonial precinct in the world comes close to Teotihuacan in size and grandeur. Teotihuacan seems to have been the dream of architects who, like our modern Frank Lloyd Wrights or Le Corbusiers, had utopian ideas for mankind and dreamed of total control over living and visual expression within their walls.

Besides some very special initial circumstances that must have accounted for the founding of Teotihuacan and the creation of an unusual sociopolitical order, Teotihuacan must have developed an ideology that helped to maintain the system for more than seven hundred years. Scholars have indulged in considerable debate about whether ideology can effect or even seriously affect major sociopolitical and economic developments. The historical materialist position is that the causative aspects of society lie in ecology and economy and that aspects such as art and religion are secondary phenomena that merely justify and mystify these realities. The idealist position holds that ideologies can be just as causal as economics in creating cultural change, since people select even practical courses of action only if these are in line with their belief systems.

The role of ideology and utopian experiments in living are highlighted by examples from recent history in which rebellion against "tradition" is historically known. The communist states of Eastern Europe are an example of a utopian ideology imposed by force and with the help of a foreign power. The ideology included everything from economics to the aesthetics of school uniforms. It is clear now, that the communist states collapsed for economic reasons: their badly planned economies were unable to compete with capitalist markets. But the collapse was not purely economic; it had an ideological component that only now is becoming clear.

Eastern Europeans did not really hate the egalitarian ideology trumpeted by the communists and are in fact quite shocked and upset by the inequalities now created by the market economy for which they are psychologically unprepared. What they hated in the communist system was the lie: the fact that the leaders preached egalitarianism but actually lived a life of conspicuous consumption like the aristocrats of feudal times. This cynicism about rulers is also true of the former Soviet Union, where communism was a local revolt against the czars and not imposed from the outside. The luxurious life of the elite and their violent and capricious extermination of their opponents, outdoing the political violence of their predecessors, undermined the system morally. There are heavy costs in ruling by fear, and people saw no point in working hard for a corrupt elite. Had the communist leaders lived as simply as they forced everyone else to live, they might have had some spiritual authority. Had they been benevolent, they might have been loved. (After all, in times past, autocratic kings knew how to make themselves loved and popular.)

The example of communist powers in the twentieth century indicates the limits of force a state can employ, the necessity for an ideology that can be believed in by the population and a ruling elite seen to be functioning benevolently toward society. It also indicates the necessity of an economic system that is competitive with the other systems coexisting in its world.

The other example relevant to the discussion of Teotihuacan is the development of the United States. The United States is an anomaly among the states of the world for a number of reasons. Unlike most Old World cultures with long feudal and royal histories, the United States was an eighteenth-century utopian experiment, born out of a very special set of circumstances never duplicated. The colonization of the Americas was, for Europeans, a great opportunity to expand into new territory and experiment with new ways of living. In most places, however, long-lived colonial cultures bound the new territories to European host countries and their political and religious systems. In the United States the "experiment" succeeded—the breaking away from monarchic rule, the creation of democracy based on eighteenth-century ideas of the rights of man, and the subsequent birth of the ideology of "equality of opportunity." Unlike the communist system, which worked by force and moral imperatives not believed in, the ideology of the United States works through the seduction of the promise of better times to come and a reasonable possiblity for ordinary people to benefit from the riches of capitalism. The seduction works: people want to come to the United States. Whereas in a communist state people were willing to be poor if that state agreed to take care of them and equality of poverty was guaranteed, in the United States people are willing to be poor, not be taken care of by the state, on the assumption that someday, by pluck or luck, they might be well-off. Despite its ideology of equality, the United States has managed to "enchant" inequality as something to admire and strive for. While the capitalist market system may be the basis of the success of the United States, it egalitarian ideology with the promise of future well-being is extremely important in creating a dynamic and positive frame of mind in its citizens.

The ideological method of the United States, which is seduction rather than force, has worked remarkably well in association with the inequalities of the capitalistic system. Like the gods of Teotihuacan, the corporate advertisers of the United States promise riches and happiness to those who play by the rules. Like the Statue of Liberty, which beckons with its torch, the Teotihuacan Goddess seductively gives water, seeds, and jades. Though some murals at Teotihuacan showed her with clawed hands and conducting the expected discipline and sacrifice of its populace, the images of abundance are more prevalent. Teotihuacan seems to have presented more images of "carrots" than "sticks" in maintaining the allegiance of its population.

Besides natural abundance the Teotihuacan elite promised order, in contrast to the greater chaos evident everywhere else in Mesoamerica. At the same time, however, the elite seem to have practiced a show of austerity that appears to have been convincing. That the elite were concerned in maintaining a show of moral legitimacy is suggested to me in the images and structures that celebrate collective values and only a modest glorification of leadership.

In sum, Teotihuacan was created as an experiment in living and was in many ways different from its neighbors in Mesoamerica—one can almost see it as a critique. This experiment may have been the result of special initial circumstances and some gifted individuals (not unlike the men the United States considers its "Founding Fathers") who set up a novel political system for a state.

Is it possible now to create the "portrait" of Teotihuacan out of its scattered elements? (By Teotihuacan I mean both the elite and the population that participated in a common culture and left material things behind.) Teotihuacan emerges as both incredibly grandiose and remarkably unpretentious in it architecture and artistic things, a combination that is highly unusual—overwhelming and disarming at once. Despite the lack of interest in inscriptions, its art and architecture are highly cerebral and intellectual and require the viewer to think. Although clearly interested in artistic forms to express a variety of concepts, the artists left behind little sign of self-conscious "aestheticism," which makes the artwork accessible. Although there is an overall insistence on order on a macro-scale, there is a great deal of variation on the micro-scale.

These aspects of the "portrait" suggest a culture that was ordered but not regimented, with a rich intellectual and artistic life that was not turned into exclusive cults, and a milieu that was both grand and everyday. By devising an "Andean" style of order over a "Mesoamerican" tradition of drama, Teotihuacan created a "balanced" culture that was uniquely placed both geographically and ideologically to be the great power of its time. It was probably as much of a mystery to its neighbors as it is to us, and unsurprisingly its images and practices were more emulated by its neighbors than Teotihuacan ever emulated them.

How and why did Teotihuacan fail? Signs of burning were noted throughout the site by archaeologists working in the 1920s and 1930s. At that time archaeologist assumed that another people had come, conquered Teotihuacan, and burned it. Recent analysis by Rubén Cabrera and René Millon has shown that the burning was restricted to the ceremonial section of the city and that Teotihuacan was unlikely to have been indiscriminately put to the torch by an invading army.[8] Current evidence suggests that Teotihuacan collapsed internally, but in the absence of a history, external invaders cannot be completely ruled out. The ceremonial areas were burned and abandoned. Slowly people moved out of the city into hamlets, villages, and small towns dotting the landscape, resuming the settlement patterns that had existed before the rise of Teotihuacan. Never again did the entire population of the valley live in a single city—not until the giant modern Mexico City grew to 16 million people in the last twenty years.

How could this collapse have come about? According to Millon's reconstruction of the last years of Teotihuacan, there is no evidence of cultural or economic decline, although Teotihuacan's contacts with other cultures were less intensive after A.D. 600. Clearly projects were going on at Teotihuacan; large blocks of greenstone were in the palaces not yet cut into masks or figures. The colossal statue of the Goddess was still unfinished in the quarries of Coatlinchan. The burning makes sense as the sign of an internal dispute, some kind of factional fighting or attempted coup d'etat. Great destruction in the palaces of the Ciudadela suggests political turmoil. In Teotihuacan, as elsewhere in Mesoamerica, ritual fires were often set when a building was renewed or enlarged, and Millon argues that such a ritual burning may have been the occasion for a political maneuver that got out of hand: the fires were greater than expected, and the fighting destroyed or paralyzed the governing elite. More evidence of an internal collapse is the fact that the ceremonial and administrative section of the city was burned rather than apartment compounds, as would be expected if invaders had set fires indiscriminately.

If Millon's scenario is correct, it suggests that the balanced system of Teotihuacan integration began to fall apart toward A.D. 700. The material evidence for this scenario is minimal. The process of moving back outside the city began before A.D. 600, although the city was not yet losing population. The presence of enthroned figurines is especially important in the Metepec phase (A.D. 600–750), suggesting either more personalized rule or greater emphasis on personalized rulership in the cults of the households. Researchers also have suggested an ecological theory of collapse: to burn the huge quantities of limestone that were needed to make all the plaster necessary to surface the Avenue and buildings, Teotihuacan may have cut down the forests of the surrounding hills.[9] This deforestation may have led to poorer retention of water in the soil, resulting in the failure of crops.

The collapse, however, was also the collapse of a social system and an ideology. In no other Mesoamerican culture was everyone collected in one vast city. Multifamily apartment compounds were never again built in Mesoamerica. Yet the people who moved away from the great city continued to grow maize and to grind it, to mine obsidian, to carve, to paint, to weave, to create featherwork. The personifications of nature continued to be worshipped in one form or another. The Storm God went on quite easily to become Tlaloc, one the the great gods of the Aztecs, maintaining his features and presumably some of his cult. Xipe Totec, the Old God, some Goddess versions of Aztec times have their roots in Teotihuacan. Animal symbols—such as the feathered serpent, the jaguar, raptorial birds, butterflies—continued in later art. It is clear that both the Toltecs and Aztecs, successor states in the Basin of Mexico that were more typically "Mesoamerican," had mythical traditions about Teotihuacan, visited and copied its images, and dug around in the ruined platforms looking for heirlooms and treasures. But if the Spanish records are correct, their knowledge about Teotihuacan was extremely limited. It was a place of awe and mystery, of old rulers, the gathering place of the gods. They had no information on its history, social structure, or religion. For the Aztecs, as for many readers of popular books, it might as well have been left by invaders from outer space.

The discontinuity between Teotihuacan and its successor cultures is therefore great. The particular form and the importance of the Goddess disappeared with the city. The net-jaguar occurs nowhere else and remains a total mystery. Whatever status the tasseled headdress signified at Teotihuacan, it too disappeared from the insignia of gods and rulers in later Mesoamerica. Similarly, the entire system of signs and symbols, body parts put together in complex combinations that are tantalizingly close to writing (but equally insistently not writing) disappeared, and with it the mind-set that created it. (Perhaps some of the codifiers of Postclassic religious codices reworked what remained of the Teotihuacan system into books, but these are already different enough so as not to be of much help in understanding Teotihuacan.) These material manifestations of what was lost are reflections of a sociopolitical order that was similarly never recreated in the later cultures. This suggests that Teotihuacan arose out of a very special set of circumstances out of which a complex and delicately balanced sociopolitical structure was created that was never again duplicated int the history of Mesoamerica.

POSTSCRIPT: THE LANGUAGE OF TEOTIHUACÁN

A Nahuatl language for Teotihuacan is suggested on the basis of the fact that no place-names in other languages survive in the Valley of Mexico, other than those of historic languages, and especially Nahuatl. Though much about Teotihuacan history was lost in the subsequent centuries, it is hard to believe that the name of such an important city also disappeared. Given what we know of the nature of Teotihuacan, some version of "The Place of the Gods" seems like a reasonable name. This issue of names includes geographic features such as rivers and volcanoes. Xitle (or Xitli) is a Nahuatl name, possibly derived from "navel" according to Doris Heyden.

If the language was not Nahuatl, some Teotihuacan names may still be preserved if they were systematically translated into Nahuatl, at least as to their original sense of meanings and word combinations.

Notes

PREFACE

1. White 1987, p. 14.

CHAPTER I

1. Bobula 1967.
2. Hevesy 1928.
3. Dioszegi 1963.
4. Von Sadovsky 1989.
5. Séjourné 1966 a, b, c.
6. Séjourné 1956.
7. Pasztory 1990, p. 181 n. 1
8. R. Millon 1973.
9. C. Millon 1962.
10. Caso 1942.
11. Armillas 1945.
12. Fraser 1962.
13. Hobbes 1991.
14. Mendelssohn 1974.

CHAPTER II

1. Lopez Luján 1989.
2. Sahagún quoted in León Portilla 1963, p. 167.
3. Umberger 1987b.
4. Jiménez-Moreno 1941.
5. See Gamio 1922, pp. 102–3.
6. Bancroft 1882, vol. 4, p. 543 n.89.
7. Charnay 1887, p. 132.
8. Hamy 1882.

9. Pasztory 1974.
10. Caso 1942.
11. Seler 1902–23.
12. Séjourné 1956.
13. von Winning 1948.
14. Kubler 1962, pp. 29 and 38.
15. Seler 1915, pp. 419–20.
16. Gamio 1922, p. 107.
17. R. Millon, Drewitt, and Bennyhoff 1965.
18. Armillas 1947.
19. Pasztory 1983a, pp. 278–80.
20. Feest 1990.
21. Nicholson 1957.
22. Pasztory 1984.
23. Lafaye 1974.
24. Séjourné 1956.
25. Caso and Bernal 1952, pp. 113–16.
26. Caso 1958, p. 75.
27. Kidder, Jennings, and Shook 1946.
28. Schele and Miller 1986.
29. See Edmonson 1974.
30. Pasztory 1983a.

CHAPTER III

1. Hodder 1986.
2. Schliemann 1989; Dorpfeld 1902.
3. Jiménez Moreno 1941.
4. Willey and Sabloff 1974.
5. Warren Barbour personal communication 1992.
6. Spence 1974.
7. Pasztory 1983a, p. 106.
8. R. Millon 1973, 1981; Armillas 1950.
9. Willey 1953.
10. Carr and Hazard 1961; Blanton 1978.
11. Sanders, Parsons, and Santley 1979.
12. For general surveys see Service 1962; Johnson and Earle 1987. For Mesoamerica see Sanders and Price 1968.
13. Wittfogel 1957.
14. Carneiro 1981.
15. Haas 1982.
16. Sanders and Price 1968.
17. R. Millon 1973.
18. Sanders and Michels 1977.
19. Santley 1989.
20. Spence 1981.
21. Clark 1986.
22. Rattray 1990.

23. Linda Manzanilla indicated a problem with the market at Teotihuacan (1992), and I questioned the pilgrimage-center concept (1992c).

24. Evelyn Rattray personal communication 1991.

25. Sanders, Parsons, and Santley 1979.

26. Sanders 1965.

27. R. Millon 1981, p. 235.

28. R. Millon 1993.

CHAPTER IV

1. For example, Séjourné called Zacuala a palace in 1959.

2. Séjourné 1966 a, b, c.

3. Linné 1934, 1942.

4. R. Millon personal communication 1970.

5. Linné 1942.

6. Pasztory 1988a.

7. Cowgill 1983.

8. Manzanilla 1992.

9. Cowgill 1983.

10. R. Millon 1992.

11. Pasztory 1988a, 1992b.

12. Sempowski 1983.

13. R. Millon 1992a.

14. Pasztory 1986.

15. Berlo 1982.

16. Linné 1942.

17. Berlo 1984.

18. Pasztory 1992c.

19. Ortner 1974.

CHAPTER V

1. Nicholson 1971; Klein 1988.

2. Spranz 1964.

3. Joralemon 1971.

4. William T. Sanders personal communication, review of this manuscript 1993.

5. Seler 1904–09, 1902–23. Seler's study of the Codex Borgia is the most detailed demonstration of his method.

6. Pasztory 1983a, p. 250.

7. Newman 1992.

8. Adams personal communication 1970.

9. Kubler 1967; Langley 1986; Pasztory 1988a.

10. Following Roland Barthes as quoted in Pasztory 1992b.

11. R. Millon 1993.

12. Caso 1966; von Winning 1987.

13. Langley 1986, p. 75.

14. Langley 1986, pp. 75–80, Pasztory 1974.

15. Pasztory 1973a, 1974.
16. C. Millon 1988.
17. These were the terms I chose to use in Pasztory 1983a.
18. Contreras 1991.
19. Pasztory 1988a, p. 70.
20. Pasztory 1992b.
21. R. Millon 1992a; Berlo 1992.

CHAPTER VI

1. Heyden 1975.
2. Manzanilla 1990 and personal communication 1991.
3. Pasztory 1983a, pp. 109–14; Matos Moctezuma 1982.
4. Pasztory 1987, p. 453; Nagao 1985, pp. 64–70.
5. Umberger 1987, p. 428–37.
6. Pasztory 1988b.
7. Sanders, Parsons, and Santley 1979.
8. R. Millon 1981.
9. I would like to thank Debra Nagao for research on volcanism and Cuicuilco. Doris Heyden, Gabriel Espinosa Pineda, Alejandro Robles, and Druzo Maldonado provided helpful information. I am especially indebted to Ana Lillian Martin del Pozzo of the UNAM Instituto de Geofisica for explaining specific points. Much of this text is based on Cordova, Martin del Pozzo, and Lopez Camacho 1995.
10. A date of A.D. 400 is given in Cordova F. de A, Martin del Pozzo, and Lopez Camacho 1994, but 50 B.C. is now considered more accurate in Martin del Pozzo, Cordova, and Lopez Camacho 1995.
11. Cordova F. de A., Martin del Pozzo, and Lopez Camacho 1994, p. 589.
12. Navarrete 1991; Schavelzon 1983.
13. Cordova F. de A., Martin del Pozzo, and Lopez Camacho 1994; Martin del Pozzo, Cordova, and Lopez Camacho 1995.
14. Heizer and Bennyhoff 1972.
15. Aveni 1980, pp. 236 and 312, and personal communication 1995.
16. R. Millon 1993.
17. R. Millon 1992a.
18. R. Millon lists all astronomical studies prior to 1981. See 1981 n. 4.
19. R. Millon 1993; Coggins 1993.
20. Many of these carved stones are still visible at the foot of the pyramid.
21. Heyden 1981.
22. Taube 1986.
23. Pasztory 1973a.
24. von Winning 1987, pp. 135–40, C. Millon 1988, pp. 227–28.
25. Taube 1983.
26. Pasztory 1976a, pp. 146–79.
27. R. Millon 1992a.
28. Sahagún 1963, vol. 11, p. 247.
29. Olivera 1969.
30. Rands 1955, p. 345.
31. Gamio 1922, vol. 1, p. 315.

32. Pasztory 1976a, pp. 167–68.

33. Grove 1987.

34. Spranz 1970.

35. R. Millon 1973.

36. Berlo 1992.

37. Berlo 1992. There is no more evidence for either argument. If they are ancestors, they appear in the form of deities, in which case the distinction is moot. I argue the reverse, that they are deities but personalized to fit family and situation.

38. Barbour considers these hollow figures males as well as females depending on the position of the leg. Berlo (1992) sees them as female. The womblike interior with small figures inside suggests feminine qualities of nurturing and gestation to me, and in that sense I consider them generically feminine.

39. Ortner 1974.

CHAPTER VII

1. R. Millon in 1993.

2. Aveni and Hartung 1982.

3. Townsend 1992.

4. Pasztory 1976a, pp. 127–38.

5. Tobriner 1972, p. 113.

6. We do not know why this figure is battered, whether it is due to sixteenth-century zeal in smashing idols or some other reason. Nor do we know why the other is well preserved.

7. Von Winning 1987, pp. 135–40.

8. Sarro 1991.

9. R. Millon 1988b sums up our current knowledge of Teotihuacan and its external relations.

10. Coggins 1979.

11. Schele and Freidel 1990.

12. Marcus 1983.

13. Coggins 1993.

14. Pasztory 1973b, Fig. 9.

15. Coggins 1993.

16. Evelyn Rattray personal communication 1991.

17. Pasztory 1974.

18. García Cook 1981, Figs. 8. 4–5.

19. Langley 1986, pp. 75–80.

20. Schele and Freidel 1990, pp. 130–216.

21. Manzanilla 1993.

22. Pasztory 1983a, pp. 152–55.

CHAPTER VIII

1. Cowgill 1983.

2. Both Cowgill and R. Millon called the Ciudadela the equivalent of Peking's "Forbidden City." Cowgill 1983; R. Millon 1973 and in conversation.

3. Caso and Bernal 1952, pp. 113–16.

4. Pasztory 1988a.
5. Sugiyama 1989.
6. López-Austin, Lopez Luján, and Sugiyama 1991.
7. Taube 1992.
8. Schele and Freidel 1990, pp. 96–129.
9. A. Miller 1973, pp. 164–65.
10. Linné 1942.
11. C. Millon 1973.
12. R. Millon 1973; Cowgill 1983.
13. Pendergast 1971.
14. Cabrera Castro, Sugiyama, Cowgill 1991.
15. William T. Sanders personal communication 1993.
16. R. Millon 1993.
17. Pasztory 1983a, Pl. 23.
18. C. Millon 1973, 1988.
19. Pasztory 1988b.
20. R. Millon 1988a.
21. C. Millon 1988.

CHAPTER IX

1. Such ideas are evident in Hardoy 1968; Stierlin 1968, 19; Heyden and Gendrop 1988; Kubler 1962.
2. Sarro 1991.
3. Christian Feest personal communication 1991. Even the geological identifications of the stones are incorrect.
4. Linné 1934, 1942.
5. Westheim 1965, p. 142.
6. Jarquin Pacheco and Martinez Vargas 1982, pp. 110, 113; Sánchez Sánchez 1982, p. 270, Fig. 8.
7. Linné 1934, Fig. 275. The drawing is a reconstruction—the original was only a fragment.
8. Cabrera Castro, Rodriguez García, and Morelos García 1982 a, b; Batres 1906.
9. Josué Saenz personal communication 1989.
10. Evelyn Rattray personal communication 1990.
11. Sanders, 1965.
12. Rattray 1990.
13. Rattray n.d.
14. William T. Sanders personal communication 1993.
15. Marvin Cohodas personal communication 1994.

CHAPTER X

1. Millon, Drewitt, Bennyhoff 1965, Fig. 95.
2. Pasztory 1974; Berrin and Pasztory 1993, cat. no. 117
3. Pasztory 1988a, p. 54.
4. Cabrera Castro, Rodriguez García, Morelos García 1982a, b.
5. von Winning 1987, vol. 2, pp. 15–16.

6. Barbour 1976, pp. 137–41, and personal communication 1984.
7. Langley 1986.
8. Langley 1986, p. 155.
9. Klein 1991.
10. Coggins 1993.
11. Barbour 1986.
12. Ball 1974.
13. Cabrera Castro, Rodriguez García, Morelos García 1982 a, b.
14. Batres 1905.
15. Rubén Cabrera Castro personal communication and visit 1983.
16. Cabrera Castro, Rodriguez García, and Morelos García, 1982b.
17. Pasztory 1988a, pp. 63–64.
18. Coggins 1993.

CHAPTER XI

1. A. Miller 1978, p. 64, Fig. 2.
2. Pasztory 1990–91.
3. Pasztory 1990–91.
4. Pasztory 1990–91, p. 120.
5. Pasztory 1988a, p. 70.
6. LaGamma 1991.
7. In 1987 George Cowgill showed me a computer-generated map of Teotihuacan that indicated evidence for mural painting distributed pretty much throughout the city. Though at first I thought the mural paintings belonged to especially rich or influential families, I rewrote my study (1988a) on the basis of the broad distribution of mural paintings. Recently, René Millon argued that mural painting was limited to a few "noble" families (1992a). More archaeological evidence needs to be presented on this issue before the case can be decided one way or the other.
8. Schapiro 1969.
9. Pendergast 1979.
10. Marcus 1992.
11. Pasztory 1992a.
12. Pasztory 1988a, pp. 189–93.
13. C. Millon 1988.
14. Pasztory 1976a.
15. Caso 1966, 1967.
16. Pasztory 1988a, pp. 137–61.
17. Ostrowitz 1991.
18. Charnay 1887, p. 146.
19. Gombrich 1979.
20. Pasztory 1990–91.

CHAPTER XII

1. Séjourné 1956.
2. Matos Moctezuma 1982.
3. Pasztory 1992a.

4. C. Millon 1988, p. 217.
5. Boone 1984.
6. Pasztory 1983b; Demarest 1984.
7. C. Millon 1988; Klein 1987; Schele and Miller 1986.
8. Mack 1987.
9. Bataille 1962; Hamerton–Kelly 1987; Girard 1977; Valeri 1985.
10. Klausewitz 1976, p. 87.
11. León Portilla 1963, pp. 113, 114, 126, 143.
12. León Portilla 1963, p. 114.
13. René Millon personal communication 1992.
14. Cowgill 1992.

CHAPTER XIII

1. Pasztory 1974.
2. Klein (1980).
3. Taube 1992.
4. Pasztory 1983a, Pl. 277.
5. Pasztory 1983a, Pl. 113.
6. Kubler 1967.
7. Sahagún 1950–78, Book 2, pp. 1–2.
8. Langley 1986, pp. 143–52.

CHAPTER XIV

1. Wicke 1954.
2. C. Millon 1988.
3. Hvidtfeldt 1958.
4. Séjourné 1956; Pasztory 1990, p. 181, n. 1.
5. Pasztory 1992c.
6. Berger and Luckmann 1966.
7. Barbour 1976.
8. Seler 1915, Pl. 10.
9. Barbour 1976.

CHAPTER XV

1. Ascher and Ascher 1981, p. 38.
2. Ascher and Ascher 1981, p. 52.
3. Pasztory 1992a.
4. Chang 1983.
5. D. Miller 1985. I would like to thank George Cowgill for bringing this issue and article to my attention.
6. Zuidema 1990.
7. Manzanilla 1992.
8. R. Millon 1988a.
9. Lorenzo 1968.

Bibliography

Armillas, Pedro. 1945. "Los dioses de Teotihuacán." *Anales, Instituto de Etnografía Americana* 35–61.

———. 1947. "La serpiente emplumada, Quetzalcoatl, y Tlaloc." *Cuadernos Americanos* 6: 161–78.

———. 1950. "Teotihuacan, Tula, y los Toltecas: Las culturas post-arcaicas y per-aztecas del centro de Mexico. Excavaciones y estudios, 1922–1950." *Runa*, Buenos Aires, pts. 1–2, 37–70.

Ascher, Marcia, and Robert Ascher. 1981. *Code of the Quipu: A Study in Media, Mathematics, and Culture.* Ann Arbor: University of Michigan Press.

Aveni, Anthony F. 1980. *Skywatchers of Ancient Mexico.* Austin: University of Texas Press.

Aveni, Anthony S., and Horst Hartung. 1982. "New Observations of the Pecked Cross Petroglyph." In *Space and Time in the Cosmovision of Mesoamerica*, ed. F. Tichy. Lateinamerika Studien, vol. 10, 25–42. Vancouver: 43rd International Congress of Americanists.

Ball, J. W. 1974. "A Teotihuacán-Style Cache from the Maya Lowlands." *Archaeology* 27: 2–9.

Bancroft, Hubert Howe. 1882. *The Native Races: The Works of Hubert Howe Bancroft.* 5 vols. San Francisco: A. L. Bancroft.

Barbour, Warren T. D. 1976. "The Figurines and Figurine Chronology of Ancient Teotihuacán, Mexico." Ph.D., Department of Anthropology, University of Rochester.

———. 1986. "Shadow and Substance: The Iconography of Host Figures Associated with Ancient Teotihuacan, Mexico." Paper presented at meeting, The Society for American Archaeology, New Orleans, April 1986. (Unpublished.)

Bataille, Georges. 1962. *Death and Sensuality: A Study of Eroticism and the Taboo.* New York: Walker and Company.

Batres, Leopoldo. 1906. *Teotihuacán.* Mexico City: Fidencio S. Soria.

Benson, Elizabeth P., ed. 1981. *Mesoamerican Sites and World Views.* Washington, D.C.: Dumbarton Oaks.

Berger, Peter L., and Luckmann, Thomas. 1966. *The Social Construction of Reality*. New York: Anchor Press, Doubleday.

Berlo, Janet C. 1982. "Artistic Specialization at Teotihuacán: The Ceramic Incense Burner." In *Pre-Columbian Art History: Selected Readings*, ed. A. Cordy-Collins, 83–100. Palo Alto, Calif.: Peek Publications.

———. 1984. *Teotihuacán Art Abroad: A Study of Metropolitan Style and Provincial Transformation in Incensario Workshops.*" British Archaeological Reports, International Series no. 199. Oxford.

———. 1992. "Icons and Ideologies at Teotihuacán: The Great Goddess Reconsidered." In *Art, Ideology and the City of Teotihuacan*, ed. J. C. Berlo, 129–68. Washington, D.C.: Dumbarton Oaks.

Berrin, Kathleen, ed. 1988. *Feathered Serpents and Flowering Trees: Reconstructing the Murals of Teotihuacan*. San Francisco: The Fine Arts Museums of San Francisco.

Berrin, Kathleen, and Esther Pasztory, eds. 1993. *Teotihuacan: Art from the City of the Gods*. New York: Thames and Hudson.

Blanton, Richard E. 1978. *Monte Albán: Settlement Patterns at the Ancient Zapotec Capital*. New York: Academic Press.

Bobula, Ida Miriam. 1967. *Herencia de Sumeria*. Serie cientifica 2 INAH. Mexico City: Muséo de las culturas.

Boone, Elizabeth H., ed. 1984. *Ritual Human Sacrifice in Mesoamerica*. Washington, D.C.: Dumbarton Oaks.

Burkert, Walter, René Girard, and Jonathan Z. Smith. 1987. *Violent Origins: Ritual Killings and Cultural Formation*, ed. R. G. Hamerton-Kelly. Stanford, Calif: Stanford University Press.

Cabrera Castro, Rubén, Ignacio Rodriguez García, and Noel Morelos García, eds. 1982a. *Teotihuacán 80–82: Primeros Resultados*. Collección Científica, no. 1. Mexico City: INAH.

———. 1982b. *Memoria del Proyecto Arqueología Teotihuacán 80–82*. Colección Científica, no. 132. Mexico City: INAH.

———. 1991. *Teotihuacán 1980–1982: Nuevas Interpretaciones*. Colección Científica. Mexico City: INAH.

Cabrera Castro, Rubén, Saburo Sugiyama, George L. Cowgill. 1991. "The Templo de Quetzalcoatl Project at Teotihuacán." *Ancient Mesoamerica* 2:77–92.

Carneiro, Robert L. 1981. "The Chiefdom: Precursor of the State." In *The Transition to Statehood in the New World*, ed. G. D. Jones and R. R. Kautz, 37–79. New York: Cambridge University Press.

Carr, Robert F., and James E. Hazard. 1961. *Map of the Ruins of Tikal, El Petén, Guatemala*. Tikal Report, no. 11. Philadelphia: University Museum, University of Pennsylvania.

Caso, Alfonso. 1942. "El paraíso terrenal en Teotihuacán." *Cuadernos Americanos* 6:127–36.

———. 1958. *The Aztecs: People of the Sun*. Norman: University of Oklahoma Press.

———. 1966. "Dioses y signos teotihuacanos." In *Teotihuacan, onceava mesa redonda*, 249–75. Mexico City: Sociedad Mexicana de Antropologia.

―――. 1967. *Los Calendarios Prehispanicos.* Mexico City: UNAM.

Caso, Alfonso, and Ignacio Bernal. 1952. *Urnas de Oaxaca.* Memorías, no. 2. Mexico City: INAH.

Chang, K. C. 1983. *Art, Myth, and Ritual: The Path to Political Authority in Ancient China.* Cambridge, Mass.: Harvard University Press.

Charnay, Désiré. 1887. *The Ancient Cities of the New World, Being Voyages and Explorations in Mexico and Central America from 1857–1882.* Trans. J. Gonius and Helen S. Conant. London: Chapman.

Clark, John E. 1986. "From Mountains to Molehills: A Critical Review of Teotihuacán's Obsidian Industry." In *Economic Aspects of Prehispanic Highland Mexico,* ed. B. L. Isaac, 23–74. Research in Economic Anthropology no. 8, Supp. 2. Greenwich, Conn.: JAT Press.

Clausewitz, Carl von. 1976. *On War,* ed. Michael Howard and Peter Paret. Princeton, N.J.: Princeton University Press.

Coe, Michael D. 1966. *The Maya.* New York: Thames and Hudson.

Coggins, Clemency. 1979. "A New Order and the Role of the Calendar: Some Characteristics of the Middle Classic Period at Tikal. In *Maya Archaeology and Ethnohistory,* ed. N. Hammond and G. R. Willey, 38–50. Austin: University of Texas Press.

Coggins, Clemency Chase. 1993. "The Age of Teotihuacan and Its Mission Abroad." In *Teotihuacan: Art from the City of the Gods,* ed. K. Berrin and E. Pasztory, 140–55. New York: Hudson.

Contreras, José Eduardo. 1991. "Ocotelulco." *Mexico desconocido,* no. 178, year 15.

Cordova, Carlos F. de A., Ana Lillian Martin del Pozzo, and Javier Lopez Camacho. 1994. "Palaeolandforms and Volcanic Impact on the Environment of Prehistoric Cuicuilco, Southern Mexico City." *Journal of Archaeological Science* 21:585–96.

―――. 1995. "Volcanic Impact on the Southern Basin of Mexico During the holocene." *Quarternary International* (in press).

Covarrubias, Miguel. 1957. *Indian Art of Mexico and Central America.* New York: A. A. Knopf.

Cowgill, George L. 1983. "Rulership and the Ciudadela: Political Inferences from Teotihuacán Architecture." In *Civilization in the Ancient Americas: Essays in Honor of Gordon R. Willey,* ed. R. M. Leventhal and A. L. Kolata, 313–43. Albuquerque: University of New Mexico Press; Cambridge, Mass.: Peabody Museum of Archaeology and Ethnology.

―――. 1992. "Teotihuacán: Action and Meaning in Mesoamerica." Paper presented at the Society for American Archaeology, Pittsburgh, April.

Demarest, Arthur. 1984. "Overview: Mesoamerican Human Sacrifice in Evolutionary Perspective." In *Ritual Human Sacrifice in Mesoamerica,* ed. E. H. Boone. Washington, D.C.: Dumbarton Oaks.

Dioszegi, Vilmos. 1963. *Glaubenswelt und Folklore der sibirischen Volker.* Budapest: Akademiai Kiado.

Dorpfeld, Wilhelm. 1902. *Troja and Ilion. Ergebrisse des Ausgrabungen in der vorhistorischen und historischen Schichten von Ilion 1870–1874.* Athens:

Beck and Basth.

Edmonson, Monroe S., ed. 1974. *Sixteenth Century Mexico: The Work of Sahagún*. Albuquerque: University of New Mexico Press.

Feest, Christian F. 1990. *Vienna's Mexican Treasures*. Vienna: Museum für Völkerkuude.

Fraser, Douglas. 1962. *Primitive Art*. Englewood Cliffs, N.J.: Doubleday.

Gamio, Manuel. 1922. *La población del Valle de Teotihuacán*. 5 vols. Mexico City: INAH.

García Cook, Angel. 1981. "The Historical Importance of Tlaxcala in the Cultural Development of the Central Highlands." In *Supplement to the Handbook of Middle American Indians*, ed. V. R. Bricker and J. A. Sabloff, 244–74. Austin: University of Texas Press.

García y Cubas, Antonio. 1871. *Ensayo de un estudio comparativo entre las pirámides egipciles y mexicanas*. Mexico City.

Girard, René. 1977. *La Violence et le Sacré*. Paris: Grasset, 1972. *Violence and the Sacred*. Baltimore, 1977.

Gombrich, E. H. 1979. *The Sense of Order: A Study in the Psychology of Decorative Art*. Ithaca, N.Y.: Cornell University Press.

Grove, David, ed. 1987. *Ancient Chalcatzingo*. Austin: University of Texas Press.

Haas, Jonathon. 1982. *The Evolution of the Prehistoric State*. New York: Columbia University Press.

Hagen, Margaret A. 1986. *Varieties of Realism: Geometries of Representational Art*. New York: Cambridge University Press.

Hamerton-Kelly, Robert G., ed. 1987. *Violent Origins: Ritual Killing and Cultural Formation*, W. Burkert, R. Girard, and J. Z, Smith. Stanford, Calif.: Stanford University Press.

Hamy, E. T. 1882. "La croix de Teotihuacán au Museé du Trocadéro." *Revue d'Ethnographie* 1:410–28.

Hardoy, Jorge. 1968. *Planning and Cities: Urban Planning in Pre-Columbian America*. New York: George Braziller.

Hassig, Ross. 1988. *Aztec Warfare: Imperial Expansion and Political Control*. Norman: University of Oklahoma Press.

Heizer, R., and James Bennyhoff. 1955–60. "Archaeological Excavations at Cuicuilco, Mexico 1957," *National Geographic Reports, 1955–60*, pp. 93–104.

Hevesy, Wilhelm von [F. A. Uxbond.] 1928. *Munda-Magyar-Maori: An Indian link between the antipodes; new tracks of Hungarian Origins*. London: Luzac.

Heyden, Doris. 1975. "An Interpretation of the Cave Underneath the Pyramid of the Sun in Teotihuacán, Mexico." *American Antiquity* 40, no. 2:131–47.

———. 1981. "Caves, Gods, and Myths: World View and Planning in Teotihuacán." In *Mesoamerican Sites and World Views*, ed. E. P. Benson, 1–40. Washington, D.C.: Dumbarton Oaks.

Heyden, Doris, and Paul Gendrop. 1988. *Pre-Columbian Architecture of Mesoamerica*. New York: Electa/Rizzoli. (Original edition 1980.)

Hobbes, Thomas. 1991. *Leviathan*. New York: Cambridge University Press.

Hodder, Ian. 1986. *Reading the Past: Current Approaches to Interpretation in Archaeology*. New York: Cambridge University Press.

Hvidtfeldt, Arild. 1958. *Teotl and Ixiptlatli: Some Central Conceptions of Ancient Mexican Religion.* Copenhagen: Munksgaard.

Jarquin Pacheco, Ana Maria, and Enrique Martinez Vargas. 1982. "Las Excavaciones en el Conjunto 1D." In *Memoria del Proyecto Arqueológico Teotihuacán, 80–82,* ed. R. Cabrera Castro, I. Rodriguez García, and N. Morelos García, 80–82. Coleccion Cientifica, vol. 1. Mexico City: INAH.

Jiménez Moreno, Wigberto. 1941. "Tula y los Toltecas segun las fuentes historicas." *Revista Mexicana de Estudios Antropológios* 5, nos. 2–3:79–83.

Johnson, Allen W., and Timothy Earle. 1987. *The Evolution of Human Society.* Stanford, Calif.: Stanford University Press.

Joralemon, David P. 1971. *A Study of Olmec Iconography.* Studies in Pre-Columbian Art and Archaeology, no. 7. Washington, D.C.: Dumbarton Oaks.

Kidder, Alfred V., Jesse D. Jennings, and Edwin M. Shook. 1946. *Excavations at Kaminaljuyú, Guatemala.* Carnegie Institution of Washington, no. 561. Washington, D.C.

Klein, Cecelia. 1980. "Who Was Tlaloc?" *Journal of Latin American Lore* 6, no. 2: 155–204.

———. "The Ideology of Autosacrifice at the Templo Mayor." In *The Aztec Templo Mayor,* ed. E. H. Boone, 293–370. Washington, D.C.: Dumbarton Oaks.

———. 1988. "Rethinking Cihuacoatl: Aztec Political Imagery of the Conquered Woman." In *Smoke and Mist: Mesoamerican Studies in Memory of Thelma D. Sullivan,* ed. J. K. Josserand and K. Dakin. British Archaeological Reports, International Series, vol. 402. Oxford.

———. 1991. "The Role of Masks in the Aztec Empire and Their Importance to Imperial Ideology." Paper presented at the Americas Society, New York, 1991.

Kubler, George. 1962. *The Art and Architecture of Ancient America.* Harmondsworth: Penguin Books.

———. 1967. *The Iconography of the Art of Teotihuacán.* Studies in Pre-Columbian Art and Archaeology, no. 4. Washington, D.C.: Dumbarton Oaks.

Lafaye, Jacques. 1974. *Quetzalcoatl and Guadalupe: The Formation of Mexican National Consciousness, 1531–1813,* trans. Benjamin Keen. Chicago: University of Chicago Press.

LaGamma, Alisa. 1991. "A Visual Sonata at Teotihuacán." *Ancient Mesoamerica* 2:275–84.

Langley, James C. 1986. *Symbolic Notation of Teotihuacán.* British Archaeological Reports, International Series no. 313. Oxford.

———. 1991. "The Forms and Usage of Notation at Teotihuacán." *Ancient Mesoamerica,* 2:285–98.

León Portilla, Miguel. 1963. *Aztec Thought and Culture.* Norman: University of Oklahoma Press.

Linné, Sigvald. 1934. *Archaeological Researches at Teotihuacán, Mexico.* The Ethnographical Museum of Sweden, n.s. 1. Stockholm.

———. 1942. *Mexican Highland Cultures.* The Ethnographical Museum of Sweden, n.s. 7. Stockholm.

López-Austin, Alfredo, Leonardo Lopez Luján, and Saburo Sugiyama. 1991. "The Temple of Quetzacoatl at Teotihuacán: Its Possible Ideological Significance."

Ancient Mesoamerica 2:93–105.

Lopez Luján, Leonardo. 1989. *La recuperación mexica del pasado teotihuacano.* Proyecto Templo Mayor. Mexico City: INAH.

Lorenzo, José L. 1968. *Materiales para la arqueologia de Teotihuacan.* Mexico City: INAH.

Mack, Burton. 1987. "Introduction: Religion and Ritual." In *Violent Origins: Ritual Killing and Cultural Formation,* W. Burkert, R. Girard, and J. Z. Smith, 1–72. Stanford, Calif.: Stanford University Press.

McKlung de Tapia, Emily, and Evelyn Childs Rattray, eds. 1987. *Teotihuacán: Nuevos Datos, Nuevas Síntesis, Nuevos Problemas.* Mexico City: UNAM.

Manzanilla, Linda. 1990. "Sector Noroeste de Teotihuacán: Estudio de un conjunto residential y rastreo de tuneles y cuevas." In *La Epoca Clasica: Nuevos Hallazgos, Nuevas Ideas,* ed. A. Cardos de Mendez, 81–88. Mexico City: Muséo Nacional de Anthropología, INAH.

———. 1991. "A Teotihuacán Censer in a Residential Context." *Ancient Mesoamerica* 2: 299–307.

———. 1992. "The Economic Organization of the Teotihuacan Priesthood; Hypotheses and Considerations." In *Art, Ideology and the City of Teotihuacan,* ed. J. Berlo, 321–38. Washington, D.C.: Dumbarton Oaks.

Marcus, Joyce. 1983. "Teotihuacan Visitors on Monte Alban Monuments and Murals." *The Cloud People,* ed. K. V. Flannery and J. Marcus, 175–81. New York: Academic Press.

———. 1992. *Mesoamerican Writing Systems.* Princeton, N.J.: Princeton University Press.

Matos Moctezuma, Eduardo, ed. 1982. *El Templo Mayor: Excavaciones y estudios.* Mexico City: INAH.

———. 1990. *Teotihuacan, The City of the Gods.* Translated by Andrew Ellis. New York: Rizzoli.

Mendelsohn, K. 1974. "A Scientist Looks at the Pyramids." In *The Rise and Fall of Civilizations,* ed. J. A. Sabloff and C. C. Lamberg-Karlovsky, 390–402. Menlo Park, Calif.: Benjamin Cummings Publishing.

Miller, Arthur G. 1973. *The Mural Painting of Teotihuacán.* Washington, D.C.: Dumbarton Oaks.

———. 1978. "A Brief Outline of the Artistic Evidence for Classic Period Cultural Contact Between Maya Lowlands and Central Mexican Highlands." In *Middle-Classic Mesoamerica A.D. 400–700,* ed. E. Pasztory, 63–70. New York: Columbia University Press.

Miller, Daniel. 1985. "Ideology and the Harappan Civilization." *Journal of Anthropological Archaeology* 4: 34–71.

Millon, Clara Hall. 1962. "A Chronological Study of the Mural Art of Teotihuacán." Ph.D., dissertation, University of California at Berkeley.

———. 1973. "Painting, Writing, and Polity in Teotihuacán, Mexico." *American Antiquity* 38, no. 3:294–314.

———. 1988. "A Reexamination of the Teotihuacán Tassel Headdress Insignia," "Maguey Bloodletting Ritual," "Coyote with Sacrificial Knife," "Coyotes and Deer," "Tassel Headdress Procession," and "Great Goddess Fragment." In

Feathered Serpents and Flowering Trees, ed. K. Berrin, 114–34, and 195–228. San Francisco: The Fine Arts Museums of San Francisco.

Millon, René. 1973. *Urbanization of Teotihuacán, Mexico.* Vol 1, *The Teotihuacán Map. Part 1: Text.* Austin: University of Texas Press.

———. 1981. "Teotihuacán: City, State, and Civilization." In *Archaeology, Supplement to the Handbook of Middle American Indians*, vol 1. ed. V. R. Bricker and J. A. Sabloff, 198–243. Austin: University of Texas Press.

———. 1988a. "The Last Years of Teotihuacán Dominance." In *The Collapse of Ancient States and Civilizations*, eds. G. L. Cowgill and N. Yoffee, 102–64. Tucson: University of Arizona Press.

———. 1988b. "Where *Do* They All Come From? The Provenance of the Wagner Murals from Teotihuacán." In *Feathered Serpents and Flowering Trees*, ed. K. Berrin, 78–113. San Francisco: The Fine Arts Museums of San Francisco.

———. 1992a. "Teotihuacán Residential Architecture." Paper presented to the Society for American Archaeology, Pittsburgh, April, 1992.

———. 1992b. "Teotihuacan Studies: From 1950 to 1990 and Beyond." In *Art, Ideology, and the City of Teotihuacan*, ed. J. C. Berlo, 339–430. Washington, D.C.: Dumbarton Oaks.

———. 1993. "The Place Where Time Began: An Archaeologist's Interpretation of What Happened in Teotihuacan History." In *Teotihuacan: Art from the City of the Gods*, ed. K. Berrin and E. Pasztory, 15–43. New York: Thames and Hudson.

Millon, René, Bruce Drewitt, and James H. Bennyhoff. 1965. "The Pyramid of the Sun at Teotihuacán: 1959 Investigations." In *Transactions of the American Philosophical Society*, n.s. 55, no. 6. Philadelphia.

Morelos García, Noel. 1992. "Discoveries in the Street of the Dead Complex." (unpublished paper.)

Murra, John Victor. 1980. *The Economic Organization of the Inka State*, Research in Economic Anthropology. Greenwich, Conn.: JAI Press.

Nagao, Debra. 1985. *Mexica Buried Offerings.* British Archaeological Reports, International Series 235. Oxford.

Navarrete, Carlos. 1991. "Cuicuilco y la arqueología del Pedregal." *Arqueologia* 5:69–84.

Newman, Barbara. 1992. "The Pilgrimage of Christ—Sophia." Paper presented at the Society of Fellows in the Humanities, New York, Columbia University, February 1992.

Nicholson, H. B. 1957. "Topiltzin Quetzalcoatl of Tollan: A Problem in Mesoamerican Ethnohistory." Ph.D. dissertation, Department of Anthropology, Harvard University.

———. "Religion in Pre-Hispanic Central Mexico." In *Handbook of Middle American Indians*, gen. ed. R. Wauchope, Vol 10, *The Archaeology of Northern Mesoamerica*, ed. G. Ekholm and J. Bernal, part 1, 92–134. Austin: University of Texas Press.

Olivera de Vazquez, M. 1969. "Los 'dueños del agua' en Tlaxcalancingo." *INAH Boletin* 35:45–48.

Ortner, Sherry B. 1974. "Is Female to Male as Nature Is to Culture." In *Women, Culture, and Society*, ed. M. Z. Rosaldo and L. Lamphere, 67–88. Stanford,

Cal.: Stanford University Press.

Ostrowitz, Judith. 1991. "Concentric Structures and Gravity as Represented in Teotihuacán Art." *Ancient Mesoamerica* 2: 263–74.

Pasztory, Esther. 1973a. "The Gods of Teotihuacán: A Synthetic Approach in Teotihuacán Iconography." In *Atti del XL Congresso Internazionale degli Americanisti*, Vol. 1, 147–59. Rome.

———. 1973b. "The Xochicalco Stelae and a Middle Classic Deity Triad in Mesoamerica." In *Actas del XXIII Congreso Internacional de Historia de Arte*, Vol. 1, 185–215. Granada.

———. 1974. "The Iconography of the Teotihuacán Tlaloc." In *Studies in Pre-Columbian Art and Archaeology*, no. 15. Washington, D.C.: Dumbarton Oaks.

———. 1976a. *The Murals of Tepantitla, Teotihuacán*. New York: Garland Publishing.

———. 1976b. *Aztec Stone Sculpture*, ed. E. Pasztory. New York: The Center for Inter-American Relations.

———. 1978. "Historical Synthesis of the Middle Classic Period," and "Artistic Traditions of the Middle Classic Period." In *Middle Classic Mesoamerica: A.D. 400–700*, ed. E. Pasztory, 3–22, and 108–42. New York: Columbia University Press.

———. 1983a. *Aztec Art*. New York: Harry N. Abrams.

———. 1983b. "Art of Aztec Mexico: Treasures of Tenochtitlan." A review of the exhibition at the National Gallery of Art. *Art Journal* 390–93.

———. 1984. "El arte mexica y la conquista espanola." In *Estudios de Cultura Nahuatl*, vol. 17, ed. C. Vega Soza, 101–26. Mexico City: INAH.

———. 1986. "Participation and Hierarchy: The Structure of the Teotihuacán Composite Censer." Paper presented at the Society for American Archaeology, New Orleans, April 1986.

———. 1987. "Texts, Archaeology, Art, and History in the Templo Mayor: Reflections." In *The Aztec Templo Mayor*, ed. E. H. Boone, 451–62. Washington, D.C.: Dumbarton Oaks.

———. 1988a. "A Reinterpretation of Teotihuacán and Its Mural Painting Tradition," and "Feathered Serpents and Flowering Trees with Glyphs, Large Birds, Small Birds with Shields and Spears with Other Fragments, Feathered Feline and Bird Border." In *Feathered Serpents and Flowering Trees: Reconstructing the Murals of Teotihuacán*, ed. K. Berrin, 45–77 and 135–93. San Francisco: The Fine Arts Museums of San Francisco.

———. 1988b. "The Aztec Tlaloc: God of Antiquity." In *Smoke and Mist: Mesoamerican Studies in Memory of Thelma D. Sullivan*, ed. J. K. Josserand and K. Dakin. British Archaeological Reports, International Series, vol. 402. Oxford.

———. 1989. "Identity and Difference: The Uses and Meanings of Ethnic Styles. In *Cultural Differentiation and Cultural Identity in the Visual Arts*, ed. S. J. Barnes and W. S. Melion, 15–38. Studies in the History of Art, no. 27. Washington, D.C.: Center for Advanced Study in the Visual Arts, National Gallery of Art.

———. 1990. "El poder militar como realidad y retorica en Teotihuacán." In *La epoca clasica: nuevos hallazgos nuevos ideas*, ed. A Cardos de Mendez, 181–97. Mexico City: INAH. 1990–91.

———. 1990–91. "Still Invisible: The Problem of the Aesthetics of Abstraction in Pre-Columbian Art and Its Implications for Other Traditions." *RES* 19/20:105–36.

———. 1991. "Strategies of Organization in Teotihuacán." *Ancient Mesoamerica* 2: 247–48.

———. 1992a. "Body Parts: Social and Religious Ideology at Teotihuacán." Paper presented at the Society for American Archaeology, Pittsburgh, April 1992.

———. 1992b. "Abstraction and the Rise of a Utopian State at Teotihuacán." In *Art Ideology and the City of Teotihuacán*, ed. J. C. Berlo, 281–320. Washington, D.C.: Dumbarton Oaks.

———. 1992c. "The Natural World as Civic Metaphor at Teotihuacán." In *The Ancient Americas: Art from Sacred Landscapes*, ed. R. F. Townsend, 135–46. Chicago: The Art Institute of Chicago.

———. 1993. "An Image Is Worth a Thousand Words: The Meanings of Style in Classic Mesoamerica." In *Latin American Horizons*, ed. D. S. Rice. Washington, D.C.: Dumbarton Oaks.

Pendergast, David M. 1971. "Evidence of Early Teotihuacán–Lowland Maya Contact at Altun Ha." *American Antiquity* 36, no. 4:455–60.

———. 1979. *Excavations at Altun Ha, Belize, 1964–1970*, 2 vols. Royal Ontario Museum. Toronto: Alger Press.

Rands, Robert, 1955. "Some Manifestations of Water in Mesoamerican Art." In *Smithsonian Institution, Bureau of American Ethnology Bulletin*, vol. 157. pp. 265–393. Washington, D.C.

Rattray, Evelyn C. 1983. "Gulf Coast Influences at Teotihuacán." Paper presented at the Rise of the Teotihuacán State conference, University of California at Los Angeles, 1983.

———. 1990. "New Findings on the Origins of Thin Orange Ceramics." *Ancient Mesoamerica* 1: 181–95.

Sahagún, Bernardino de. 1950–78. *Florentine Codex, General History of the Things of New Spain*. 12 books in 10 vols. Trans. Arthur J. O. Anderson and Charles E. Dibble. Santa Fe, N.M.: The School of American Research and the University of Utah.

Sánchez Sánchez, Jesus E. 1982. "Zone Central del 'Complejo Calle de los Muertos.'" In *Memoria del Proyecto Arqueología Teotihuacán, 80–82*, ed. R. Cabrera Castro, I. Rodriguez García, and N. Morelos García. Colección Científica, vol. 1, no. 132. Mexico City: INAH.

Sanders, William T. 1965. "The Cultural Ecology of the Teotihuacán Valley." Ms. on file, Dept. of Anthropology, Pennsylvania State University.

Sanders, William T., and Joseph W. Michels, eds. 1977. *Teotihuacán and Kaminaljuyú: A Study in Prehistoric Culture Contact*. Monograph Series on Kaminajuyú. University Park: Pennsylvania State University.

Sanders, William T., Jeffrey R. Parsons, and Robert S. Santley. 1979. *The Basin of Mexico: Ecological Processes in the Evolution of Civilization*. New York:

Academic Press.

Sanders, William T., and Barbara Price. 1968. *Mesoamerica: The Evolution of a Civilization.* New York: Random House.

Santley, Robert S., 1989. Janet M. Kerley, and Raúl Olivarez. "Obsidian Working, Long Distance Exchange, and the Teotihuacán Presence on the South Gulf Coast." In *Cultural Adjustments Following the Decline of Teotihuacán,* ed. R. A. Diehl, 131–52. Washington, D.C.: Dumbarton Oaks

Sarro, Patricia Jan. 1991. "The Role of Architectural Sculpture in Ritual Space at Teotihuacán, Mexico." *Ancient Mesoamerica* 2:249–62.

Schapiro, Meyer. 1969. "On Some Problems in the Semiotics of Visual Art: Field and Vehicle in Image-Signs." *Semiotica* 487–502.

Schavelzón, Daniel, 1983. *La Pyramide de Cuicuilco.* Mexico City: Fondo de Cultura Economica.

Schele, Linda, and David Freidel. 1990. *A Forest of Kings: The Untold Story of the Ancient Maya.* New York: William Morrow.

Schele, Linda, and Mary E. Miller. 1986. *The Blood of Kings: Dynasty and Ritual in Maya Art.* New York: George Braziller; Fort Worth, Tex.: Kimbell Art Museum.

Schliemann, Heinrich. 1989. *Ilios, the City and Country of the Trojans: The Results of Researches and Discoveries on the Site of Troy and Throughout the Troad in the years 1871, 72, 73, 78, 79: Including an Autobiography of the Author.* Salem: N. H. Ayer.

Séjourné, Laurette. 1956. *Burning Water: Thought and Religion in Ancient Mexico.* New York: Vanguard Press.

———. 1959. *Un palacio en la ciudad de los dioses,exploraciones en Teotihuacán 1955–1958.* Mexico City: INAH.

———. 1966a. *Arquitectura y pintura en Teotihuacán.* Mexico City: Siglo XXI Editores.

———. 1966b. *Arqueología de Teotihuacán: La cerámica.* Mexico City: Siglo XXI Editores.

———. 1966c. *El lenguaje de las formas en Teotihuacán.* Mexico City: Siglo XXI Editores.

Seler, Eduard. 1902–23. *Gesammelte Abhandlungen,* 5 vols. Facsimile edition. Graz-Austria: Akademische Druck-und Verlagsanstalt, 1960–61.

———. 1904–09. *Codex Borgia. Eine altmexikanische Bilderschrift der Bilbiothek der Congregatio de Propaganda Fide,* 3 vols. Berlin. Spanish translation; Mexico City: Fondo de Cultura Económica Comentarios al Codice Borgia, 1963.

———. 1915. "Die Teotihuacán—Kultur des Hochlands von Mexico." In *Gesammelte Abhandlungen,* vol. 5, 405–585. Facsimile edition. Graz, Austria: Akademische Druck-und Verlagsanstalt, 1960.

Sempowski, Martha. 1983. "Mortuary Practices at Teotihaucan, Mexico: Their Implications for Social Status." Ph.D., Department of Anthropology, University of Rochester.

Service, Elman R. 1962. *Primitive Social Organization.* New York: Random House.

Smith, William Robertson. 1969. *Lectures on the Religion of the Semites.* New York: Ktav Publishing House. (Original edition 1927.)

Spence, Michael W. 1974. "Residential Practices and the Distribution of Skeletal Traits in Teotihuacán." *Man* n.s. 9, no. 3:262–73.

———. 1981. "Obsidian Production and the State in Teotihuacán." *American Antiquity* 46, no. 4: 769–88.

Spranz, Bodo. 1964. "Göttergestalten in der Mexikanischen Bilderhandschriften der Codex Borgia-Gruppe." In *Acta Humboldtiana*, no. 4, *Series geographica et ethnographica*. Wiesbaden: Franz Steiner Verlag.

———. 1970. *Die Pyramiden von Totimehuacan Puebla (Mexico).* Wiesbaden: Franz Steiner Verlag.

Stierlin, Henri. 1965. *Living Architecture: Mayan.* New York: Grosset and Dunlap.

———. 1968. *Living Architecture: Ancient Mexican.* New York: Grosset and Dunlap.

Sugiyama, Saburo. 1989. "Iconographic Interpretation of the Temple of Quetzalcoatl at Teotihuacán." *Mexicon XI* 4:68–74.

Taube, Karl. 1983. "The Teotihuacán Spider Woman." *Journal of Latin American Lore* 9, no. 2:107–89.

———. 1986. "The Teotihuacán Cave of Origin: The Iconography and Architecture of Emergence Mythology in Mesoamerica and the American Southwest." *RES* 12:51–82.

———. 1992a. "The Temple of Quetzalcoatl and the Cult of Sacred Wars at Teotihuacán." *RES* 21: 53–88.

———. 1992b. "The Iconography of Mirrors at Classic Teotihuacán." In *Art, Ideology, and the City of Teotihuacan*, ed. J. C. Berlo, Washington, D.C.: Dumbarton Oaks.

Tobriner, Stephen. 1972. "The Fertile Mountain: An Investigation of Cerro Gordo's Importance to the Town Plan and Iconography of Teotihaucan." *XI Mesa Redonda* 2, 105–15. Mexico City: Sociedad Mexicana de Antropologia.

Townsend, Richard F. 1992. "The Renewal of Nature at the Temple of Tlaloc." In *The Ancient Americans: Art From Sacred Landscapes*, ed. R. F. Townsend, 171–85. Chicago: Art Institute of Chicago.

Umberger, Emily. 1987a. "Events Commemorated by Date Plaques at the Templo Mayor: Further Thoughts on the Solar Metaphor." In *The Aztec Templo Mayor*, ed. E. H. Boone, 411–50. Washington, D.C.: Dumbarton Oaks, 1987.

———. 1987b. "Antiques, Revivals, and References to the Past in Aztec Art." *RES* 13: 63–106.

UNESCO, 1958. *Mexico, Pre-Hispanic Paintings.* Greenwich, Conn.

Valeri, Valerio. 1985. *Kingship and Sacrifice, Ritual and Society in Ancient Hawaii.* Chicago: University of Chicago Press.

Von Sadovszky, Otto. 1989. "Linguistic Evidence for the Siberian Origin of Central California Indian Shamanism." *Shamanism Past and Present*, vol. 1, ed. M. Hoppal, 165–85. Budapest: Ethnographic Institute, Hungarian Academy of Sciences, and Fullerton, Calif.: International Society of Trans-Oceanic Research.

Von Winning, Hasso. 1948. "The Teotihuacán Owl-and-Weapon Symbol and Its

Association with 'Serpent Head X' at Kaminaljuyú." *American Antiquity*, 14, no. 2: 129–32.

————. 1987. *La iconografía de Teotihuacán: Los dioses y los signos*. 2 vols. Mexico City: Universidad Nacional Autónoma de Mexico.

Westheim, Paul. 1965. *The Art of Ancient Mexico*. Garden City, N.Y.: Doubleday. (Originally published in 1950.)

White, Hayden. 1987. *The Content of Form: Narrative Discourse and Historical Representation*. Baltimore, Md. Johns Hopkins University Press.

Wicke, Charles R. 1954. "Los Murales de Tepantitla y el Arte Campesino," *INAH Anales* 8:117–22.

Willey, Gordon R. 1953. *Prehistoric Settlement Patterns in the Virú Valley, Peru*. Bureau of American Ethnology Bulletin 155. Washington, D.C.

Willey, Gordon R., and Jeremy A. Sabloff. 1974. *A History of American Archaeology*. San Francisco: Freeman.

Wittfogel, Karl A. 1957. *Oriental Despotism: A Comparative Study of Total Power*. New Haven, Conn.: Yale University Press.

Zuidema, R. Tom. 1990. *Inca Civilization in Cuzco*. Austin: University of Texas Press.

Index

Schmitt